Maid IN *India*

STORIES OF INEQUALITY AND OPPORTUNITY INSIDE OUR HOMES

TRIPTI LAHIRI

ALEPH

ALEPH

ALEPH BOOK COMPANY
An independent publishing firm
promoted by *Rupa Publications India*

First published in India in 2017
by Aleph Book Company
7/16 Ansari Road, Daryaganj
New Delhi 110 002

ISBN: 978-93-84067-33-5

1 3 5 7 9 10 8 6 4 2

Printed and bound in India by Replika Press Pvt. Ltd.

For
Ma, Baba, Smita

CONTENTS

PROLOGUE

ONE RECENT NOVEMBER, I MET up with a handful of friends in Goa for the destination birthday celebration of one of our group. It was amazing that all of us—working and in our late thirties—could make it. But then, it wasn't a very typical group. Only a few among us were married, even fewer had children. One of these few asked the birthday girl if it would be okay if she came with her three-year-old and live-in nanny in tow. This was a rare chance to spend time with both her friends and her child. 'Of course,' said our host.

Before the Goa trip, our friend hadn't travelled a great deal with the nanny, although she often travelled overseas for work. Sometimes, if she was spending a chunk of time at a university with good day care, she would take her daughter; other times, on shorter research trips, her daughter and the nanny would stay home with her husband, a very involved father by any standard, while she travelled alone.

On our first night, reservations had been made at an elegant waterside restaurant. Initially, I and probably the others, with the blithe unconcern of the childless, imagined that nanny and child would remain at the hotel while the adults went off to eat at restaurants. But it was inconceivable to the mother to leave her child in a hotel while she went out. So, the nanny and the little girl, quiet and well-behaved, as little girls in India often are, came along with us.

Initially, I viewed this development with a trepidation formed by past observation. In today's India it is not unusual to see, often in largely empty restaurants, a couple seated with their child at a table for four, while the help is dispatched to sit not one but two tables away. Or, a nanny dandling a child on her lap at a nightclub while her employers and their friends drink cocktails as it creeps towards midnight, her hours of sleep dwindling since she is no doubt expected to be up and ready for another day at sunrise. Or, for example, amid children playing in a neighbourhood park, seeing a plump, light-skinned boy on a swing crook his finger at the petite darker woman standing nearby and utter a single word: 'Push'.

I knew my friend to be progressive and well-intentioned, but now that I thought about it, had we ever met in situations where her ideals were under pressure, where I had to watch her decide between what was right and what was convenient? In any case, when it comes to domestic help, many progressive people have a blind spot. Professors who study and critique feudalism and the serfdom of rural peasants, underpay and overwork those very rural peasants when they hire them in the city as maids; feminists who are fighting the patriarchy nitpick and circumscribe the autonomy of their maids to such a degree that the maid becomes too nervous to proceed without asking a million questions, upon which she gets a scolding for being so irritating; as journalists, including those who cover strikes and the mistreatment of labour, we rarely stop to consider if our own homes are good places to work—I doubt most of us could confidently say the answer is 'yes'.

With a sinking heart I wondered if I was about to take part in the pageant that seemed to be increasingly emblematic of class relations in this new post-liberalization India—in which one set of people sits eating and drinking overpriced western cuisine, an extravagance made possible by the wide array of opportunities, both legal and illicit, now available to them—while another set of people, usually a great deal leaner, and in most cases female, sits apart from them, often before empty plates.

But it seemed my trepidation was unfounded. After a wander around the restaurant with her charge, the nanny joined us at the table. Our friend asked her to take a look at the menu to see what she'd like to order. All seemed well. And then the next wave of guests arrived to join us.

Some of the guests were older—the birthday girl's mother and other relatives among them—and suddenly it became clear to all of us that some serious seating management was going to be required. Nobody put it into words, but everybody there knew that many of the new arrivals would no more consider it appropriate to eat this celebratory meal while seated at the same table as the help than Lady Grantham of *Downton Abbey* would. Some of the older people—

and they were not so old, mind you, it was perhaps a generation's difference—were of a time when 'camping' meant having a servant sleeping at the doorway of your tent in case you should call for a bottle of water in the night. Their feelings weren't unusual, it must be said: they were the norms of most elite Indians, including in my family.

We each tried in our own ways to rise to the occasion, to balance the competing demands of making welcome the nanny, a soft-spoken, educated woman from Jharkhand who bantered with her charge in English learned on the job, while at the same time not making our friend's relatives, some of whom were hosting us, uncomfortable. Through a complex telegraphing of meaningful glances, us 'younger' folks moved over to one end of the long table to sit with the nanny in order to allow most of the others to be separated from her by a cordon sanitaire of our own class. This seating arrangement allowed us to share with her the dishes that had been ordered for the whole table, without drawing too much unwanted attention to that breach in the class rules for dining in India: the help eats leftovers, and she eats later.

Meanwhile, at an adjoining table, the presence of a family of Russians sounded a helpful warning note about the perils of dining out with children sans nanny. Their children ran around noisily, climbing up the wooden poles that supported the thatched ceilings over each table hut, as the grown-ups, oblivious, chatted and drank copiously. Our child was a model of good behaviour, thanks to the shared ministrations of her solicitous caregivers. All in all, I was relieved by what seemed to me our exemplary handling of the situation: hadn't we quite fairly balanced our more modern sensibilities with the older folks' class snobbery?

But the next day it turned out that this arrangement had not been to everyone's liking. My friend, who was hosting the gathering, was worried that one of her family members, unusually silent, had had his enjoyment of the evening marred by being seated opposite a person who, to him, was just a servant. At other meals out, the seating arrangements were duly tweaked further. On one of the last days, though, as we walked to breakfast at one of the relative's homes, the birthday girl's mother, a gracious and impressive, if occasionally intimidating, woman in her seventies, called up my friend to inform her tensely that the nanny was seated at the breakfast table in the living room. The older guests had made their peace with sitting together with the nanny at meals out at a restaurant—out in the world, one must make peace with brushing elbows with all sorts—but this breach, in such a sacred place, the family table in the home, was the last straw.

My friend was completely unnerved. I felt rather nervous myself. Now what? Certainly, neither of us was capable of delivering a lecture on how times had changed to her doughty and elderly mother, recently recovered from an illness. When we arrived, however, we did not find the nanny being waited upon by the lady of the house as she tucked heartily into cold coffee, fried eggs and Goan sausage, and implanting, by her example, revolutionary ideas into the minds of the live-in help who always ate in the kitchen. Rather, she was sitting next to her charge, trying to get her to do possibly the most trying and time-consuming of all parenting tasks: eat another bite. How could she do so without sitting at the table? Ought she to stand next to or behind the child, rather than beside her? Her employer didn't think so. Still, it was not her house. And though our friend may have resented how put out her hosts were by where the nanny was sitting, being mindful of what she owed the woman, she was also mindful of what, as a guest, she owed her host. And then there was what she owed her friend.

The nanny, too, was hardly a stranger to navigating a wide range of social milieus and beliefs and ideas about the proper etiquette between maid and employer, or to the fact that her position and the respect accorded her yo-yoed up and down from one house to another. She was likely an expert at reading a room and making sure she (almost) never put herself in a position where she could be rebuked for transgressing social boundaries. Borders between countries are marked out by fences and guards, but borders between classes are marked out by where you may sit, where you may go to the bathroom, and where and with whom you may eat.

And thus, before our friend could take measures to quell the silent tensions seething in the room, I heard the nanny ask sotto voce where she should eat breakfast. Our friend replied equally softly, 'In the kitchen.' She departed, and the class sanctity of the table was restored. We continued with breakfast, with our sausages and fried eggs and cold coffee, all of us pretending the morning had not been roiled by subterranean tremors.

INTRODUCTION

THE SPIDERWEB

IN 2009, IN INDIA'S NORTHEAST, a woman agreed to send her oldest daughter to Delhi with a man full of promises. 'Uncle' was to take the girl far away from the machetes and the bows and arrows of the angry young men who roamed the villages around the relief camp where the family had landed after violence broke out in the area. He was to take her to safety.

That same year, a woman living in a bungalow near the sixteenth-century fort, Purana Qila, a part of which now houses the Delhi zoo, was preparing for her first solo travel experience, to Australia. All her life she had scarcely passed a moment alone; it was a life spent first in the embrace of her own family, and then, after marriage, that of her husband's. She wanted to know that she could do this.

Neither of them could have known it back then, but the paths of the woman in the leafy Delhi neighbourhood of Sunder Nagar and the woman in Assam would cross, dramatically, thanks to the gossamer networks that spiderweb across this dusty, sprawling capital, linking tycoons and refugees, politicians and orphans, India's one per cent and her 99 per cent. In a wealthier country, the ways in which the lives of the impoverished and the affluent are enmeshed are often made invisible; in India, that intertwining is plain to see. We see each other at traffic lights, sometimes at school. Most often we see each other at home: our homes, that is, the homes of the one per cent, into which a significant slice of the 99 per cent enter as servants.

India has always had servants in some form or another—a casual glance at epics and rulebooks thousands of years old makes that clear— but once they swirled much more tightly around a particular point on the map. In that solar system they orbited a local zamindar or man of influence. Like called only to like: a family would have help from their district, if not their village. It was a relationship governed by the strict hierarchies of caste, tempered ever so slightly by the shared foundation of being born and reared on the same soil. Now help is unmoored from these confining and yet protective networks. And what was once a trickle has turned into a steady stream of women and men leaving their villages for the great unknown—usually one of India's five largest cities, Delhi, Mumbai, Chennai, Bengaluru and Kolkata—set in motion by changes that began occurring more than two decades ago.

The government's slightly looser hold on the economy in the 1980s, and especially after 1991, coupled with astonishing advances in communications meant there was suddenly an array of jobs and business opportunities that you didn't have to be a swot to get. You could be a construction worker who lived, ate and shat in the rubble of the home you had just helped demolish; you could ferry little plastic bags of instant noodles and other snacks cooked in the searing heat of a street stall to a new type of office-goer, living too far from home and family to come bearing a packed tiffin for lunch; you could drive a taxicab or an autorickshaw to ferry a different kind of new worker—women—back and forth. As taxing as these new jobs were, they beat the most common alternative—a fall into the abyss signified by no job at all.

Together, these chances drew many more people to cities than in the past, and in neighbourhoods churning with migrants, new alliances formed and the universe expanded. A man from Uttar Pradesh married a woman from Jharkhand; two boys from Chhattisgarh and Bihar became the best of friends. And they might say to each other, why don't we go into business? If you can get girls, I can find them places. Because suddenly, everybody who came into money was asking for girls—not red-light area type girls, though there was that too—but someone to come to their home to cook and clean, to fetch them glasses of water and play with their children.

These girls and women—freed from the families they leave behind, and yet restricted by the homes in which they reside as servants, at once powerless because of their age, gender, language and ethnicity and also powerful as the fulcrum on which an entire village family's hopes rest—are the focus of this book. Although India (and labour organizations) include jobs mainly done by men—such as driving or serving as a watchman—in tallies of household help, the relationships these men have with their employers, performed for the most part in public, are fundamentally different from those that develop between women and their employers, unfolding as they do behind closed doors and away from the world.

Two-thirds of all domestic help employed by families are women and that share rises to 80 per cent if workers whose duties take place outside the house are excluded. That is almost the exact opposite of the state of affairs at the start of the twentieth century, when women supplied just a third of household help; until the 1970s or so, cooking and housekeeping, when done for pay, was largely the province of men. These days, it is one of the most common jobs that women do outside the home, at least in cities, where the most recent figures show domestic work absorbs more than 8 per cent of urban female workers, compared to less than 1 per cent of male workers.

If Kolkata, as the former capital during colonial times, is where people looked to understand Raj-era British and Indian attitudes to servants, Delhi is where we should look to understand where they stand now, in the vastly different and more ambitious India that has emerged in recent decades, and that is still being shaped by the striving of millions of young people. Delhi, the nation's capital, is one of the country's richest cities and certainly its most powerful. If any place in the country should be a model, it ought to be this one, where the highest court in the land sits and tells the state what it owes its citizens, and its citizens what they owe one another. Instead, like its weather, Delhi, in its social mores, is a city of extremes, its people veering wildly between generosity and meanness, and tending more often to the latter. The state of relations between sahibs and servants in this wealthy, powerful Indian city is a way to gauge what kind of people we Indians are away from the public gaze, what we think we owe the people who by some unlucky chance have landed on a spot far down on the class totem pole. The answer to both of these questions, most of the time, is rather sobering.

♦

The steady upward curve in the numbers of people employed

as servants in India since the start of the new millennium isn't the continuation of a long-standing trajectory, it's the reversal of one. Despite the conventional wisdom among the Indian elite that 'everyone' has servants (and has always had them), the practice of having help actually began dwindling in twentieth-century India, just as it had in America and Britain from around the 1950s onwards.

In India, as in Europe and America, the keeping of servants followed a dramatic boom-and-bust trajectory up until around 2000, with large numbers of people working as help in the early twentieth century and extraordinarily few by its middle. In India, the large numbers of help in the early twentieth century were at least partly due to the presence of British colonial officials who employed large numbers of help, especially in the pre-1911 capital of Calcutta (the British, in turn, claim to have been inspired by the Mughals). Earlier, under the rule of the East India Company, hiring excesses were such that at one point the company issued strict guidelines on how many servants the young male employees it shipped out could hire. One eighteenth-century household, probably not typical, had more than a hundred people serving four officials, counting everything from palanquin bearers and carriage drivers to cooks and porters.

The picture was quite different by the middle of the twentieth century. For America and Britain, that change was bracketed by war; for India, war and independence from Britain signalled the beginning of the decline in household servants. In all three places, that change also coincided with the 'diminishing fortunes of the [very] richest' people, at least for a while, and an increase in prosperity and opportunity at other points of the class ladder. (In recent times, of course, a tiny portion of the globe's richest have reversed the trend, with some of them pulling far ahead of their fellow members of the 1 per cent club to produce growing numbers of multimillionaires and billionaires whose rise has been both the source of angry populism and, in some cases, leaders who represent that ire.)

After World War II, which was followed in just two years by India's independence from Britain, and the division of the subcontinent into two nations, the number of people working in domestic service in India waned dramatically due to the end of the Raj, war economies, and the reversals of fortune many families experienced at Partition.

Nearly seven decades after Independence, refugees on either side of the border and their descendants reminisce about how they fled to safety with just the clothes on their back, leaving behind large homes and servants (we never have heard what happened to the servants). After Independence, the number continued to decline, as if India, in the first years of becoming a new nation, was making good on the promises of self-abnegation that were such a large part of the freedom movement shaped by Mahatma Gandhi. If Britain saw the numbers of servants drop from 250,000 in 1951 to 32,000 two decades later, during the same period, the number of servants in India shrank by half, to less than 700,000. In 1971, India had about a quarter of the number of servants recorded in the Census of 1911.

But a quite different pattern has emerged since the socialist-era 1970s. In the past two decades, the keeping of servants has experienced resurgence, even as the word itself has been excised from vocabularies. In this, too, India is part of a larger phenomenon, an alteration taking place simultaneously in many parts of the world. According to international labour groups, as of 2010, there were more than 50 million such workers globally, an increase of nearly 20 million from 1995, most of this made up of women. There are now more than 40 million female domestic workers globally. By default, this means that the number of families able to employ domestic help has surged too. And yet, as we embrace an institution we can only enjoy thanks to the presence of inequality, we shy away from calling the people we hire servants, reaching for more egalitarian words by which to discuss the people who handle our cooking, cleaning and children while we do other kinds of work.

So, American families hire West Indian and Nepali housekeepers and nannies made available to them by the joint forces of global poverty and immigration, while Swedish families hire Filipinas as au pairs, and offer them financial incentives if they will leave the country without falling pregnant and claiming residency. Meanwhile, India's newly affluent benefit from the huge disparities that divide India by importing rural tribal women to the city as 'helpers', 'childminders' and 'housekeepers'. At Delhi's elite Gymkhana Club, a sign that barred 'maids and ayahs' from setting foot in the front lawns was replaced, sometime in 2015, with one with the words 'personal attendants'.

They are still barred, of course, but much more politely.

For much of India's independence, only a very tiny share of people could afford to have servants. But in the last two decades, Indians who are experiencing, at long last, a new level of prosperity are increasingly able to hire people to aid in carrying out the astonishing amount of housework that life in India seems to entail at any income level. In the decade after liberalization in 1991, the number of maids, drivers and nannies in India doubled. Their ranks doubled again in the decade that followed. Particularly for the growing numbers of women who work in urban India, 'work-life balance', depends increasingly on having help.

The help, strangely, except for the most elite ranks of these workers, do not often reach for the same words their employers have adopted. At least in India, many workers continue to use the word 'naukar'—servant—to describe their job, and call their employers 'malik', sometimes translating this word into English as 'owner'. If at times, this book swerves from the sanctioned words in favour of the verboten ones, it is to be accurate to the words people use in telling their stories, and to capture the true flavour of the relationships they describe.

◆

As their fortunes soar, the rich and rising classes of Indians have had to work hard to keep the India of poverty and privation at bay. They live in bubbles composed of beautifully kept bungalows to which they invite their friends, or they go on outings to malls in air-conditioned cars whose windows glide up, creating a hermetic seal at the touch of a button. But to live this beautiful life, affluent Indians must invite the other India into their homes, to clean those bungalows, drive those air-conditioned cars, and keep their children away during those long soirees.

And so the poorest districts of West Bengal have emissaries stationed at Gurgaon condos with names like Western Heights and Central Park; the Maoist areas of Jharkhand's Gumla and Khunti districts have dispatched ambassadors to the diplomatic and bureaucratic circles of the capital; and a young woman running from Assam's many conflicts can sometimes find, unexpectedly, a safe harbour in a well-appointed bungalow in the heart of Delhi.

As in the US military, it is possible to follow a 'don't ask, don't tell' policy, it's possible to remain carefully unaware of exactly how this person who has come to be at your service represents oh-so-many failures on the part of the Indian state over oh-so-many decades. But many times, despite all efforts to the contrary, that wall is breached and the other India and its problems spill forth into these beautiful homes, setting in train a series of collisions that can create something ugly—or something precious.

◆

Around 2011, Neera and Pavan Varma hired a young woman through the mediation of Masterji, a man whose free entry into homes all over the city courtesy of his inchee tape and mastery of the sewing machine, allows him to easily broker new relationships (and break existing ones). The Varmas, who live in a Sunder Nagar bungalow with wind chimes hanging from the balconies, have both worked for most of their lives. He is a British-educated electronics engineer who runs help centres for electronics giants across Asia. She worked for the country's largest state-run bank, and kept her job even after coming to live with her husband's family, despite the fact that, at that time, few married women did. Her own mother had worked as a school principal, says Neera, who wears her dark hair in a shoulder-length bob. And so she withstood for a long time the pressure most married women face to quit.

The Varmas wanted to help their new maid, Chutki, a diminutive gap-toothed young woman from Assam, open a bank account to deposit her salary, rather than banking it for her as many employers do (sometimes forgetting altogether to hand it over when the time comes to part ways). They found themselves with a chicken-and-egg problem because, in order to open a bank account, the young woman needed some form of ID. But Chutki, who, like others in her family, had journeyed from relief camps in Assam to homes in West Bengal before finally coming to Delhi, did not exist on paper at all. She had barely gone to school, and had lived and eaten in the homes of others since the time she was ten and began working as a maid, she does not drive, therefore she had no school certificate, no ration card, no driver's licence.

Chutki's employers suggested she apply for the Aadhaar Card, a new government ID that Indian banks, notoriously circumspect about opening new accounts, were suddenly accepting. But when Chutki went to apply for an Aadhaar card, the registration officer asked her to provide some other form of government ID first. Neera's banking experience helped her find a workaround.

'When I have an account, I can have it joint with anybody,' says Neera. Step one: open a bank account at your own bank, and add the new maid's name to it. She begins to exist, even if in just a vague shadowy outline.

Then, using the joint account and a letter of introduction vouching that Chutki lived with her, Neera opened a fixed deposit account in the maid's name. Now, the woman had a document in her name alone with a supporting Delhi address. With this, she went back to the Aadhaar office, which appeared satisfied with these financial documents. They took her photograph, scanned her iris, and pressed her fingers into the fingerprinting glass. In a few weeks, she received her Aadhaar card in the mail at her employer's address. Now she had an ID with an address *and* a photograph. She was a fully realized person, on paper.

Pavan Varma finishes the story with a beam. 'With that Aadhaar card, she comes back to the bank and says, "*Now* can you please open my account?"'

In India, there are still so many things in everyday life for which you need to 'know someone'. For the rich that someone is usually a notch or two below themselves in class, a person, usually referred to, a little unkindly, as a 'tout', with expert knowledge of how a particular court or government department works. When it comes to the working class, though, it is usually the rich, their employers, who they turn to as fixers to provide entry into the system.

Neera, in her late fifties now, says she grew up with the idea that, as an employer of domestic help, this assistance was part of the deal. Her father, a personal secretary in the Prime Minister's Office when Jawaharlal Nehru was leading the country, and her mother, did the same for their own workers. 'That was how my parents raised me,' she said. Pavan followed her lead.

Eight years ago, just after India passed a law prohibiting children thirteen and under from working as maids, the Varmas' driver brought his ten-year-old brother-in-law to them and asked them to find him work. Neera and Pavan declined and instead they invited him to stay in their servants' compound and enrolled him in school. He is now in his last year of secondary school, and practises English with guests who come to the house to meet the Varmas. Another time, the daughter of a maid died during childbirth, married too young despite Neera's lectures to the young woman's mother on the subject. Her children have ended up at the Sunder Nagar house, to be taken care of by their grandmother, still working at the Varmas' bungalow.

In recent years, Indian domestic workers and employers have begun to speak wistfully of having a more cut-and-dried contractual relationship, 'like in the West', where high salaries are paid for timely, efficient work, and personal entanglements, so inconvenient at times, are eschewed. But the building of networks with the rich and powerful remains one of the most important fringe benefits of domestic work, a chance for women and men to find the kind of patrons who are still vital to helping their children become confidently middle class. Spots in schools and universities, jobs even, can rarely be secured by money alone. Networks matter. It is only the most educated and savvy workers who would choose a high salary alone over the services of a guide to walk with them through India's many circles of bureaucracy to get into school, get into college, find a job, or, in the worst-case scenario, to navigate the entrails of the city's criminal courts.

Pavan tells me with pride that none of the children of their servants now work as servants. In fact, both the daughters of a man who worked for their family for decades have gone on to become doctors.

'And they're married to doctors!' he tells me. 'They have gone from lower class to middle class.'

In India, it is easy to judge what makes a bad employer. But it can be harder to decide if someone is a good employer. By the standard of pay, the Varmas are not among the more generous of Delhi employers. At the time we met, Chutki was earning about 6,500 rupees a month, much less than the 10,000 rupees then typical across much of South Delhi for live-in help, or the 15,000 to 20,000 rupees that expats pay for housekeeping. But if the Varmas don't pay high salaries, they do help secure school admissions, pay for school fees, and turn a blind eye to any number of visiting relatives staying in the servants' block and being fed from their kitchen. They act as a miniature welfare state, a vital role in a country where most have little access to a safety net.

♦

Whoever named Sunder Nagar contented himself with merely affixing the word 'pretty' to the neighbourhood's name, which is accurate enough as far as any Delhi neighbourhood deserves that appellation. But whoever named Uttam Nagar, a bustling neighbourhood in West Delhi, can certainly be accused of false advertising. Rather than inserting 'Best', into the name, Average Nagar, or Congested Nagar, would have been more truthful choices. The paint on the two- and three-storey homes here has for the most part turned a dun-grey colour. The homes here are small and sit slap up against each other. A couple of them would fit comfortably into a typical family plot in Sunder Nagar and they are rarely built with living quarters set aside for servants, as wealthier homes tend to be. But even so, maid brokers, who mark one of the biggest changes in the hiring of servants in India in past years, flourish here.

The shops in Uttam Nagar stock the staples of price-conscious lower-middle-class life: large jute sacks of cut-rate basmati rice that nevertheless hope to evoke the extravagance of Mughal emperors with names like Kohinoor and Red Fort. A large poster looks like it may be asking for votes for the man emblazoned on it, but actually it is advertising his forty years in the grocery business and his excellent prices. A small sign on a private doctor's clinic tells you in (a highly economical) six words everything you need to know about the health of the upwardly mobile in the city: 'Sugar testing! Pregnancy test! Nebulizer available!'

It is 2014, the weekend after India elected a new prime minister, Narendra Modi, and Om Prakash Verma (no relation to the Sunder Nagar Varmas) is watching the frenzied footage of the victory parade of supporters of the Hindu nationalist Bharatiya Janata Party in the Indian capital. He is sitting in his front room, which is almost completely filled by a sofa and a bed covered with a bedspread printed with sunflowers.

The sixty-two-year-old Om Prakash Verma, wearing a blue shirt and a checked lungi, and his wife do their own housework. Not so long ago he bought an expensive mop with a built-in spinner for 2,000 rupees with which he cleans their three-room house. In your sixties, he explains, it's not so easy to get down on your hands and knees with a roughly woven pochha to wipe the floor. His wife does the cooking as she always has. But for a brief while the family—or at least one branch of it—had joined the ranks of many new middle-class Indians who have live-in help.

Verma was a 'colonizer'. He would put together 8 or 10-acre properties in West Delhi, cut them into individual plots, and sell them on commission on behalf of the farmers who owned them. This was in the late 1980s, as the world was inching towards the moment when tanks would cross the border between Iraq and Kuwait. Those tanks sent oil prices soaring in India, eating into the crude-importing country's foreign reserves, and leading to the decisions in 1991 that many economists believe marked a decisive turn from socialism and raised the curtain on India as a stage for global business. But Mr Verma knows that entrepreneurial zeal, at least the sort focused around land, existed well before that moment. For a time, Mr Verma became a man to know in this part of Delhi. Once he attended a birthday party at a Delhi farmhouse at which a prime minister was present. Then things took a downward turn.

Mr Verma's strained growl of a voice is the audible marker of the thing that put the brakes on his dream of becoming 'rich at high speed'—throat cancer. He stopped colonizing. As an entrepreneur, he had no health insurance, and no pension. Perhaps he remembered with a pang the job in the postal service he quit to make his foray into real estate, a move that distressed his government clerk father. He was forced to sell the land he had acquired for himself in the course of his colonizing. That's what happens when you have cancer and are the breadwinner of the family—and have a daughter you're duty-bound to get married. Things improved when, through a matrimonial ad, the family found a woman whose stars matched the slightly unlucky astrological aspects hanging over Mr Verma's younger son. Not only that, their prospective daughter-in-law had a staff position as a trauma nurse at the country's largest public-run hospital. By this time, Mr Verma had a new appreciation of the value of a government job.

'Salaries used to be 10,000 to 15,000 rupees, now it's 50,000 or 60,000,' says Mr Verma. It also used to be that, when a daughter-in-law came, the in-laws could relax. But when your daughter-in-law is earning more than your son, things play out a little differently. Mr Verma's younger son had been working in sales for the multinational food corporation Nestlé but he was a temp worker on contract, not a full-time employee like his wife. The new daughter-in-law did not come downstairs from their 300 square-foot second-floor apartment to cook and clean for her in-laws, she cooked for herself and her husband. And her in-laws accepted this, if grudgingly.

'We never think we are doing our own work when our daughter-in-law should be doing it. If she doesn't understand her duty what are we to say?' said Mr Verma. 'We don't want to compel anyone to do our housework.'

When the couple had their first child, Mr Verma's son watched the boy after his wife returned to work. But after their second son was born, the couple brought home a girl from Jharkhand to their flat for 1,800 rupees a month. Many Indians may wonder why they didn't rely on the built-in babysitting resource on the ground floor: the grandparents. But if a daughter-in-law can renege on her traditional role of being a devoted servant to her in-laws, then they too can resist providing the anytime, anywhere babysitting many Indian grandparents provide. These familial reciprocal arrangements can be claustrophobic, creating debts and obligations—turning to the market may have seemed a more liberating, fuss-free option to Mr Verma's daughter-in-law. And live-in help was being temptingly advertised everywhere by that year: in flyers delivered with the newspaper, on posters on walls, on the internet.

It's not what Mr Verma or his sons grew up with. Nor is it what his daughter-in-law grew up with. He tells me more than once that marrying into his family and moving to Uttam Nagar was a step up for her, that she hails from a 'mix-up type colony', a settlement of jhuggis. No one there would have had a servant. More likely, some of the people in her old neighbourhood might have been servants.

'These days young people are rising up so fast, their status and their parents' status is no longer the same,' said Mr Verma.

In recent decades, millions of families have moved into the terra firma of the upper ranks of India's middle class, defined by some economists as the ability to spend above $20 per family member a day, measured in purchasing power parity, or at about 40,000 rupees a month for a family of four (when someone in India describes themselves in English, and in a certain kind of accent, as middle-class, you can safely assign them to the ranks of elite). Those Delhi residents who do remain in domestic work are themselves at least lower middle-class, meaning a family living on at least 15,000 or 20,000 rupees a month, and expect salaries that first-time employers of help are unwilling to pay. Yet despite this apparent demand-supply problem, enough women are taking up domestic service that, from less than 1 per cent in 2000, their percentage jumped to 2 per cent of total female employment in just slightly over a decade. At times, when droughts and other crises send more women out of their villages to look for jobs than usual, the share of working women in cities who are employed as nannies, maids and cooks in private homes can occasionally cross 10 per cent.

How did this happen when many of those who were servants need no longer be servants? The market stepped into the breach, pairing someone from the new middle class with someone from among the millions of Indians who are still extremely poor. It might pair, for example, a family with conservative Haryana Jat roots in Delhi to a teenage tribal girl whose Hindi is rudimentary, whose housekeeping skills have been honed in a village hut—where life is lived largely outside—and who has no way of knowing that in a house with more than one room, you are expected to knock when you see a closed door. The market, like politics, is a whimsical matchmaker.

The junior Vermas had imagined someone different, someone more citified who would slot easily into their household and make it run more smoothly, not someone who was homesick, and whom they had to cajole into staying put. These were perhaps tall expectations, given the men and women behind the ads for servants were competing largely on price, at monthly salaries that were about the cost of the Vermas' state-of-the-art mop. But then, the Vermas were new to the world of live-in help. They were aghast at the prices asked by Delhi cooks and cleaners: 5,000 rupees, even 10,000 rupees. It seemed to them that if a skilled nurse with years of experience at the country's top hospital was worth 50,000 rupees, then shouldn't 2,000 rupees be adequate for an unlettered girl who would spend her day playing with a child?

On practically the very first day, the maid sent to the Verma home told the family that she didn't want to be a maid, that she had been hustled into coming to the city, and that her parents were looking for her. Alarmed, the family sent her back, giving the broker an earful.

'These guys push them into coming, or they buy them, I don't know how they bring them here,' says Mr Verma. 'You could call what they do human trafficking.'

◆

The most recent official figures claim India has around 3.5 million domestic workers. That total, which includes chauffeurs and security guards but wouldn't include childminders or cleaners who describe themselves as self-employed rather than the employee of a family, is clearly an underestimate. But, as with most things, no one really knows the true figures. The head of a new government skills council set up to improve working conditions for domestic help estimates the number to be around 20 million, the *Wall Street Journal* has reported. That is certainly an overestimate given that the female workforce in urban India—where domestic workers are concentrated—is about 22 million, many of whom work in health, education, construction and other occupations. A recent report from consulting firm KPMG forecasts that the ranks of domestic workers will be nearly 8 million in 2017, but doesn't explain how it arrived at that figure. There are about 18 million households in India whose monthly spending puts them in the top 5 per cent by consumption (and therefore, by correlation, also at the top in terms of income). But it's not likely that all of these households are employers of domestic help, given that membership in this class begins at about 11,000 rupees and 25,000 rupees of spending for a family of four in rural and urban India, respectively. It's likely that the number of households who employ help in India number no more than five to seven million, which means the numbers of women and men working as cooks, cleaners and childminders could be in the range of the KPMG estimate.

Linked as it is to inequality, the demand for servants is also driven by changes that are welcome and beneficial. Indians are becoming better off. More women, at least in urban India, are experiencing the freedom to study further and to work outside the home. At some points in the recent past the female workforce as a whole shrank—particularly in rural India—but from the early 1990s to now, the story of Indian cities has been one of steady growth in the numbers of working women. The number of women in cities of working age increased some 40 per cent between 2001 and 2011, while the numbers of those women who were employed increased by over 70 per cent during the same decade. And it is this development, even more than the greater general prosperity, that is driving the urban demand for maids and nannies. Because for Indian men to work or lead full lives outside the home, paid domestic help was never a requirement. As one Bengali woman pointed out in a 1924 essay, 'For the sake of their family life and for their own advantage they have kept women as servants...the term "goddess" is nothing but an elaborate joke!' Men, regardless of caste or class, have always had a servant—a woman who was, literally, one of the family.

In the third book of the Mahabharat, Draupadi retires with another woman, Satyabhama, to a chamber for some girl talk. Satyabhama, Krishna's wife, is trying to hold on to her man, but is finding it mighty hard what with all the milkmaids about, batting their eyelids at the blue-skinned, flute-playing avatar of the god Vishnu. She asks Draupadi the secret to her happy marriage with the five Pandava brothers: is it a love potion or a spell? A particular kind of kajal? Some anti-ageing product? Beauteous Draupadi is not amused. A husband whose wife gets up to such tricks begins 'to dread her like a serpent ensconced in his sleeping chamber', she says.

'One cannot obtain happiness here by means that are easy,' Draupadi tells her friend, who probably begins to wish she hadn't said anything in the first place, because now Draupadi, possibly India's first domestic goddess, recites a litany of all the things she does to win her matrimonial family's undying love and loyalty.

'I never bathe, or eat or sleep till he that is my husband hath bathed, eaten or slept, till, in fact, our attendants have bathed, or eaten or slept,' says Draupadi. (Now multiply by five.) 'Whether returning from the field, the forest, or the town, hastily rising up I always salute my husband with water and a seat. I always keep the house and all household articles and the food that is to be taken well-ordered and clean. Carefully do I keep the rice, and serve the food at the proper time.'

Draupadi's views are reiterated in many other Hindu texts. These ancient works elaborate that while prayer, study and tending the sacred fire are a man's route to racking up good karma, and eventually nirvana, for a woman, caring for her husband, mainly through caring for her home, is the route to spiritual freedom, as religious scholar Julia Leslie writes in her analysis of an eighteenth-century work on the ideal Hindu woman. Perhaps this traditional view of housework—as not merely women's work, but an almost sacred calling—is what explains why India has long had one of the most skewed distributions of household work between men and women in the world.

A 2014 Organization for Economic Cooperation and Development report on how men and women in some two dozen countries spend their days found that Indian women do about thirty-five hours of housekeeping chores a week compared to two hours a week for Indian men—in other words, they do about fifteen times more housework than Indian men, the worst such ratio in the report. Indian women also did more unpaid housework than women in any other country featured in the report. It must be said, things are pretty bad in Turkey as well—there, women do twelve times as much housework as men. At the other end of the spectrum, in Sweden, women do just three hours more of housework a week than men. British women do twice as much housework as their men, while American women do 1.5 times more.

Still, thirty-five hours of housework a week is likely a vast improvement compared to what women had to do in the past, when it was much more common for families to follow complex rules for preserving ritual (as well as actual) cleanliness that made housekeeping both a confining and highly time-consuming affair. For example, if you left the kitchen in the midst of food preparation and went to a less clean part of the house, you had to bathe and change again before returning to the kitchen.

Indian villages had a system where people of different castes carried out work for the local landowner—say cutting his hair—in return for grain. But very often these were personal services or work that had to be done outside, like washing and feeding animals. The top work, and particularly the cooking, was always done by the women of the home because of the abiding fear of contamination, and this could be onerous in joint families of old.

'There were eight maidservants in the house, but all of them lived outside the household,' wrote Rassundari Devi in her memoir, *Amar Jiban*, published in 1876 and believed to be the first autobiography in Bengali. In it, she recalled cooking for as many as two dozen people each day. 'There was nobody to do the household chores in the inner quarters. I was the only one.'

In the early twentieth century, in fact, indoor housework was so clearly reserved for the women of a family or else those of a 'decent' caste, that *Harijan*, the weekly founded by Mahatma Gandhi that was dedicated to writing about efforts to advance the rights of 'untouchables', now better known as Dalits, would report on cases of people from communities usually shunned by caste Hindus being hired as servants as a mark of progress. One 1933 headline proudly reported that four landowning families in Tamil Nadu's Tanjore district had hired Harijans as servants.

Just as work outside the home in India has traditionally been marked by a caste system that put one group of people permanently at the service of others, within the family, too, there is a caste system. Men being Brahmins in their own homes, regardless of their caste, are naturally excluded from any work at all. The work is done by women, but not by all the women in a household equally. And this is where the sharp rivalries between women begin. In general, it has been the junior-most woman, usually a new daughter-in-law, who has been at the service not just of men, but also other women who can pull rank on her. Among women, the ability to hand off housework to another woman, has long been both a prerequisite of and a marker of advancement.

A mother-in-law's authority is fairly accepted, she need do little to prove it. There can only be one mother-in-law (or only one that counts anyway, the mother of the man). But other women in the family must generally jockey with one another to lighten their own load and make someone else's heavier. For younger women in the family—a sister, or a daughter, or a wife—the arrival of a new woman into the family is a chance to elevate her own status. This is why in India, you learn to parse sisters-in-law pretty early on. A wife's sister is a completely different order of sister-in-law from a husband's sister, or nanad, who is obviously senior; the jethani, the wife of the oldest brother in the family, outranks the devrani, or wife of the youngest brother in a family.

Even highly acclimatized British memsahibs acquired this knowledge, and used it as a yardstick during the Raj to measure how well or how poorly an Indian acquaintance was treating them. In her autobiography, Flora Annie Steel, the wife of a Scotsman in the Indian Civil Service, described a visit to a Muslim princess. The princess, dressed to Steel's eyes in a dirty outfit, greeted her while 'chewing and spitting paan in a most unceremonious style and after a while actually had the cheek to tell a woman, whose look betrayed her sweeper caste, to sit down beside me'. Offended, Steel rose to depart, delivering this message in courtly Urdu to another woman present, 'She has treated me as she would not dare to treat her youngest sister-in-law.' By way of explanation for British readers, Steel, or perhaps her editor, added in parenthesis, 'the height of rudeness'.

Thanks to the march of women's rights in India, the benefits of which have so far accrued to some more than others, women who might encounter one another within the same household have far greater opportunity to recalibrate their status than before, which leads to more conflict, and less female solidarity. A young woman who has married into a family need no longer defer to the seniority of a husband's older sister, or a long-time elderly retainer of her in-laws in a multigenerational haveli, as she once might have. In some cases, she may no longer be as deferential as she might once have been to her mother-in-law. If she arrives with enough money or the right kind of job, or even just a greater feeling of entitlement, she may be able to divest herself of housework or make someone else do it. That someone might be a senior sister-in-law, or even a mother-in-law. Or that someone might be a maid.

Whoever it is, she will behave with her in much the same way that mothers-in-law and sisters-in-law used to behave with a new wife: she will stand at her elbow and point out everything she does wrong. She has to. The borders between the categories of wife and cook, mother and nanny, sister-in-law and maid are now even more porous than many women would like to admit, more jalis than walls. The right to criticize and scold is a marker that you have ascended in the family hierarchy, and in a hierarchy so apt to shift—rare though it is, some women have risen to the status of madam in families to which they entered as maid—you cannot forego any stamp of authority.

◆

Knock firmly enough to not be mistaken for background noise but not so loud as to seem peremptory. That would not do at all. Don't keep knocking. Give madam time to answer before you knock again. Listen carefully at the door between knocks in case she is calling for you to enter.

'Knock twice, not three times. If someone banged your door hard wouldn't you get cross?' says the trainer, Preeti, a young woman in her early twenties who has a bachelor's degree in political science, a degree that is no doubt useful in preparing the group of women she now instructs on the art of being a superior maid. 'Madam gets cross too. Knock on the door lightly like this and ask for permission to come in.'

Suddenly, there is a loud bang on the door, startling Preeti who is in the middle of coaching a diffident woman who alternates between too-soft and too-loud knocking. The kudawala has come to pick up the garbage, which he asks for in a sullen tone, with apparently little care for how his knocking is received. Much giggling ensues among the women at this fine example of how not to knock.

The knocking class is taking place at a small house in a suburb of Gurgaon (the city was recently officially renamed Gurugram but few people use that name) rented by The Maids' Company, a firm set up like so many others to try and earn a profit from the demand for help, though it hopes to do so in a more ethical way. They want to do good, in addition to doing well. In return for wages pegged to the local minimum wage, a rarity for maids, the company tries to take the rough edges off the young Bengali and Bihari migrant women it recruits and reduce the amount of time madam will have to spend showing someone how the home of an upwardly mobile family works.

For the most part, Preeti's instructions highlight the vast differences between the lives of the maids and their would-be employers. Every once in a while, though, she draws parallels between the lives of her apprehensive recruits and their imaginary employers. In relation to each other, they may not be equals; but in relation to their husbands, to men in general, they are equally unequal.

Lovely and her friend Renu are two teenagers who arrive in the middle of the knocking class—they immediately stand out from the other maids who are mostly older and married—both look rather like memsahibs, or the children of memsahibs, themselves. In fact, when Lovely went home to her village around Eid a few months earlier, many in the village, clocking her jeans and figure-skimming tops and carefully threaded eyebrows, believed her to be one. For family members, on the other hand, who know she is a maid in the distant city and not a memsahib, her attire at times evokes dismay. 'What is it you are wearing?' a great-aunt once asked Lovely, eyeing her blouse and cropped pants. 'Capris,' Lovely informed her. 'Hai Allah,' came the response. 'No chunni?'

The other women at The Maids' Company wear their oiled hair tied tightly back, red sindoor in their partings to signal their married status, and are dressed in slightly frumpy, loose-fitting salwar kameez or saris with loud prints. Lovely and Renu wear their hair long and loose, like the madams do, and have carefully tailored outfits. Lovely talks nineteen to the dozen—her younger sister already works as a nanny for The Maids' Company, and it was Lovely's idea to bring her friend Renu here, as well as change her own job, since her long-time madam is being obstinate over a raise. 'They'll spend 5,000 rupees on themselves at a club in one night,' she vents to me later, 'but if we ask for 2,000 rupees more, it's too much money.'

Renu, with her round baby face, fair skin and light-brown hair, looks like a college student and it transpires that she is, for her this is a way station. She wants to work till she saves enough for her tuition fees that increased suddenly, soon after she joined college. It turns out she too is married, even though there is no sindoor in her brown hair. She clearly has mixed feelings about being here, she feels it a bit of a comedown, and as the interviewer presses her about what sort of work she's willing to take on, her reluctance becomes more apparent.

'When the baby is sleeping what will you do?' asks the interviewer, a woman in her late thirties.

'I'll do odd jobs around the house,' says Renu.

'What odd jobs will you do? Will you knead atta for rotis? For twelve hours, you won't only be doing childcare, especially if the child goes to school for three or four hours. And tell me what you won't do.'

'Sweeping and mopping,' Renu responds swiftly.

'For sure, there will be a cook and cleaning woman. But suppose she goes on holiday. Would you do the sweeping then?'

Renu mulls this over, looking increasingly grave.

'I guess I could do that. But I won't do toilets.'

Lovely senses this may not go over well and tries to persuade her that rich people's toilets are different. 'They're so clean,' she says with enthusiasm. 'They even drink their tea in there!' But Renu is not convinced.

Yet it is Lovely who drops out after a day or two—her madam comes around on the raise, perhaps having sussed out salaries in the market. Preeti doesn't know that and she broods on Lovely's absence, feeling she may have been too hard on her in the training, trying to mimic the kind of situation she might encounter in a home, where frequent carping or a sharp tone aren't uncommon. It seems a young city-bred woman won't accept either with the equanimity of an older migrant, particularly one with young children to think about. They think they deserve better.

'That day I scolded her. And she wasn't feeling well also,' says Preeti. 'I wanted to see how she would react, if she was capable of handling a scolding. Her work was very good but she can't listen to criticism. She really feels it. Her attitude is, "Take me as I am."'

◆

Soon after I moved to Delhi in 2005, my parents retired and began embarking on the project of setting up a household with enough staff to provide round-the-clock care for an invalid—my grandmother. After attempts to hire a live-in person locally failed, my parents turned to a Bengali maid agent to supplement their part-time staff. I was puzzled and fascinated by his work, and how he found the women he brought us in exchange for a fee. Did he go door-to-door? Or go to villages that had suffered some kind of calamity? I hoped one day to travel with him to the source of the maids that my parents hired and trace the thread that connected my parents' home in East Delhi to a distant West Bengal village.

However, by the time I began working on this book in 2012, this

broker said he had all but retired from that work, citing a newish rural
employment programme as one among many reasons he had come to
find recruiting rather challenging. So I followed other threads across
the city of Delhi to villages in Jharkhand, West Bengal and Uttar
Pradesh, and then back again, until I had seen how a chance encounter
in a village could form the beginning of a long chain that connected
a village to a broker, and a broker to a sahib or madam. I saw, too,
how sometimes that connection ended in a crime, and sometimes
it ended in a small or large step up the class ladder. Despite having
reported across India for years, I was finally able to understood what
poverty was in a much more tangible way, not only as a class or a
social condition, but as a specific relationship between the number of
hours worked and quantity of food that could be eaten as a result,
and how the difficult alchemy of turning large numbers of the first
into a large quantity of the second was fuelling the desire of many
families in villages to see their daughters become maids.

♦

To be a servant in India today is in many ways an enterprise with a
much more uncertain outcome than in the past. If the relationships
that prevailed in the past between sahibs and servants in Indian cities
were plotted on a graph, I suspect they would make for a fairly flat
line, with small variations from one household to the next. In the past
the reward for being someone's servant was mainly reliable room and
board. But now these relations make for a much more jagged line, full
of peaks and troughs.

A job as a servant in India, even at the lower end of the salary range,
can, on the one hand, provide a very real opportunity of extracting
a family from the ranks of the millions of extremely poor. But it
could also be a portal into near enslavement. Nowhere is that more
true than in Delhi, the city state which has a per capita income that
is three times the national average.

Through luck and the right networks, a woman might circulate
in a micro-economy populated by foreign-returned Indians and expats,
or affluent and progressive local families, in whose homes she can
sometimes earn as much as 30,000 rupees a month plus room and
board. Overtime and other perks can bring her earnings close to that

of a nurse at the All India Institute of Medical Sciences (AIIMS) or a professor at Delhi University. Such a job would allow her, before she retired, to own a home of her own, educate her children, and help them become firmly white-collar.

An unluckier woman, or more likely a young teen, might be recruited by an aunt or a brother-in-law or another relative close enough to win the confidence of her parents, but not so close that they would be genuinely concerned about her fate once they had collected the fee for finding her. Once in the city, they would probably leave her in the hands of a broker, barely an acquaintance, who would in turn place her in a home whose address might never be passed on to her parents. She might not see her village again until her family, alarmed by the fact that she had not returned for festival after festival (or sent money), would borrow train fare from friends and neighbours to come to the city to look for her. It's a sequence of events that has happened often enough that a small group of non-profits founded in the last fifteen years focus largely on reuniting parents with girls taken to the city to be maids.

Cut off in this way from the outside world, many of these young women have become victims of violence ranging from beating to sexual assault in the homes they work in. Increasingly, and disturbingly, it is women—the same women who have been freed to have careers outside the home by the help they have hired—who are the perpetrators of this violence and who appear as villains in newspaper stories about abused maids. In one, a public school teacher is arrested for beating her maid to death. In another, a thin and wizened girl is found at the home of the spokesperson of a multinational, her ears so swollen that doctors diagnose it as a boxer's injury. In a third, a trauma nurse at AIIMS is accused of giving her maid a black eye.

Some blame what appears to be an increasing level of violence against maids as a sign of the inability of women to wield power over others as well as men always have. New to this whole power business, women lack finesse, they claim; where one slap would suffice, they rain down a barrage of them. Others blame the nouveau riche or the 'new middle class' for the trafficking of girls to the capital, the forced work and miserly wages, the beatings and even the killings of domestic workers.

Occasionally, much, much more rarely, the transgressions go in the other direction. A lone elderly man or woman will be murdered by a newly hired servant. A family is tied up by the newly-hired unvetted help dispatched by a maid broker, and beaten and robbed. Or, the most common of these reverse class transgressions—upon a death, a much trusted and loved old retainer will unexpectedly come forward with a will that the family knows nothing about, bearing the unmistakable if shaky scrawl of the now deceased family member. If the old retainer is a woman, she may even tell authorities she was the deceased's 'all but in name' wife.

For the most part, these dramas remain hidden until they have built to a climax and end up on the front pages of newspapers, or in courtrooms, reminding us briefly that despite the promise of its clean, carefully kept, dust-free interiors, the home is no refuge from the rage and conflict we think of as belonging, along with dirt, to the street.

◆

In trying to understand what is happening in our homes, we find ourselves unconsciously expressing old prejudices. The new middle class, after all, is the old poor made good. They have 'forgotten their place'. The women, too, have forgotten their place, crossing the Lakshman rekha, the line that divides the good woman at home from the bad women in the world. If she can be unwomanly in this regard, then it is no surprise that she lacks self-control in her anger.

But if this parcelling out of blame is based on longstanding prejudice, it is not entirely misplaced. The newly empowered and newly enriched in India are not bursting with compassion and generosity for others, for the most part. And this should be no surprise. When the government and the law have little to tell you about how to treat people that you find yourself in a position of power over, then you allow yourself to be guided by what you have seen done before, what you still see others around you doing. It is the old rich and the old powerful who have taught the newly rich and the newly powerful that it is the ability to mistreat, to talk down, to shout, to waste the time of others—*and to get away with it*—that truly distinguishes India's haves from its have-nots.

The relations most Indians have with their servants grew out of the feudal rights of rural landlords over people who owed them service in return for being tenant farmers, or who owed them service because of their caste group. As such, they are dotted through with signposts that signalled the superiority of the employers over the people who worked for them. We eat first, they later, often out of food portioned out for them; we live in the front, they in the back; we sit on chairs and they on the floor; we drink from glasses and ceramic plates and they from ones made of steel and set aside for them; we call them by their names, and they address us by titles, sometimes formal, sometimes familial: sir/ma'am, sahib/memsahib, bauji, maji, didi, aunty, baba.

The gulf between what we say we believe in, as members of the country's elite, and how we actually live is so immense that it doesn't even merit being called hypocrisy. Hypocrisy requires at least some awareness of the great distance between one's actions and one's claims. And nowhere else is this distance so visible—and yet we seem blind to it—as when we are at home. Not that we lack sincerity in those battles we do wage, and the causes we think worthy of taking up; perhaps it's more a matter of difficulty knitting together the multiple identities we inhabit in the course of our day and through our lives, through which we are sometimes the oppressor, and sometimes the oppressed.

Across Delhi, for example, as many of us became wealthy enough to redevelop modest homes into much larger ones, we did not increase the amount of space we were willing to give to live-in help in those homes. Instead, the help's quarters often shrank and made way for sprawling marble bathrooms, walk-in closets and gigantic living rooms where the people who rent or buy these new apartments—people like us—discuss with our friends, who live in similar kinds of houses, how India can lift herself out of poverty. Meanwhile, the servants live in a boiling tin shack of 60 square feet on the roof. Adults like to joke about the difficulties their toddlers face in grasping the concept of sharing, but most grown-ups clearly haven't mastered it either.

Such jarring contrasts between word and deed are everywhere. In homes built with public funds for the government employees of a nation whose Constitution commits to fostering equality and fighting caste discrimination, the bathrooms have separate doors through which the toilet cleaner is expected to enter; across the capital you will find

homes frequently have 'service lanes', back alleys, to be used by the
help so they don't appear at and sully the front door.

People who claim to be free of caste bias don't allow women who
clean bathrooms to cook for them, citing hygiene. And left-leaning
professors at elite Delhi universities, who usually lament the effects
of privatization and unfettered capitalism on the Indian workforce,
suddenly highlight the importance of paying the 'market rate' when
they think a friend is paying her maid too much. Closer to home, and
more painfully, I noticed that in my own family, which was tolerant
of a wide array of cross-caste and cross-religion marriages, including
that of my parents, separate crockery was put aside for maids and
other service workers, again for 'hygiene' reasons.

The new masters—the new rich, and newly empowered women—
are drawing on this long history of how masters treat servants in
India. But why then, if masters are behaving the way masters always
have, do we feel as if something has changed, as if relations are
more prickly, more prone to erupt into conflict than they were in
the past? When Indian social relations were more static, they may
have conveyed an appearance of greater peace and social harmony,
even if this placidity was one of brutal oppression of one group by
another, and the acceptance of this oppression. In times when women
accepted the total domination of men, the young accepted the total
domination of the old, lower castes the total domination of upper
castes, or servants the total domination of masters, the surface calm
might have persuaded those sitting in positions of privilege that all
was well with the world. A society in motion, which offers the chance
for reinvention and advancement, meanwhile, can look disturbingly
disordered.

Masters may be behaving as they always have, but the people
playing those roles are not the same as they were in the past, and
the people who find themselves slotted into the role of servants, for
now, eyeing the changes in who gets to be a master, no longer believe
that that is all they can be. Many employers may still be vastly richer
than their help, but that is by no means true of all employers. For
some, one catastrophe would lose them their place among the ranks
of the middle class. Meanwhile, for some domestic help, it would take
just one well-settled child to allow them to consider having domestic

help of their own. A growing proportion of the people who are in domestic service come from all different points of the class and income scale, sometimes much closer to the lower ranks of their one-per cent employers than to the very bottom ranks of the 99 per cent.

These workers have expectations that are more expansive than those of workers of the past, and they no longer consider themselves far beneath the people they work for, sometimes referring to their newly middle-class employers with open contempt. 'These people have 25,000 or 30,000 rupees a month, that's all,' said one domestic worker at a rights group meeting in West Delhi, speaking of her employers. Another, at the same meeting, sniffs, 'At home my employer hangs around in an old, torn petticoat. If she doesn't have anything better to wear herself then what will she give to you?' On the other hand, the wealthy families of South Delhi are spoken of with almost fondness, as one woman says, 'Those people know how to keep servants.'

The cadre of aspirants to being the new masters is growing. But the spoils that can land you in such a spot—the good schools, the good colleges, the good jobs—are finite. And so, the effort to get somewhere can put you on a collision course with someone else who wants those exact same things. Things will get worse for some, and better for others, and it's not quite as clear as it used to be who these winners and losers will be. Against these shifts, someone else's gain can feel like your loss—a rising tide doesn't actually raise all, it submerges some.

People always imagine the class struggle to be something that takes place outdoors, in streets, with masses of workers waving placards and storming the factory gates. Perhaps some battles, especially those that involve only men, or specific segments of the working class, take place in that way. But when the battles are of women against men, women against other women, and servants against masters, then it is the home, not the streets, that becomes the front line. But these conflicts, which come to a head in the capital and other buzzing, growing cities like it, don't begin there. Their seeds are planted thousands of miles away, when a family in a farming village or a relief camp turns its gaze towards the distant capital in the hope of something better.

PART I

Harvest

ATHGAMA, JHARKHAND

THE GUMANI RIVER COMES DOWN from the Rajmahal Hills of Jharkhand, where hundreds of years ago a son of the Mughal emperor Shah Jahan set up a rival kingdom against his younger brothers. One of those younger brothers was Aurangzeb, at whose court the Italian traveller Niccolao Manucci wound up working as a physician in the seventeenth century, affording Manucci the opportunity to share many of his observations regarding Indian servants in his memoirs (unlike what might be expected of a foreign traveller writing about India today, these were mostly pejorative of the help and sympathetic to their masters).

It's now fashionable to revile Aurangzeb, but if not for his predatory style of ruling—he took much of the Deccan from Southern rulers—the India of today might be substantially smaller than most nationalistic Indians would like it to be. Aurangzeb's regnal name, Alamgir or 'he who seized the world', tells you everything about how the sibling rivalry between him and his aforementioned brother ended. This brother, Shah Shuja, was unwise to take on a man with such a name, and his venture was unlucky from the start. The worst of it was when a fire burned through the zenana taking with it Shah Shuja's favourite wife, or perhaps his least favourite wife (possibly both, since more than seventy women died in the fire, according to some accounts). After Shah Shuja's huge army of chainmail-clad elephants proved no match for Aurangzeb's military strategy, the older brother fled to Arakan in Burma where he was apparently assassinated.

All that's left of Shah Shuja's time in this part of India is a small marble hall in the drab district capital of Rajmahal. Its scalloped arches overlook the broad grey expanse of the Ganga, so very near the end of its long journey to the Bengal delta. By the time the Ganga reaches Rajmahal, it has already absorbed the Gumani River under a different name. Over here, the fused river is wide and treacherous after the monsoon rains; British indigo dye planters and their wives often fell from boats and drowned as they rounded the little mahal.

But as temperatures soar after the December rice harvest and Christmas celebrations, the rivers retreat. The Gumani shrinks into a little silvery, snakelike thing, uncovering a blanket of fine golden grains on its banks. The people in Athgama, whose farmlands stretch to the river, call this githil or balu. In the city, the builders call it ret. The English newspapers call it sand, and have bestowed on its harvesters the epithet 'sand mafia'.

Until a few years ago, the people of Athgama village had only two harvests. In March, they cut the wheat that ripples in a golden wave towards the low hills in the distance. Farmers with spare money rent the services of a thresher for an hour or two, filling 50-kilogram sacks to the brim with flaxen kernels, leaving chaff in the fields to be gathered for kindling by women. A month later, they round out the winter harvest by picking and drying the purple-flowered chana dal, known here as bhoot. Then there will be no more planting till the rains come. In November, they cut down the rice that grows lush in a year of good rains, a green carpet that is punctuated by gently curving date palms, like so many colons strewn across the landscape. But in recent years they have discovered another harvest—the golden dregs of the Gumani River.

One warm April day, I sit on the Gumani banks with the entrepreneur—or sand mafioso, as some would have it—who brought this much-needed work to Athgama. Most days, during the time of the sand harvest, this young man, about twenty, is to be found here, wearing his work uniform of bright blue shorts and a threadbare white shirt with an American eagle on it. Sometimes he cradles a baby belonging to a woman working down on the bank in one arm, his account-book on his lap. Other times an infant is left sleeping beside him, as he jots down numbers next to the names of the people who have loaded each tractor. He makes these notes in tiny but tidy handwriting learned not at the local public school but at a school run by Christian missionaries in a neighbouring town.

As we speak, he watches the bank. A tractor that appears to be departing without paying for its load of sand sets off a hail of shouts and his deputies on the bank run to intercept it by planting themselves in front of the vehicle. I'm reminded of parking attendants in Delhi, who position themselves by the rear right tire of cars as they reverse, to prevent unscrupulous sorts from leaving without paying. The reward for such vigilance is generally 20 rupees; on some occasions the price is a crushed foot.

In the distance, in a field that can be seen from the river, the sandman's parents are cutting wheat, their land among the last to be shorn. His father owns around three-fourths of an acre—about the same as most people around here—but it's a good location because it means that when rains are scant, the family can come down to the river and haul water up its banks to their fields. In Athgama, three-fourths of the families qualify as poor, owning less than an acre of unirrigated land. Whether your land is irrigated or unirrigated plays a role in your poverty designation by the government. The wheat and rice harvests wrested from these small parcels, generally worth the equivalent of an income of 70,000 rupees a year, have to feed five or six people.

In Athgama, to eat is to eat rice. Breakfast is puffed rice with chopped onions and tomatoes and a drizzle of mustard oil. Lunch and dinner are a heap of rice with a little dal, a few spoonfuls of fried potatoes or chopped tomatoes, if they're in season. Calculating about seven to nine cups of cooked rice a day per person—about 1,400 to 1,800 calories, which is rather conservative if your days are spent farming rice, wheat or sand—a family of five will need around 1,000 kilograms of rice a year when children are young, and more as they grow.

In India, rice yields an average of about 300 kilograms of rice for a bigha of land, or 1,200 kilograms to the acre. In much of Jharkhand, there isn't irrigation—and little sign of this improving much (a mammoth irrigation project for the state first conceived in the 1970s has still not been completed)—or the money to spend a lot on fertilizer or other things that might boost yields. Many districts do far less well than the Indian average even when rains are decent. With most families in Athgama farming about three bighas, they might get 600 kilograms in a pretty good year or 900 kilograms in an excellent year. The second harvest of wheat helps some, but even so, when other work is available—no matter what it is—everyone takes it.

When he was seventeen or so, our sand entrepreneur, a tall man whose teeth gleam remarkably white when he smiles (and he is prone to smiling often despite what seem to me the dire straits of this village), heard that other villages on the Gumani's banks were miraculously making money out of dirt. Rocks into money, he had heard of, yes. For decades Jharkhand has harvested rocks from the hills, which are trucked out of the state. Wood from the trees, yes. But the sand on which he and his father squatted as they soaped themselves to bathe in the Gumani—that was a new one. He went to a neighbouring village and asked people there how Athgama could get in on the sand business. He was told how, even though it meant more competition for those already reaping this harvest.

He collected 50 to 100 rupees from families in the village to pay for dirt to level out a road down to the bank. Then he sent three or four boys to the nearest big town to advertise, by shouting till they were hoarse at the town's main chowk, that Athgama was selling sand: come and get it. The tractor-trailers started coming, cutting across farmers' fields in the neighbouring village to get to Athgama, rolling down to the river bank by 6 a.m. each day. On an okay day, Athgama might get seven or eight tractors driving down here, each with a 14-foot trolley attached behind it, each taking away 8,000 or 9,000 kilograms of sand. On a good day, two dozen tractors and even a truck or two might come down, and the river could yield up to 40,000 kilograms of sand.

Suruj Kujur is among the workers on the riverbank when I visit. Like the other women, she has tied her faded red sari high enough to leave her calves bare. She walks over to the men who have been digging up the sand and loads a basket with perhaps 25 or 30 kilograms of sand. She squats a little, bending at the knees, to allow the men to pick up and lower the basket onto her head. Then she straightens up and walks over to the trailer where she empties the basket. She might do this as many as seven times to fill one of the tractor-trailers, by herself carrying approximately 200 kilograms for each of these wagons. When this wagon is full, about ten minutes later, she and the other people loading it have each earned four rupees.

On the April day that I have come down to the banks, notebook in hand, twenty-three tractors and two big trucks in all arrive, and by 5.30 p.m., Kujur has hauled more than 4,000 kilograms of sand, all on her head. At the end of the day, when the money is distributed, she gets 110 rupees. This is the same amount that the entrepreneur pays himself, and his two sisters, who are also working alongside everyone else. All in all, a third of the village is represented here today. Meanwhile, the farmers in the neighbouring village, whose fields provide a shortcut for the tractors, get 850 rupees without showing up at all, because they own that land. Is it any wonder that families fall out in their quest to inherit land?

I've come to meet Kujur because previously I had met her daughter in Delhi, and I wanted to follow the skein that knots this distant village to the capital. I know a little bit about where the young women who work in the homes of my parents and extended relatives end up, but what are they leaving behind? Everyone knows they're leaving behind poverty and unimaginable hard work. But it's one thing to know this as an abstraction, and another thing to see it in reality—especially when the big trucks arrive. The trucks are gaily painted with an eclectic collection of insignia: the words 'Mother's Blessing' float above a little painting of two huts while a crescent moon embraces a star. For a single truck of this size to be filled, thirty or forty people must empty their baskets of sand into it more than a dozen times each. In the meantime, its driver snoozes in the shade of the axle.

Kujur hardly takes a break while loading these trucks. Just once she pauses for a sip from a puddle that has been dug near the river to allow clearer water to seep through from below. Almost no one stops even for that drink of water, even though it is very hot, nearly 40 °Celsius, and there isn't a cloud in the sky or a single tree between the river and the truck, and they must be parched. Perhaps if they did stop, they might not be able to start again.

This work is even harder because the trucks can't come all the way down to the river as the tractors do, for the makeshift road might give way under their weight. The unreliability of sand, and the need for a critical mass of it to keep rivers on their course and support the weight of bridges that span these rivers is the reason that environmentalists are deeply concerned about the extraction of sand from Indian beaches and riverbanks. But it's also true that this trade is what puts food in the mouths of Kujur, her children, and many more like them.

The trucks park a little way up, near a dried-up well, perhaps 100 metres away from where three or four men are digging up the bank and loading baskets. As the sand in the truck gets higher, men set up a gangway of planks resting on the lorry's back gate. Then, leaning forward, Kujur runs up this gangway to empty the sand into the back of the truck. She has to run so her momentum counteracts the weighty basket on her head that could tip her backwards if she went more slowly.

Over an hour, Kujur manages to heave more loads over to the truck than most other women, although there is no reward to her for doing so. Nineteen times she empties a basket into the truck over an hour. After an hour of this, Kujur has earned 14 rupees. After twelve hours of this, the soreness settles deep into Kujur's neck and back. Each load of sand carried on the head feels as if it knocks her neck deeper into her body, the pain settling around the cervical vertebrae where her neck meets her shoulders. Or so I imagine.

Her Hindi is rudimentary, my Santhali consists of three words, the word for 'hello' and two words for sand. More importantly, her free time is non-existent. She has absolutely no 'free' moment to spare in her day, even for her children, let alone a half-hour window just to talk to me. Can I in good faith make the argument that she should carve out time for the abstract good that might accrue from people in faraway Delhi understanding what the life of the mother of one of their maids is like? What I know of her life, I know from following her around, a journalistic technique I would never be allowed to deploy with an Indian of my own social class. She doesn't know the words in my language to tell me to get lost, and I don't know the words to understand them in hers.

She wakes up at 4 a.m., like most people around here. By 5.30 a.m., after washing her face and changing into a faded sari, she has left to go down to the river, a fifteen-minute walk. The only days she doesn't go to the river are the days on which she gets wheat-cutting work in neighbours' fields. Once at the bank, she will work there for the next twelve hours, for as many days as she can get work, which is usually until the monsoon comes.

Like her mother, Kujur's youngest daughter's morning unfolds to a strict timetable. By 5 a.m., nine-year-old Sanjali is lighting twigs, placing them carefully in the hollow base of an earthen stove, which from a distance looks like a swelling in the ground next to their hut. Then she puts a metal pot with water and yellow chana dal on the stove; soon the water is bubbling ferociously as she squats nearby peeling a large clove of garlic. After the dal is ready, she packs some of it into a small bowl, which she places into a pan filled with rice, tying the whole thing up into a neat little cloth bundle.

Jharkhand is a mining state, and coal crops up in almost every household chore around here. Sanjali washes the previous night's dirty dishes using a blacking mixture made from charcoal and straw. Early in the morning, women walk over to the train tracks to pick up scraps of coal that fall from freight trains heading to Kolkata. Mixed with dung and water, and shaped into laddoo-sized balls, they keep a fire going so that the kindling collected from the forest can last longer. Floors are refreshed by lipai, wiped over a few times a week with a mix of charcoal, cow dung and water. Needless to say, this carbon-based housekeeping is a far cry from the world of hand sanitizers, liquid-gel detergents, antibacterial floor washes and self-wringing mops that newly recruited maids must quickly become familiar with. Except for the tractors that come for sand, life here is fuelled mostly by manpower.

By a little before eight, wearing a faded checked shirt and white skirt embroidered with pink anchors, same as yesterday, the little girl pulls the reed door of their temporary hut shut (the ceiling of their earthen home next door collapsed months earlier). Then she places a little coil of cloth on her head like a coolie at a railway station. She puts the pot of food on it, and sets off towards the river.

Her oldest sister, Fullin, used to do the cooking when Sanjali was younger. A few years ago, the city's demand for maids, like its need for sand, came to be felt here too even though the train station is far, at least in terms of time not kilometres. It takes a couple of hours at least to get there, with most of this time spent waiting in the next village, a few kilometres walk away, for a shared auto to be filled up. Through a woman acquaintance who lived near the local police station in Athgama, Fullin found work in the city. This was after their father, Furley, suffering from mirgi or epilepsy, didn't get up again after one seizure. She worked at first for an elderly couple near

Defence Colony in Delhi and then as a nanny for a family in Noida. Until quite recently, she worked for the spokeswoman of the Indian arm of a French multinational, in an upper middle-class neighbourhood where journalists and academics have apartments, including several friends of mine. Until, that is, her employer was arrested for allegedly locking Fullin in a bathroom, not feeding her, and beating her, with a broom, a pan, or any item that came to hand.

After Fullin went to Delhi, the sister younger than her but older than Sanjali took over the cooking. But soon this sister too went away to work as a maid, this time to Mumbai. When she came back on holiday one year, two more girls, one of them as young as eleven, went back with her to Mumbai. A master at the local school where Sanjali is enrolled expects that soon enough the little girl will follow in her sisters' footsteps.

In her best month—September—Sanjali went to class for three weeks. In April and March, when her mother is down at the river, she manages just three or four days since she must cook and deliver her mother's lunch. Not that she's missing much. Just two schoolrooms are in use, with the lower grades gathered together in one, and the upper grades in another, to go over strangely dissonant lessons. On one day, the text is about the importance of eating a varied diet, such as fresh fruit, meat and milk, items rarely seen in abundance here. Most days there is just one teacher to shuffle back and forth between both classrooms, the others are off on election duty or census duty or some other duty. One of the teachers has spent much of his career at this school trying to get a transfer. When the children first join, they hardly speak Hindi, and two of the three teachers don't speak Santhali.

Sanjali is hardworking, she's small, she's quiet. Her only experience of the working world is what her mother does: twelve hours of back-breaking labour a day. When she has a spare moment, she goes next door and washes dishes for her grandfather and step-grandmother, without even being asked. Just the sort of person a Delhi family would love to hire—and now they can, thanks to enterprising intermediaries with relatives in these village who turn up every now and again.

Not that it's a hard sell. On my short visit, although I am an entirely unknown entity, and although everybody knows the cautionary tale of what happened to Fullin working in Delhi, whispering and pointing at her scars, more than one girl, as young as nine or ten, says to me, 'Take me to Delhi. I'll work in your house.' If you're willing to be at someone else's beck and call, and wait upon them, you can have a fan, light, television and earn twice as much as you would hauling sand for a day. I could easily set up as a maid broker, I think; after all, so many of my friends on hearing that I'm travelling to Jharkhand have said, only half in jest, 'Find me a maid.' And that is how this village has added a fourth harvest to the other three: the girls.

This harvest is being reaped all over India, or at least in those places where the cost of food for a month or half a month is roughly equal to what even the stingiest family in an Indian metropolis is willing to pay for help. It's being reaped in villages across the states of Jharkhand, Bengal, Bihar and Orissa, as well as in the still rural pockets swallowed by growing cities. Unlike the predictable harvests of rice, wheat and sand, pegged to the monsoon, this harvest is reaped erratically, at a moment of crisis. A father dies, or a mother is lost and a father remarries; a parent falls ill and the family falls into debt; a wedding must be paid for; and that is how a young girl or a woman, or occasionally a boy, ends up in the city.

VARANASI, UTTAR PRADESH

USHA PAL'S FATHER OPERATED BY the philosophy that being good to your son-in-law is the best way to be good to your daughter. A worker at the state-run electricity company in Varanasi, he helped his daughter's husband go from contract worker to staff utility repairman some twenty years ago, ensuring him a decent wage and benefits. Her father also left Usha a small herd of buffalo. Further good fortune: her three oldest children are all boys. Women have been whisked into prosperity on less robust foundations than these. But, for her, it all came unstuck because of an untrustworthy sister-in-law, the woman her husband fell for.

How did she find out? The money her husband gave her for housekeeping dropped dramatically. They started fighting. He started hitting her. She was the one wronged, so naturally he was the one lashing out. Even though his family sided with her—she continues to live in the part of Chittopur occupied by his brothers and cousins—he began living with the other woman in another part of Varanasi.

The paths in Chittopur, a herding village marooned in this ancient city of 1.4 million, have an extra layer of paving over the asphalt—a yellowish-green mixture of dung leavened with bits of chaff that the buffalo have eaten and extruded. Walk along the cream-and-maroon boundary wall of the Banaras Hindu University that borders one side of the village, and you will find the alley that leads from the university road to Usha's home. Veer left, by a large cattle shed which is home to some eight or nine gleaming buffalo, while another dozen lie on a patch of open ground between this shed and her home. A soaring pile of dung patties, which sell for 3 or 4 rupees for a bundle of twenty, marks the tin-roofed home of Usha and her daughter, Renu Pal.

They were a family of six, four men and two women. Now they are just two women. Usha's sons, for the most part, have turned out to be as unreliable as her husband. Everyone says have boys: boys stick around; girls get married and leave you. But it is Renu who is the reliable one, cooking and cleaning before she goes to school. The boys have been like dandelions: a few puffs of adversity and they drifted away.

Usha's oldest boy had no knack for learning. He can't even write his own name, his mother says. One day he got a job working at a tea stall near a hospital in the next neighbourhood over, Lanka. Then he started sleeping there, so he could hang out late at night with other boys like him, playing cards and pooling money for a little drink. He comes home every two weeks or so, and gives his mother 200 or 300 rupees.

She doesn't blame him for not doing more, she knows her son is disappointed. He was supposed to get married. That would have settled him. But with no education and no prospects—a job at a tea stall is one thing if you're eleven or twelve, but not at twenty-two—girls of his family's station and caste wouldn't be enthusiastic about him as a prospective husband. A girl like his sister, Renu, probably expects to marry someone who's finished high school, if not college. So why would any of her friends or neighbours look at him?

Her middle boy, Dinesh, is doing better. He studied up to class ten. Then he got into government service on the back of his football skills—different government agencies have sports teams that play against one another and if you're not good at exams that's another way into a steady job. The agency that hired him has sent him to a college to study, he practises for the agency's team at the same time.

Her youngest son, Ram, again wasn't one for school, despite the sibling he is closest to, Renu, being a diligent student. Ram and his sister Renu, who are close in age, have a deep bond, a love that usually manifested itself in constant squabbles, at least when they were younger. Renu has a scar by one eyebrow where he poked her with a knife when they were five or six. They were in the same class for a while at a local private school. Passport-size photos show them looking solemnly at the camera, dressed in brown and white striped ties and button-down shirts. But a schoolmaster there started hitting Ram and he lost interest in school. 'My parents have never beaten me. How come he's beating me?' he said, according to his sister. When his mother would insist he go to school, he would depart with his schoolbag and then toss it down the moment he was out of sight and spend the day with other kids who were playing hooky, his sister said. For a while after dropping out, he tended the buffalo his mother had got from her father and sold the milk. Those that remain, that is. Over the years, the small herd of livestock dwindled, dying rather than multiplying.

Ram grew up into a wiry boy, with a hint of his mother's features crowned by a shock of thick black hair that stands almost straight, like a cartoon character who has just stuck his finger in an electrical socket. Then, Ram Pal too vanished. He sent word through someone that he'd gone to a wedding in Delhi, and that he'd be back soon. Days passed before his mother was able to talk to him on someone else's mobile phone.

'Ma, I lied,' he said. 'I'm working.'

She felt a sharp stab of guilt. When she looks back, yes, she may have said to him in a moment of anger, a moment of frustration, 'Don't just sit around. If you're not going to go to school, then go get a job.' But she didn't mean for him to go so far away to find one.

'Son, come back,' she told him. 'Work around here.'

Her husband has been contributing more money to the household he abandoned after she threw his money back at him one month saying, 'It's fine. We'll just eat stones.' It's true she'd been falling sick often, but that's why she needed her son close by, not off earning money far away. But he convinced her not to worry. Didn't he come back all right after going to Pune the year before to work in a heater factory with his friend? That was even further away. Didn't he earn 10,000 rupees from that stint? In fact, it was with the same friend, a young boy called Ali, with whom he was always hanging about, that he had gone to Delhi. His friend, though, came back soon enough, and headed back to Mumbai to look for more factory work. He didn't care much for cooking and waiting on people. But Ram had stayed on. The people he was working for were connected and he saw the job as a stepping stone.

He gave her the personal cell phone number of the politician he was working for, a Member of Parliament, and she sometimes called asking the sahib to connect her with her son. The politician was nice to her on the phone, real polite, she says. He would tell her, 'Your son's a good boy.'

Ram Pal tried to explain to his mother what he had learned when he wasn't in school. He'd learned that to get ahead, you needed more than an education, which in any case he didn't have. In other words, what he had probably learned was that a job in the capital, where the country's powerful reside, was worth a dozen jobs in a town mainly dedicated to the past.

'Ma, if I stay around small people, I'll learn small things,' he told her. 'With big men you learn big things.'

MAMATA COLONY, WEST BENGAL

IN THE DISTRICT OF MALDA, nearly 350 kilometres from Kolkata, there is a tiny settlement whose residents don't dare to bestow upon their fledgling village one fixed appellation, perhaps fearing, like a mother who won't name her baby too soon, that a presumption of permanence might invite the evil eye. Instead, some call it Mamata Colony, after the mercurial chief minister whose largesse helped create it. Others call it Hathkola Colony, after the hand pump that is just about the only public utility the village has apart from the highway that borders one side of it and gives it a third name—Beesmail. The village is conveniently located behind a bus stand at the 20-mile mark from the start of the highway. Lovely Khan just calls this place, where her parents and youngest siblings live, Colony. Whatever its name, it is the offspring of villages round about here, in this corner of West Bengal.

After coming to power in 2013, Trinamool Congress party workers all over the state began to set up new villages to thank their supporters, and to accommodate people whose parental villages were beginning to feel increasingly crowded as grandchildren began to grow up and in turn, marry and have children. Colony arose on an acre of land the party seized from a local teacher whom they accused of encroaching upon public land, pointing to public records that showed the land was held by the government under a decades-old land redistribution programme. One of Colony's forebears is the village of Mahanagar, just across the railroad tracks, which is where Jahanara, Lovely's mother, grew up.

In Jahanara's old village, many homes have a cow or two tied up outside. The thatched huts are spotless, their earthen walls decorated with embroidered cloth hangings, often made by women as part of their trousseau, or posters that show rosy-coloured babies against a backdrop of the great mosque at Mecca. Huge barrels in inner courtyards contain rice for the year. In many homes, a cradle hangs from a ceiling, and a baby sleeps in it. It's a beautiful place of rice fields and mango trees and little man-made ponds where children can swim.

Lovely's father's village, which also sent its overflow to Colony, is a few kilometres away. That's the place where she spent her childhood, and where her father squandered his inheritance on business ideas that never went anywhere. Lovely's grandfather had been a village chief. He owned a lot of land, which Lovely's father inherited. He grew up to be a well-educated drinker and dreamer who wasn't very excited about farming, and didn't know how to do anything else well, she says. One time he took up selling fish, another time he thought he might be able to make money off amateur theatre productions. After all these endeavours failed, he decided to start over in the city, taking his family with him.

The day Lovely moved to Delhi she sobbed till her bright eyes were red and swollen. She wouldn't get into the van that had come to her village to take her family past the mango groves to the railway station in Malda town. Finally her cousins had to drag the nine-year-old out of the hut and load her into the van. Soon after the family got to Delhi, or rather its southern border, where a bustling city called Gurgaon had come up, Lovely learned her father had sold their home, the one she had to be dragged out of. 'He sold it cheap too,' she says.

One day, not long after they moved to the city, when Lovely was playing in a park in Gurgaon's DLF Phase-I, a neighbourhood name typical of this alphabet soup of a city, a guard at an office nearby asked her if she would like to earn some money sweeping. She would, she responded.

'It seemed like two-and-a-half lakhs to me,' said Lovely of the 250 rupees she earned each month. When Lovely first came and put money in Jahanara's hands, her mother told her not to work. She enrolled Lovely in a local school, but Lovely's schooling in Malda had left her several years behind city girls the same age. She felt embarrassed to sit in a classroom with girls far younger than herself and she soon stopped going. Jahanara had her hands too full—literally—to keep track of Lovely. She'd already had six children by the time the family moved to the city, the youngest not yet a toddler. Soon after settling in a tin shack in Gurgaon's Chakkarpur neighbourhood, Jahanara had another daughter, and exactly a year after that, a son. Eight children in all, not counting the daughter who died in an accident long ago while playing next to a bubbling pot of rice on the stove, back in Malda.

In Malda, Jahanara had set out one day to get the operation that her sisters, each as illiterate as her, had undergone. None of them had more than two children. She is the only one with a large brood. But her in-laws, well-educated and prosperous enough to have some free time to immerse themselves in the Quran, had different ideas. 'The Book says it's a sin,' she was told, as they brought her back from the bus stop where she was waiting with other women to go to a nearby sterilization camp.

So, while Jahanara took care of her youngest children, her oldest daughter took on more work. 'If you have time to play, you have time to work,' a middle-class aunty once advised Lovely, and she took it to heart. Childhood—as in a protected, cared-for period of life reserved for play and study—is a luxury the upper class can afford, not the poor.

A decade after moving to Gurgaon, Lovely's parents began to talk about returning to Malda. Life for a family of ten was proving to be exceedingly expensive in Gurgaon. Even with one son married and in his own room, and another mostly on the street, hanging out and smoking pot with his auto-rickshaw driver friends, they were still eight to a room, and just two earned salaries to meet the family's expenses: Lovely and her younger sister, fifteen-year-old Rina, who had got a well-paying job by claiming to be older than she actually was. Their father had hurt his knee in a street accident and had difficulty walking. Back home, he could make some money as a contractor, putting together groups of men to come to the city to work, earning a commission for each head, and the girls' salaries would go farther. Lovely thought about it, even gave Jahanara the money to buy a little handkerchief of land back home in the new settlement her mother had heard about.

By this time Lovely was working for a middle-aged woman she regarded as a surrogate mother. The woman's husband spent most of his time in Saudi Arabia, working as an adviser to a prince, according to Lovely. The woman's children were away in the US and England studying. Lovely's role was part maid, part friend. Lovely's sister was also earning well as a nanny, bringing home around 10,000 rupees a month. They told their mother to go on without them, the two sisters would stay behind and continue working. Lovely was nearly eighteen at this point, and a bona fide city girl. Her sisters, except the very youngest who insisted on staying with their mother, felt the same way. The family split up. Four daughters stayed in the city, along with a brother who was never home. The two older sisters kept working. Between the two of them they thought they could make sure the two sisters next in line after them didn't repeat their mistakes, that they finished school, and maybe got office jobs.

'Don't worry about us,' Lovely told her mother. 'Rina is a strong girl. And I'm strong too.'

Those of them who returned—Lovely's parents and youngest sister and brother, both Delhi-born—are living in a shack whose walls are made of palm leaves. Like them, many of Colony's buyers are migrants, some of whom have returned for good from wherever they migrated to and some who are building for a future retirement. The women have put aside some money from years of being maids in Delhi or Mumbai and their husbands have put aside some money from years of construction work in Kerala or Rajasthan or Gurgaon. Many of the women seem much more uncertain of the wisdom of this homecoming than their husbands, and speak wistfully of the city and of working for money.

Jahanara's children have adapted quickly back to village life. When they need to go to the bathroom they squat to the right of the shack, in easy view of the neighbours. Meals are sparse, with a small serving of fried potatoes and rice making for a typical lunch. Two years after returning to the village, Jahanara hasn't been able to build a toilet with the money Lovely periodically sends. Instead, just like in the city, the money disappears on barely noticeable improvements, like an extra layer of thatch or dirt to level the ground, or it goes on food and medicines to treat her youngest son's occasional asthma attacks.

At night, a complete and utter darkness falls on Colony making a trip outside the pools of light that circle each hut fraught with danger for the women. Each little landholding is likely smaller than the apartments in which these women have cleaned and cooked when they lived in cities. The entire village, which doesn't have any public services besides that hand pump, could probably fit in the gated Gurgaon complex of Lovely's employer ten times over. In the apartment in that complex, Lovely takes a shower, with running hot water and privacy. She and her sister have threatened their mother that unless she builds a bathroom with the money they send, they won't come visit again. With the bathos of a Bengali mother from the movies, Jahanara says, 'If I die, they won't come for my funeral if there's no bathroom.'

When I leave Colony, a young woman who is especially nostalgic for her days working as a maid in Delhi dispatches her father to sit with Lovely's mother and me at the local railway station. He asks me what I think of this place. I think of the tall rice rolling in a green wave from here to the next village, the brown-eyed cows and the embroidered wall hangings and say, 'It's beautiful.' But he seems hurt, as if I am trying to trick him with my answer. He gestures at the deep blackness that surrounds the station at night, barely a light winking here and there, and says, 'This is not beautiful. Delhi is beautiful.'

DOPARIA, WEST BENGAL

GOLBANU BIBI HAD ALWAYS TOLD her son, 'As long as I am here you needn't work. If you work, I will run away.' Sajan Ali did as Ma said, taking occasional bricklaying jobs secretly but for the most part spending his days taking his son to school, relaxing at home or heading over to the tea shop off the Kalyani Highway at around five to shoot the breeze with other men. And right up until 2011, she kept her end of the bargain, paying most of the family's bills. From her earnings as a cook, she gave her son 4,000 rupees a month, which paid for her grandson to go to a private school. Every two or three months she bought huge 25-kilo sacks of rice for the family.

Sajan remembers his mother always being very fearful and overprotective. When they would go in a train if he happened to sit by the window, she would make him change his seat to the middle, which she thought was safer. Once she saw a bus run over a young man who was heading to work on a motorbike, and he says she became more protective than ever.

'When I was eighteen, I was like a six-year-old child,' he says.

Perhaps because she couldn't be around as much as she would have liked, she worried about him all the more. Almost as long as Sajan could remember, his mother had worked. His father fell ill with breathing difficulties when he was still a little boy, and his mother, a moon-faced woman, began to work in households in Kolkata to bring him and his sister up. Like so many mothers around here, she was gone from early in the morning till late in the evening. Like so many grandmothers too. Sajan's grandfather was a sharecropper, and his grandmother too had worked as a maid.

Later, when he and his sister were older, their mother was always gone, living in the home of doctor employers in Kolkata's Salt Lake area, and coming to see her children once a week, on Sunday. Although she gave up keeping the Ramazan fast in the home of her Hindu employers, who thought her to be Hindu and knew her as Rakhi, she would come home for Eid. Lunar holidays thankfully come together and Durga Puja often elides with Eid in such a way that no one would wonder about the faith of a woman who takes a few days off at around this time. (Kolkata employers of that time hadn't adopted the pragmatism of today's Delhi employers who often prefer Muslim maids, knowing they won't ask for days off during the frenzy of cleaning around Diwali.) At Eid, she would buy Ali clothes and cook kheer.

But in 2011 she and her employer fell out. She had worked at that home for years but they deprived her of her Durga Puja bonus that year; for her part, she didn't show up to work for a week or more so she could attend Sajan's wife's sister's wedding. When she went back to the house in Kolkata where she worked as a cook, they told her they had found someone else. She stayed at home cooking for her son and his family, looking always for a new job. A year went by.

She began frequenting the home of a retired jute mill weaver, whose wife had been working for many years in Gurgaon, pleading with them to get her a job. The weaver says that Golbanu bibi said she couldn't stay at home much longer, that she wasn't getting enough to eat, that her family wasn't treating her well; her son says the weaver's account is a lie.

The weaver's wife spoke to her contact in Delhi, a smooth-talking man named Deb Kumar, who lived in Karol Bagh, in a building populated by Bengali goldsmiths. 'Bring her, I can find her a job,' he told the weaver's wife. And suddenly, Golbanu bibi was gone from Doparia. Sajan Ali had kept his part of the bargain—he didn't work, or if he did, he did so secretly, hiding the construction contracts he occasionally took on—but his mother was unable to keep her promise to stay in the village with her family.

In Delhi, Golbanu bibi, or rather Rakhi, started working in one household for a week or two but didn't seem to care for it. She asked Deb Kumar to move her and soon she was working in a large bungalow alongside Ram Pal, of Varanasi, for the politician. Like Ram Pal, she tried to soothe her family back in the village with white lies. Sajan got a call from her. 'It's just a visit,' she said. 'I'll be back in fifteen days.' At first, they spoke twice a day. Then the phone calls became more infrequent, and finally they ceased. A year would go by, and the festivals would roll around again before he knew anything of his mother again.

In West Bengal, Sajan's story is not unusual. Many men stay home while their wives and mothers go out and work as maids. They spend their time at adda, hanging out, where in freewheeling conversations about life, the universe and everything, men cast aspersions about women who go to Delhi to work. The driver who has brought me here joins in their conversation with hearty agreement. His belief, shared by many of the men around here, is that of ten women who go out to work, two are doing ek numbari ka kaam—honest-to-goodness work—while the rest are doing do numbari ka kaam, which could be any underhanded crooked work, but generally translates to lying-on-your-back-kind-of-work when used about women.

It seems petty to belittle their achievements and taint the earnings that these women bestow on the men they love. But that's how envy works. The men may have been the ones blessed with an education, or more loved by their parents than their sisters. But when they grow up, finding steady work is not so easy. Now that he is the main breadwinner, Sajan Ali might like to take on more work, but with difficulty, he gets construction work twelve or fifteen days a month. There isn't enough work, or at least not enough of the kind of work that is men's work. It is the women, strangely, who despite their little education and little training, except in how to do lots of housework, on whom they must depend.

KOKRAJHAR, ASSAM

AT SUNSET, AS CHRISTMAS EVE approaches, men wearing military fatigues and masks walk into five Santhali hamlets, deep in the forests near the Bhutan border. One village is a 5-kilometre walk through forests from a main road. Another is a 7-kilometre walk through jungle from the nearest school. Some of the fields nearby, planted with mustard and sesame to be pressed for oil, are already blazing yellow. The floss flower shrubs that grow extravagantly along the roads, in fallow fields, and whose sap, people here say, can staunch a bleeding wound, are covered in bluish-white spidery blooms, perfuming the air. Once native to Florida, the shrub settled here long enough ago that the Santhals know it in their own tongue as randhuia, the Bodos as bangri lewa. When the randhuia blooms, village markets also blossom joyfully with large gleaming stars, tinsel and ruffled shiny frocks for little girls. But these Christmas visitors, these unknown men, bring no gifts.

The masked men ask for water. The women serve them from cool clay pots. And then the men open fire. More than seventy people, including eighteen children, are killed within minutes. Although the identity of the attackers was disguised, the following day, houses in Bodo villages, easily distinguishable from Santhal ones by the wooden cross-beams that give their homes a vaguely Teutonic air, are set on fire in retaliation. A photograph in an Indian daily shows young men with bows and arrows looking at the plumes of smoke. By January 2015, more than 200,000 people are displaced. Some of them soon go back to their own villages, while others add to the tens of thousands for whom a relief camp or a hut of black tarp spread over stacked loose bricks has become a permanent home.

This episode of violence, described in a 2015 report by the Delhi Solidarity Group, is by no means the worst of the ethnic clashes that have taken place in Assam over the past two decades. In 2012, hundreds of thousands were displaced when Muslims, believed to be illegal migrants from Bangladesh, and Bodos fought. But the worst of the gondogol, as everyone here calls the troubles, was in 1996. Ask anyone what happened and why it happened, and the answer is always a sheepish smile and a mutter, 'What can I say?' What is for certain is that many people were born and grew up in these relief camps. And around the same time, girls, and boys too, started to leave for other parts of the country in large numbers. Because of the violence, the places where girls could be left in safety while their mothers and fathers worked dwindled. Schools shut. Trusted neighbours vanished, some of them dead, while others migrated. Parents thought, what awaits our child here? Starvation, maybe. Rape, maybe. Death by shooting, or by a bow and arrow, even.

Digambar Narzary, the founder of a local non-profit against trafficking, tells me that when he returned to Assam after completing his master's in Mumbai, he was struck that there seemed to be so few teenagers at the camps and ravaged villages he visited. Then, weary mothers, babies in their arms or at their breasts, explained: Uncle took them. Aunty took them.

Sometime in 2009, Uncle took a girl from Assam, from a village in Kokrajhar district—among the three districts in the state worst affected by ethnic violence. For reasons that will become clear later, you cannot know her name. Instead, you can call her, as her family and neighbours often did when they felt too lazy to use her name, Mae. Girl. Only if there were many girls about might someone ask, which Mae? And then someone would tack her name, the name of a bird, on to the front or the end to explain. Mae came to Delhi sometime between the third and fourth cycles of ethnic violence after her family could not think of what else to do with her.

Mae was no more than a toddler when the 1996 gondogol broke out. It was a May afternoon when Pano and her husband heard that Bodo men had set fire to the nearby market and were heading for their village. The couple picked up a few things—and Mae—and ran through the fields, which were squishy and muddy from the rains. Many times Pano slipped but they kept going. For a year, the family along with neighbours camped about 10 kilometres away. Then for their safety, the government distributed the people to different state-run relief camps guarded by a paramilitary battalion. Government officials took pictures of parents with their children to determine how much relief rations they ought to get. A picture taken in 2000, in Safkata relief camp, shows Mae's father with a slew of children. Actually, though, the rest of the children were not theirs. Displaced families quickly learned to make the most of the meagre relief allotments by borrowing extra children when it was their turn to be registered for relief. Mae, in a purple dress, looking about five or six—though the card lists her as nine—is in the front.

For a while, her family had sent her, their eldest daughter, to the home of a relative. She had started attending temporary classes set up at a local school. The little money her mother could save from fishing and selling bundles of firewood at weekly markets went towards buying more food or a new tarp to replace one that was in shreds. Her father, ill with tuberculosis, could hardly breathe, let alone work. The family heard that a girl in the hut across the road, Melo, went to Delhi for a year and come back with money. She had gone with a man from Jharkhand whose chief characteristic appeared to be his fondness for drink. It turns out the Uncle from Jharkhand is going to take her back for another year of work and this time Mae goes too; she and her mother think it will help pay for her father's treatment. Uncle takes them and two girls to New Bongaigaon. There, they board a train to Delhi.

If Mae truly was nine in 2000, she might have been seventeen or thereabouts when she first arrived in Delhi. If she was five, as she looks to be in the photograph, she would have been fourteen. Was she excited to go? Maybe. Melo, who had been to Delhi and was not scared, would surely have told her friend of the fans and television and the lights, so many lights, of the city. Was she afraid to go? Maybe. Pano says her daughter was a quiet and timid girl, not a talkative chatterbox. In Delhi, Uncle hands her off to the couple who will put her to work. The woman, Merry, teaches her how city sweeping and mopping is done and in a week she is judged to be trained. The husband, Benoi, runs a placement agency out of a room rented cheaply in a West Delhi market. They place her in a Punjabi businessman's house to be a maid. Suddenly, she is living with strangers, strangers who may or may not, as many Delhi families do, judge their maids to be slow and stupid because it takes them several moments to understand instructions issued in a language that they did not grow up with.

No one calls Pano, or any of her relatives, to tell her where Mae is, to give her the address of her daughter's employer, or his phone number. It's true that this isn't an easy task, since Pano doesn't have a cell phone. But her neighbours do. Then again, the agents never trouble themselves over niceties like this and it would be most unlike the average Delhi family to lose sleep over whether their new teenage maid is able to get in touch with her family or not. For the most part, we Delhi employers privately think that 'these people' don't feel about their families the way we do about ours, because, after all, just look at how many relatives they have. In fact, as far as the typical Delhi family is concerned, the less a maid has to do with her relatives, the more convenient it will be for us: so many requests for leaves for weddings, deaths and festivals avoided. That is the advantage of the out-of-town maid who is cut off from her own family.

But eventually Melo's father helps Pano track down a phone number for the home where her daughter is working. A year has passed by the time mother and daughter speak for the first time. Pano is happy to hear her daughter's voice but the calls are not entirely satisfactory. The employer never allows Mae to speak to her mother for more than a few minutes. Other times Pano calls the exact same number and asks for her daughter only to be told, 'There's no one of that name here.' Pano asks Chutki, her youngest sister and Mae's aunt, who is also working in Delhi, to look out for her daughter.

Still, three years after Mae left, there is more gondogol: more than 70 are killed and 400,000 displaced. Despite the unsatisfactory phone calls, there is some consolation in the fact that Pano's daughter is far away from the troubles, in the relative safety of the city. There is no way for Pano to know, for example, that the maid broker who put Mae to work at the businessman's house—or at any rate a man with the exact same name and profession—has been arrested at the border in connection with the vanishing of a teenager from Jharkhand, another girl who had come to Delhi to be a maid.

But we are getting ahead of ourselves. And we are privileging the dramatic, a common journalistic technique. We are so fearful of the everyday, fearful that you, the reader, will be bored at being told that most of the women and young girls who come to Delhi as maids aren't fleeing the colourful violence of possibly being hacked to death with a machete or mown down with automatic rifles one Christmas Eve or being pierced through the heart with a handmade arrow. The vast majority are fleeing a far more mundane kind of violence.

They are fleeing the daily violence of having to earn a handful of rice or dal by bending over thousands of times a day, sickle in hand, to chop scratchy bundles of wheat. They are fleeing the everyday violence of carrying loads on their heads, for two rupees or four rupees a go, dozens of times a day, under a blazing sun, to earn the grand sum of 100 rupees. But it's not as gloomy as all that. One Delhi maid broker explains the exodus with great simplicity. 'Those who don't have enough to eat, they come to fill their stomachs. Those who have enough to eat, they come to send their children to school.'

PART II

CHORE BAZAAR

THE MOTHER OF ALL MAID BROKERS

BUSINESS EDITORS MAY KNOW THE last closing share price and market capitalization of India's top firms, but Sunita Sen knows their true bottom line: what their CEOs pay the help, what they feed them, and just how many servants each family employs. For her, a particular bungalow on the erstwhile Aurangzeb Road or a mansion on Prithviraj Road is not associated with the politician with a tendency for putting his foot in his mouth or that businessman whose invisible hand is all over the budget. Instead, Mrs Sen thinks of them as the places to which she sent the nanny from Orissa, the cook from Uttarakhand or the nurse from West Bengal.

Elite Indians can employ rather a large number of servants. A family of four can easily have an equal number of help. For a brief period, I, an able-bodied person with no children, had two or at least one-and-a-half—a part-time cook and cleaner, and a driver. But after having driven myself for five years, I couldn't help being a terrible nag from the back seat and the driver dropped me after two weeks, to the relief of both of us. Policing myself around one employee I could handle, two was just too stressful. My parents, in their seventies, had about five when my bedridden grandmother was still alive, not counting the day and night nurses. The five included a driver, three women to do the cleaning and laundry generated by two apartments and an invalid, and a cook to prepare meals for the eight to ten people that had to be served lunch and dinner daily because of this staffing arrangement. But these numbers pale in comparison to the staffing of families in what must be the top one per cent of the one per cent, according to Sunita Sen.

There's that family who founded a leading hospital chain frequented by medical tourists from Afghanistan and Pakistan. 'They have twenty-two servants,' she tells me. There's that major real estate developer around the corner from the posh hotel whose birthday parties are sometimes entertained by top-tier American pop stars ('twenty-seven servants'). There's the telecom mogul who probably paid crores of rupees for his Lutyens-style bungalow ('at least fifteen'). Voter rolls confirm these numbers, showing as many as thirty-five to forty registered voters at some bungalows, with a variety of last names from different parts of India, and associated with different religions, making for remarkably cross-cultural and multi-faith households. With that many adults, the numbers of people, including children under eighteen, living at these residences could be as high as seventy or eighty. A few of the bungalow residents append 'SQ'—short for servants' quarters, as the housing complexes in the back gardens of these sprawling homes are known—to their voter's ID but most are more circumspect, just listing the house number.

We are sitting in Sunita Sen's living room in South Delhi and drinking tea out of black teacups engraved with silver flowers—they match the cushion she is resting against in her pleather armchair—as she tells me how she came to be the person that the people who live at Delhi's toniest addresses call in a panic when the nanny elopes or the cook doesn't return from 'a short trip to the village' and is then rumoured to be working for more money elsewhere. It is from this house, in a low-rise, middle-class apartment building in a back road in Delhi's Chhattarpur area, that Mrs Sen, and a few others like her, began the freelance matchmaking businesses that would eventually lead to the rise of the massive 'placement' industry that helps the capital and other large cities extract maids and nannies from the remotest of villages.

Friends of mine have described Mrs Sen, a short, plump Bengali woman, as a formidable force in the world of Lutyens' bungalows and Chhattarpur 'farmhouses', a world whose inner workings she knows so well, she has become rather blasé about them. Most of the capital's residents pass these homes covetously, craning for a glimpse into them. But Mrs Sen is not impressed. For starters, she tells me this about the mansions with the most servants: their servant bathrooms are always filthy.

'Because a lot of servants are there, everybody is using, girls, boys,' says Mrs Sen, her hair pulled back in a low ponytail, coughing as she talks, hugging a brown cardigan around herself on a still chilly January day. 'If there are four [loos], and there are twenty-five servants, you can well imagine?

'Who will make it clean? She will say "you do it", he will say "you do it". It is better to have flats like us. We have two bathrooms, one for the girls, one for the boys. And weekly one person cleans it.'

Mrs Sen's neighbourhood is surrounded by the personal residences of affluent businessmen and lawyers, some of whom are also her clients, and one of whom constructed the building in which she and her husband bought a flat early in their marriage. Some of these homes lie empty until winter, when they are rented out by their owners as venues for weddings and the occasional concert. Not far away is the mansion of deceased liquor baron Ponty Chadha, killed in a shootout, in whose home she has placed nannies and drivers ('no worker ever wants to leave that house,' she tells me). The boundary walls and gates to these homes are even higher than those in posh South Delhi areas. This landscape of tall, nearly indistinguishable metres and metres of wall is no doubt why young girls from villages who are placed in Delhi homes as maids have such a difficult time explaining to their family members exactly where they have ended up. The sort of landmarks that allow you to orient yourself in a village—the primary school, the hand pump, a temple or church—are widely scattered, and often themselves behind walls.

The walls of Delhi aren't all created equal, they too can serve as markers of class and status. The walls in older neighbourhoods where families still occupy the homes their parents built are low enough to see over, reminders of a time when the world outside the home seemed less threatening, and families did not mind if passing street vendors could look over the walls and into their homes. Although, with the wisdom of hindsight one has to ask, was it truly a gentler time? Or was it just a gentler time for those at the top of the food chain, when a million mutinies had not yet begun to erupt, forcing the 'haves' to build higher walls.

These days, bungalows that are home to people with a lot of money are shielded by walls easily a dozen feet high. The stand-offishness these walls connote is softened slightly by virtue of their being wreathed with bougainvillea creepers and malti flowers carefully nurtured by gardeners over decades. *We want to keep you out,* the walls seem to say, *but here's something to look at because we know you're there, on the outside.* But around here, in Chhattarpur, the walls are tall and unadorned. The people inside, they really don't care what you think.

Despite being outside these walls herself, Mrs Sen was among the first to read the tea leaves about what the people inside them wanted, driven in part by the necessity of having to give up a job she clearly loved. The daughter of a government scientist from Kolkata, she grew up in northern India where her father was posted, which may have injected a dose of entrepreneurial spirit into her, despite coming from a part of India not generally associated with a love of business. After being passed over for an air-hostess job because of her short stature, she fell back on her secretarial course and joined a crafts-exporting business in Delhi that also stocked shops in five-star hotels with sandalwood tchotchkes and Kashmir carpets. There she made herself indispensable. She didn't just type letters and answer phones. Taught to drive by her father, she delivered goods, went to banks to deposit payments, and even picked up her boss from the airport. 'In an export house, you are peon, you are driver, you are secretary,' she tells me.

She gave half of her significant salary—10,000 rupees at the time—to her mother, a woman who had completed at best two years of school growing up in a plantation in eastern India. Mrs Sen was the first woman in her family to have a job, and she was proud of it. But when she married, her in-laws weren't impressed by her dedication to her work. 'They used to tell my husband, "We had seen so many girls from our village..." They were very homely type, working with the mother-in-law, doing all the household chores and all that,' Mrs Sen recalls. They would tell their son, 'Your wife doesn't have time. She's always ready to go to office.'

Supported by her husband, Mrs Sen kept working for several years, hiring a maid and a cook to do the chores her in-laws would have liked her to do. But finally, she decided to leave her job to spend more time with her daughter, who often fell ill, a decision that she still remembers with pain. As her daughter grew older and more robust, and spent longer hours at school, Mrs Sen found herself lapsing into depression. 'After working so hectic it was very difficult for me to sit home.'

Then she hit upon an idea that would allow her to work and set her own hours, so she would still have time for her family and could not be accused of neglecting her home for a job. At a certain point in a social evening, the conversation invariably turns to the help. But where some saw only the self-involved carping of India's upper middle class in such chatter—in one of his books, V. S. Naipaul heaps scorn upon a woman who is lamenting that the demolition of a local slum has lost her a maid—Mrs Sen saw a business opportunity.

Mrs Sen began by placing ads saying that she was looking for people from West Bengal, Assam, Chhattisgarh and Jharkhand to bring her girls who wanted to work. People who were themselves working in Delhi as maids, who in any case were bringing relatives to the city when they heard of a job going for them, now brought them to Mrs Sen for the 200-rupee finder's fee she paid. When she first started, she placed four or five workers a month, now she places fifteen or twenty. She gets a dozen calls every day from people looking for domestic help. Even as we speak clients call her up, haranguing her about not yet having sent them anyone. 'Madam, if no one has come to me, then how can I call you and tell you anything?' she says to one woman. Then, trying to mollify the caller, she adds, 'You know how these people are. They just keep making promises. They know they'll get a job whenever they come so they take their own time.'

To another caller she says, 'She didn't call you? She called me this morning saying she had a very bad sore throat and she would start from tomorrow. I told her to call you!' Thanks to a vile combination of fog and pollution common in winter, almost everyone has sore throats or hacking coughs like Mrs Sen's.

In the late 1980s, Mrs Sen's belief that she might be able to make money finding maids for people probably seemed outlandish to her friends and acquaintances. There were just a smattering of other concerns offering this service. They included a group run by nuns in South Delhi; a Punjabi lady; and later, a retired military gentleman in the Bengali neighbourhood of Chittaranjan Park joined their ranks. At the time, domestic workers were mostly hired through word-of-mouth. A friend's driver's wife or neighbour's maid's sister-in-law might be looking for a job. Civil servants who moved into a government flat, which came with attached quarters for domestic help, often found the people working for their predecessors were keen to stay on so they could hold on to the housing, even if the civil servant's wife wasn't offering a salary. People with relatives in a small town or village could always get cheap help—the child, perhaps, of someone working for their relatives back home.

Perhaps Mrs Sen was prescient, or perhaps she was just lucky. But at the time she set herself up as a maid broker, demand was about to ramp up and the old systems of hiring began to steadily prove less than satisfactory, driven in great part by alterations in city planning. As the city expanded and real estate prices began to creep up in the 1980s, newer housing developments were often built by housing societies formed by professional groups who could get access to subsidized land and financing. On the growing edges of the city, apartment complexes became a more common sight than the detached or semi-detached houses of earlier decades.

For those detached homes, the Delhi planning authority had dictated that rooms for domestic help built as part of private residences be at least 100 square feet, and up to 250 square feet, not counting a kitchen, bathroom or any outdoor space. That version of the capital envisioned two families, not equal by any means, but still living each in its own way a complete life, side-by-side, and interdependent.

But the authority didn't require that the new apartment complexes coming up in the 1980s and after to make such arrangements. In fact, ostensibly to prevent excessive congestion, any units built for help would be subtracted from the total building area allowed in these housing societies. That led most complexes to eschew making provisions for servants. If the families who moved into these new homes wanted to have live-in help they would have them sleep in the living room or kitchen, others made do with part-time help hired from the shacks that crop up wherever poor migrants believe there are jobs to be found.

As the economy speeded up in the 1980s and 1990s, young professionals moving to the capital to study or work often eyed the somewhat comfortably proportioned (and undoubtedly more economical) servants' quarters in older Delhi homes as ideal starter apartments, leading to the eviction of domestic help. In the new millennium, these homes and their quarters have been redeveloped into large, marble-laden apartments, and the space earmarked for the use of the help has diminished into a tiny room, mostly likely on a hot roof, built from materials vastly inferior to the ones used in the main home.

All of this was very good for Mrs Sen. But it was necessary for her to be strategic in order to be successful. People who were one or two generations into city life wouldn't agree to be live-in workers in homes where they might be asked to sleep in the kitchen or on the stairs. And, in many cases, people who had come to the city as servants in the 1970s had worked their way into purchasing homes of their own. Or, if they had been living in informally built settlements that the government tore down as part of its periodic redevelopment efforts, they had been given a handkerchief of land in some distant corner of the city as compensation. Newer migrants, with a little wherewithal, found that what was available on the rental market, even in a slum, was often an improvement on what employers were willing to provide, since it allowed for family life.

To find live-in workers, it was increasingly necessary to reach out to ever-poorer parts of India, to people for whom a mattress or a carpet under a fan that worked all night would be a luxury. Many employers living in cities—now second or third-generation city-dwellers themselves—no longer had such remote connections. But Mrs Sen, through her network of agents, did. As others copied her, they created a new niche in the economy: the placement agency. Thousands of these agencies exist now, in every large Indian city, charging a fee that is usually equivalent to a month's salary to supply domestic help.

In recent years, again reading the tea leaves, Mrs Sen has rejigged her business. She says she began to find it more and more difficult to recruit young women who are willing to do only housework. When she asks women what sort of job they're looking for, they almost all say 'babycare', and are happy to explain why. They tell her, if they are in charge of an affluent family's baby, 'Wherever the baby will go, I will accompany. In summers, baby will always be in the AC room, I will be there. She will be going in the AC car, so will I. She will be going to the malls, so will I. Whatever she will eat, I will eat.' Many of the nannies she places report back to her that they spend their days trailing ma'am and her children through malls.

Now she no longer supplies cleaners, occasionally supplies cooks and mainly focuses on childcare, made up of japas, who are short-term nurses for infants, and nannies, whose pay can be double or triple that of a cleaning woman. Depending on her level of experience, a japa can earn at least 20,000 rupees for forty days of work beginning just before or soon after a baby is born. The most experienced and reassuring ones might be paid more, with expectant mothers tying up their services months in advance through word-of-mouth or online forums. After the japa's forty days are done, Mrs Sen provides nannies whose salaries, in early 2014, were around 16,000 rupees and upwards a month, increasing every year.

In South Delhi, even the well-off typically pay about 10,000 to 12,000 rupees for full-time, live-in housekeeping help. In the East Delhi complex where my parents and other retired diplomats live, 7,500 rupees is typical; outside that complex many families in the area likely pay much less. Only a very tiny group of expat employers are likely to top the wages sought by Mrs Sen, offering somewhere between 20,000 rupees to 35,000 rupees to the English-speaking help they hire, with an even smaller number paying above that.

Mrs Sen's clients can afford the fees and salaries she expects, of course, and many families are ready to pay more. These employers tend to have incomes of at least 25 lakh a year and in many cases, more like 50 lakh a year, making them a rarefied fraction of India's elite. But water finds its own level, and families who are not yet part of the one per cent but who still want full-time help need not fret. There are now multitudes of Mrs Sens, a few of them even more expensive, but most of them far, far more economical.

Childcare is where the money is, Mrs Sen tells me, because while women are taking on roles outside the home, most men are not taking on more work within the home. 'No, no. None,' she says, when I ask her about this. At least none among the class that she caters to. 'So you have to have somebody,' explains Mrs Sen. 'It is very difficult for the mothers to, you know, go to office without any kind of help. So that is the reason it is going up and up.'

India's domestic help market has seen adaptations like this before. By the 1970s, water carriers, so numerous at the start of the twentieth century, numbered less than 1,000 thanks to the advent of municipal water supply. By 1931, about two decades after the Ford Model T first drove out of a factory, Delhi recorded the existence of about 1,500 motor car cleaners and drivers (a decade later a few women were found doing this job). These workers would eventually displace the tens of thousands of horse grooms and coachmen common at the start of the twentieth century. Some professions do make a comeback. In 1901, the Census report noted with satisfaction that the numbers of household gatekeepers appeared to be declining, calling it an occupation that is 'fast disappearing with improved efficiency in the protection of property by police'. Of course, it didn't. Like the demand for nannies, the appearance and disappearance of different kinds of help, is a sign of the times.

Mrs Sen's daughter, now in her thirties, is among the growing group of mothers who go to office. She works in the finance department at the consulting firm McKinsey & Co., often till past seven. That's why the only unbreakable appointment on Mrs Sen's otherwise flexible schedule is departing at lunchtime to pick up her grandsons from school. She will watch over them, with the help of two maids, until her daughter gets off work.

EK NUMBER KA KAAM

IT'S NOT UNCOMMON FOR FIVE-YEAR-OLDS in India to bully their parents. Generally, though, the little tyrants tend to be boys. Many girls learn at an early age to talk less, run less, eat less. Not Santosh Srivastava's little girl. She is one tough little cookie, issuing a series of commands and complaints as I attempt to interview her father. 'Papa, this phone isn't playing the cartoons,' she shouts at one point. 'Okay, just hurl it on the ground,' he suggests amiably. At another point, the little girl begins punching her father in his stomach, shouting, 'Fatso! You've become a real fatty, eating and eating.' Will this elicit a spanking or a scolding? Not at all. At these remarks, Srivastava, a chubby-faced young man in his twenties clad in shorts and a yellow T-shirt, just beams fondly.[14]

Our interview is punctuated with shrieks of 'Papa!' at ever increasing decibel levels. Srivastava is solo parenting at the moment; his wife is visiting her family in Jharkhand. She calls on his mobile phone repeatedly, likely missing her little girl, prompting Srivastava to ask his daughter rather tentatively, 'Don't you want to speak to your mother, she's called so many times?' But the little girl hangs up on her mother, calls loudly for Maggi ('Papa! Papa!'), and enquires when the lady will stop with her tedious questions.

Then she returns to her cartoons, casting a baleful glance in my direction. I am cowed and rush through my remaining queries as she tucks into two steaming platefuls of instant noodles. ('Papa, salt!')

Three decades after Mrs Sen first began recruiting girls as domestic help in Delhi homes, she has lots of competition from people doing similar work—most of them half her age and from rather different social circumstances. A search on the Delhi government's database of registered commercial establishments for agencies that provide domestic workers throws up more than 1,000 results. Srivastava and his wife, proprietors of the S. K. Group Placement Service, located opposite a slum in southeast Delhi, are among them. These middlemen (and often women) are usually former cooks and drivers and nannies who've cottoned on to a bizarre fact about India's domestic service market: you can earn more for finding someone a maid than you can by working every day as a maid for three months. Or six months. Or, if the employers are particularly kanjoos, for a year.

Realizing this, Srivastava retired as a cook at the age of twenty-one, seven years ago. He had been in domestic work for about a third of his life when he quit it. He started when he was thirteen, after a truck heading out from the local sugar mill near their Uttar Pradesh village knocked his father off his motorcycle. Srivastava, who was riding pillion, spent two months in the hospital. His father died on the spot.

He had been a good student, he says about his younger self. But when he was better he didn't go back to school. Instead, he went to Delhi to work for a doctor, a friend of his father's. He was the oldest of six siblings and with their father gone, the responsibility for all of them was his. His earnings of 1,000 rupees a month paid for extras like cooking oil, spices, notebooks and pencils for his youngest siblings; their food came from the fields. The sister born after him dropped out of school too and waited for her brother to save enough for her to get married.

Over the next eight years, he worked his way up to a salary of 10,000 rupees, cooking for a family in Jangpura. He began 'living out' in a nearby neighbourhood called Kotla, a warren of one-room tenements in a locality known for its suppliers of marble and teak by the square foot, German-made faucets, sculptural light fixtures and domestic help to the wealthy neighbourhood of Defence Colony just across the road. There, in his friends' circle of cooks and maids, he fell in love with a Christian woman from a village in Jharkhand. In their home, a 100-square-foot room on the third floor of a tenement with a bathroom and kitchenette in the corner, there is room enough for two faiths. On one wall hangs a picture of the holy family while a little Hindu altar is on another wall. Even though Mr Srivastava did not convert, his family was against the marriage. He told them to mind their own business. 'Forget about me,' he told them. 'But I'll still send you money,' he quickly added. 'Don't worry about anything else.'

'I have married according to my own thinking; I have planned according to my own thinking of what I'm going to do next,' says Mr Srivastava. 'If I lived according to their thinking, maybe I wouldn't be able to do everything that I'm doing.'

In 2008, after hearing all their friends complain about either the employers or the agents they had worked with– the ratio is two complaints about employers for every eight complaints about recruiting agents, he says—the couple decided to give the business a try themselves. His wife already had some experience: she had done some recruiting on trips home for a man running a placement service out of their neighbourhood.

They left Kotla, crowded with such maid recruiters, for Taimoor Nagar in Southeast Delhi, where they live on the better side of the drain that bisects this area. They live on the third floor in a building whose walls are grimy and splashed with crusty, rust-coloured paan stains. An enormous truck tyre rests on one landing, perhaps stored by its owner. Outside, wild black-bristled pigs nuzzle the garbage spread like a bedcover over the black waters of the drain. It is from this place that Mr Srivastava runs the business that quadrupled his income. He is just back from his village, where he was overseeing the completion of a two-storey brick home for his mother and siblings to live in. If the numbers he's giving me are correct, he's earning more than a lakh a month, putting his little family in India's top one per cent (a group whose threshold starts far lower here than in other countries, but more on that later). From near disaster—which the death of a father often signifies—to where he is now, that's a whirlwind ride.

And, he emphasizes, he's doing ek number ka kaam—honest work—not do numbar ka kaam, as most agents do. When young women turn up in the city asking for a job, he calls their families in villages to make sure they are in the know and also to check the ages of the job seekers. He distributes salaries the way his workers ask for them. If they want monthly payments, that's what they get. If not, he keeps meticulous records for workers who have asked him to hold their monthly payments for them until they go home, rather than trying to fob them off with 10,000 rupees when the eleven-month contract is over and it's time to settle accounts. He lobbies with employers for better food and for working hours not to greatly exceed ten hours a day. He has worked with local police and a child rights group to help find children brought to the city to work, and consulted with the city government on possible regulations for brokers.

Mr Srivastava's area of operations stretches from Delhi's suburbs to Kashmir, he says. But there are two areas from where he now generally declines to entertain enquiries. In South Delhi, they don't stint on money, but the homes are too big and the expectations too high: 'Too much overtime,' he says. In Punjabi Bagh, they want to pay as little as 2,000 rupees a month, and although they no longer say it as baldly as in the past, they want children. They always claim it's because the girls won't have any real work, they'll just be companions for an elderly mother or a toddler. But Mr Srivastava believes it's because children put up with a lot before they run away. They don't know any better.

Mr Srivastava offers three categories of workers: housekeepers, specialists, and health attendants. In the housekeeper category, he has three sub-categories. For a woman fresh from the village, he sets the salary at 5,000 rupees a month for sweeping and mopping, doing the dishes and washing clothes, for a day that likely starts at 7 a.m. and ends at 10 p.m., with a two or three-hour rest gap in the afternoon. He has to train her a little, as do her employers, since her experience in the care and upkeep of a mud floor and thatched walls don't translate at all to city housekeeping. Someone with a bit more experience, who knows how to make a bed and use glass-cleaner and polish silver and brass statues, gets between 6,000 and 8,000 rupees. An experienced person, whose skills range from laying a table with an assortment of cutlery and glasses, to using a microwave and a washing machine, gets 10,000 rupees. His specialists include cooks and nannies. A cook who can only do North Indian food can start at 12,000 rupees for a full day, while those who know Chinese, South Indian and pasta as well, can ask for 15,000 rupees and up. The Srivastavas charge a commission of 25,000 to 30,000 rupees for every person they place in an eleven-month contract, and they place perhaps four or five people a month.

It's not all profit, of course. He and his wife have travel expenses a couple of times a year, escorting workers back to their villages or from them, both for their safety, and, I suspect, to prevent poaching by other recruiters. His wife is in Jharkhand right now because she took some workers back in December, and then decided to stay on and spend Christmas and New Year's with her own family in Latehar district.

Apart from the room they live in with their daughter, the Srivastavas rent two other rooms in their tenement, which provide room and board to workers who are in between jobs. One of the workers in transit, a petite girl from Jalpaiguri in West Bengal who is headed home, makes a cup of tea for each of us, and I wonder whether one perk of being a domestic work recruiter is never having to do your own housework. But Mr Srivastava says he doesn't have a problem with housework. 'I sweep and mop this place. I cook my own food, I wash my own clothes,' he says. 'I like doing my own work.'

This, fortunately for him, is far from the norm, otherwise Mr Srivastava would not be in the business he's in. I ask him how long he expects to be able to live off supplying maids, and cooks and drivers to India's affluent. 'Lifetime,' he responds, without missing a beat.

ONLINE MATCHMAKING

WHEN IT COMES TO CHORES, most Indians who can afford it firmly believe another human is still the best labour-saving device. It turns out research on machines backs this up. An experiment to train a robot to fold laundry found that a toddler could fold a small square towel in ten seconds, while it took the robot half an hour to do the same. As the *Wall Street Journal* put it, 'The difference between picking up a lace nightgown versus unravelling a pair of crumpled jeans knotted with other clothes is a calculation that requires massive computing power and a soft touch.'

There are all sorts of labour-saving technologies now available in India—from washing machines and vacuum cleaners to roti makers. But Srivastava is not worried by all this. Labour-saving devices powered by technology won't lead Indians to forego domestic help, he says. 'I know a family...they have a machine for every task, washing dishes, washing clothes, even then he wants domestic workers,' says Mr Srivastava, referring to the head of the family. 'He needs someone to run those machines.'

Not that Indian families are resistant to the possible efficiencies that technology can bring to the universe of domesticity. Not at all. But they don't want to use technology to replace servants; they want to use it to *find* them. India has always been a little oblivious to the fact that there's supposed to be a more or less impermeable border between the traditional and the modern, between the old-fashioned and the cutting-edge. Which is why women take contraceptive pills so that they can avoid menstruating during religious functions and ultrasound machines are used (unlawfully) during pregnancies to identify and eliminate unwanted girls. And so, if you want a hardworking serf at the lowest possible price, you no longer scour your ancestral fields— which in any case have all been sold to real estate developers to be turned into apartment complexes. Like hopeful but hard-nosed brides and grooms, you go online.

Indian online classified pages list a wide variety of maid brokers, many of whom, like corporations providing broadband and other services, promise that prospective employers need only send a text message or missed call to have an executive show up on the doorstep, suitable candidates in tow. On the web directory JustDial, placement agents have uploaded videos explaining their services over a soundtrack of digital synthesizer beats. 'I have been providing drivers and maids for five years,' says one man from Bihar. Some effort has gone into his video, which pans from him thumbing through through a file with a serious expression while seated at a desk decorated with a laughing Buddha and green bamboo in a vase, to a tidily dressed young woman and man seated on a bench and looking hopeful. It is several notches up from several of the other placement agency videos, in which paan-chewing women wearing garish red lipstick, their eyes vacant, and seated on beds promise wonderful domestic help in monotonous drones. Those videos offer an insight into why so many people say such unsavoury things about the services some placement agents and the women they are in charge of are actually providing.

A slew of online job portals like Babajobs and Nanojobs, which once focused mainly on white-collar job seekers, are now helping place domestic workers without the intervention of a broker. The sites offer clues to the wide range of salaries prevailing across different areas of the city, and what employers are looking for. On Babajobs, people in Delhi seeking domestic cooks are generally willing to offer 10,000 rupees a month. Many, strangely, offer far less for childcare than for cooking, generally around 8,000 rupees a month, but sometimes just half of that. A professor at a local business college, for example, is seeking a maid for six hours a day for 3,500 rupees a month while a single mother in Uttam Nagar asks for a full-time live-in maid who will clean and do childcare for the same salary, a job that twenty-two people have applied for despite its low wages. The ads seeking childcare are often devoid of much detail apart from the child's age, and can almost uniformly be summed up as 'Woman wanted very badly!'

Cities deemed more 'corporate', like Mumbai and Bengaluru, offer higher salaries. On Nanojobs, maids in Mumbai who are seeking live-in jobs online rarely ask for less than 10,000 rupees, and many ask between 12,000 and 14,000 rupees. On Babajobs, a 'travelling senior executive' in Bengaluru offers a salary of 15,000 rupees a month along with health and life insurance and twenty-five days off a year, asking for someone with a 'pleasing personality' capable of supervising the cook and the part-time cleaner, and 'smooth execution' of dinner parties.

But rather than connecting directly with workers online—a fair number of prospective employers seem to be suspicious of servants clever enough to operate a computer and surf the web—many employers are trying to recreate the old 'word-of-mouth' system on social networking sites like Facebook. On such sites, members post photographs of women who have worked for them, and ask whether other members know anything about these maids. I would be horrified if this was how a potential employer planned to check my past—and certainly, many of the maids look rather sullen in the photographs—but on sites closed to the public until a moderator approves a request to join, such requests elicit candid if hard-hearted responses.

When one woman seeks information on a Gurgaon-focused Facebook maid-referral site about a worker she recently let go, another woman posts a comment telling her that the lady resembles her previous maid, who had tuberculosis. The first woman writes back, 'No wonder she was so weak. Had less appetite. Always stole n drank milk.' Another woman blacklists a maid because when the woman quit, she searched the woman's bag and found it full of her lipsticks and nail polishes, which she confiscated although, tainted as they were by her servant's touch, she had no intention of using them. 'Though I took it back from her I was left with no choice but to put in bin.'

Despite the moderator's attempts to deter people from commenting on looks, they do, which is where things get really strange. On various occasions, women claim to recognize women as their former maids, more frequently than one would expect even for people living in condo complexes near one another. Given that the maids in question are often from different states and ethnic origins than the employers, I wonder whether some of these aren't a case of racist ignorance—as happened when an older white man famously mistook the Indian-American actress Mindy Kaling for Pakistani Nobel Peace Prize-winner Malala Yousafzai. My suspicions deepen when, in one such exchange, an employer posts a photo for comparison. The commenters agree it is the same woman. But to my eyes, they don't look like the same woman at all, even if they both look as if they could hail from West Bengal's Darjeeling area, home to many ethnic Nepalis.

Another time, an employer posts a photograph of a plump young woman, who looks North Indian and is relatively light-skinned compared to some of the other photographs posted of women from eastern India. She is wearing glasses and a short kurta in muted colours rather than the kind of bright, multi-coloured nylon sari many workers wear. Several people chime in 'pretty!' or 'she looks like from a good family!' and insist she's not a maid. One offers this caution: 'By body language she did not looking like a maid, you must check her id proof.' The group moderator intervenes and asks people not to say that some women look like maids and others don't, but most people don't understand what she's trying to say and defend their words as merely being complimentary.

Apart from hiring and references, these forums also offer women a chance to compare salaries and discuss the appropriate etiquette towards servants. On a group aimed at connecting moms, an acquaintance tells me, a long discussion broke out one day on whether the help should be allowed to use the house washing machine for their own clothes. Some say absolutely not. Others think a live-in maid should be allowed to use the machine—as long as she makes sure to wash her clothes separately from family laundry, a laundering practice that dates back at least to the Victorians.

But most of all, these groups end up being a place to vent about maid woes, which for many only truly seem to have begun when they embarked upon motherhood. Some women share alarming stories. One woman reports being stopped by an elderly couple in the mall who tell her they recognize her nanny, whom she has been very happy with, as the woman who locked them in a room and cleaned out their house—not with a broom, but with the help of her husband and other men. Another reports discovering the nanny she hired and tried to give a fair chance to had hit her child.

Many mothers urge the installation of CCTV cameras in homes, especially when one woman, who is clearly extremely stressed, asks whether it's safe to leave her infant with a woman who appears to suffer from extreme PMS and mood swings, and who she has only just hired. 'Your baby is at risk every time she cries or, in some way, irks the nanny,' warns one group member, while another urges the woman to consider day care. 'Tell me of one that will take a baby under the age of six months', the original poster pleads. 'I am more than ready,' she says. Motherhood, without a 'mom or mom in law to stay in with you on a long term basis [is] a very scary prison to be caught in.'

It is only rarely that the class solidarity that is generally firmly in evidence online breaks down. When one woman gives a bad reference to a worker, complaining about her for flirting with guys on the phone, another member responds, 'They need their time and during that time whether they talk to one boy, 5 boy [sic] or no boy is none of my business.'

Another time, when a photograph of a maid that has been posted for vetting appears to show a girl in her mid-teens, several call the poster a lawbreaker; in response, a few members leap to her defence. 'As if people have kept the birth certificates of the maids…there must be thousands of underage maids in Gurgaon and Delhi,' says one woman in a post. Another woman chastises her. 'Let's not take our civic responsibility so lightly…we want rules and laws but not when they come in the way of our convenience. Our society is becoming a dangerously selfish place.'

The law, though, doesn't actually back civic-minded people who think that if you want to help impoverished young people, you should pay for them to attend school rather than hiring them. It sides with the people who want to hire teens to work in their homes, adopting a reasoning that many child rights activists hate to hear—that parents need the income from their teenage children. The groups trying to reduce child labour say that by sending teens to work, parents lock themselves and their children into poverty for another generation. But the state hasn't been convinced. The law only bars hiring a maid under the age of fourteen, a change first brought about in 2006. In 2016, that ban was watered down when a loophole was inserted into the main child labour prohibition law allowing children under fourteen to work for family members, which is in any case how many children first become servants in their teens, by working for distant relatives in the city. And despite efforts by rights groups to urge people to hire women eighteen and older, many employers actively seek out teens.

At one point I come across a portal that offers a fairly lengthy list of agencies that supply maids. This list spurred more than 300 comments posted from 2010 to 2013 from people 'urgently' seeking maids to take care of children or elderly parents, or do general housework, or do all three at once. A post by a man from Haryana looking for a 'full time semi-trained girl' of 'age around 14/15 years' to take care of his toddler while at the same time doing other household work is pretty typical of the requests. No one seems to think it odd that this internet discussion is taking place on a website run by nursery school chain Shemrock, which advertises its devotion to 'the social, emotional, spiritual, physical, motor and cognitive development' of children.

In a country as given to red tape and regulations as India, it's astonishing that there are hardly any rules regulating the recruitment of domestic workers, particularly given how young so many of them are. In 2014, Delhi made a start on the process, issuing an executive order with rules for placement agencies, but it hasn't been fully implemented. The Delhi Labour Department and Delhi Commission of Women, which was to help administer the order by perusing placement agency records for labour violations and to identify the people families say are missing, didn't respond to interview requests. In this vacuum, the demand for maids at any cost—or rather, at the lowest cost possible— is spurring crimes that range from trafficking to being kept in near slavery-like conditions. Worse, all this takes place behind the closed doors of a home. Occasionally, though, some of the malpractices do come to light.

In 2007, an outfit calling itself the Adivasi Sewa Samiti, or Tribal Welfare Society, brought a teenage maid to Delhi and placed her with a couple. There, her employers' driver allegedly raped her and she became pregnant, according to court records. Instead of reporting the matter to the police when the crime was brought to their attention, the couple that had recruited the teenager sold her baby to a childless family for 23,000 rupees. After an exposé by a cable news channel led to an investigation and legal proceedings, a lower court ruled that the baby boy could stay with the couple that had purchased him. Shocked by the ruling, a city agency, the Children's Welfare Committee, asked a higher court to intervene. On this court's orders, social workers contacted the young girl's family in Jharkhand and told them what had happened to their daughter; the family in turn told the authorities that they weren't at all interested in having her return home. The city government finally agreed to hire her as a 'house aunty' in one of its facilities, where her child could live with her.

At the close of the case, the court expressed grave concern about the numbers of very young girls who could be seen taking care of children across Delhi and urged authorities and neighbourhood associations to work together to combat this. But such calls have been unable to shatter the strange looking-glass perception that prevails among the prosperous. In this world view, workers who ask for more money and more rights are greedy thieves—'extortionists' is a word one hears often—who need to be put in their place. It is employers who are the true victims, who are always being taken advantage of, and let down by their ungrateful workers, and the maids and their handlers who are the villains.

'Someday I will get someone who will be as reasonable as we are,' writes one woman on one maid referral Facebook group, drawing on the language of workers' struggles without a trace of irony. 'It's a fight against a smaller version of corruption...we all should unite and fight against them.'

'SERVICE, NOT SERVANTS'

I FIRST HEAR ABOUT THE Maids' Company while eavesdropping on a conversation that its founder is having at a party. Gauri Singh, a Punjabi woman, began to follow in her parents' footsteps after school, like many young Indians. Her parents were both architects who had founded their own firm in Chandigarh, and worked on prestigious projects that included a naval base in southern India. She went as far as completing an architecture degree before veering off in her own direction. After graduate school in London for development studies, she worked for the Gujarat-based development group SEWA, which focuses on informal women workers. Several years later, she started a small microfinance group aimed at women in the city of Ludhiana in Punjab. Many of her clients were maids, and they gave her an idea for a new venture, which she is telling a mutual friend about at this party we are both at circa 2011.

Later, we become friends ourselves. But all I know at that point is that she is stylish and lives in a beautifully designed house, in a nice part of town, a combination that invariably prejudices me against people I don't know very well. So when I hear her describe her current work, training and placing women in cooking and cleaning jobs in Gurgaon, as development work, I scoff silently to myself: how can supplying maids to well-off Indians possibly qualify as development?

A year later, I come across Gauri's website for the business, The Maids' Company. It's cheerful, with a cartoon logo of a smiling woman with a lopsided bun holding a frying pan, a broom and other sundry implements. A calculator on the website allows prospective employers to price the cost of four, six, eight, or twelve hours of cooking and cleaning, with rates pegged to the minimum wages in the state of Haryana. I am trying to figure out how people should decide what a fair salary for their cook or cleaner is—something I find myself grappling with even years after I began employing help as I careen wildly between wanting to be better than my peers, and yet finding myself worrying, as so many of my class fear, that I am being 'taken advantage of'. On forums dedicated to offering guidance to new arrivals in Delhi, both foreigners and returning Indians, fights frequently break out over the issue of what the right wage is, and people of the same class and affluence can arrive at quite different amounts.

Like many labour markets in India, domestic help seems to simultaneously suffer from feast and famine. At dinner parties, guests complain that it's difficult to find reliable help. And yet, according to the Census, between 2001 and 2011 India added an average of 13.5 million people a year to its workforce. They are mostly men and most of them lack the certificates to allow them to get even the most basic of white-collar jobs. As a result, women often must dip in and out of the labour market to supplement a husband's income with work she has been trained to do since she was a child. There are many of these women, and they might undercut one another by 100 or 200 rupees a month when the need for a job is dire. That's the feast. The mismatch comes about in part because employers' expectations aren't in line with what they're willing to pay. At the prices they want to pay, they can most easily get inexperienced help, migrants who are still invested in the village, and who will need to go home at harvest and festival time for several weeks, after which they may or may not come back. If you want someone who doesn't require a lot of training, who can make her own decisions about how long to stay at a job and who is invested in putting down roots in the city and therefore staying in a job—that means paying more. A lot more. The smartest, most experienced, and most trustworthy women—who can manage your life if you wish and escort your children to play dates without you being there—are much fewer in number and highly sought after. That's the famine.

When we meet in a coffee shop in August 2012, Gauri tells me that she believes that if she can fix many of the common complaints people have about maids—that it takes so long to train them to the ways of city housekeeping, that people are late or take time off without warning, that there's high churn—then she can in turn fix the employers. In particular she hopes to fix the pay scale, which shocked her when she began carrying out surveys.

Gauri's surveys of women working in Gurgaon in 2011 showed that women were averaging 5,500 rupees a month for a full day's work, usually around ten to twelve hours, even when employed by people at the top of India's income ladder, working at the multinationals and IT firms that are commonplace to this still scruffy-looking Haryana city just across the border from Delhi. At the time, she calculated that the minimum a family of four could get by on was 10,000 rupees, or about $1.60 per person a day (in purchasing power terms, it's the equivalent of about $7 a person). She and her two most trusted lieutenants, one of whom followed her from SEWA, decided to peg the salaries they negotiated to the state of Haryana's minimum wage, which meant asking employers to pay about 50 per cent more than they were used to paying, as well as committing to annual increases.

A year into starting, Gauri had recruited about seventy maids and was refining the business model, hoping to eventually take it nationwide, perhaps even have the workers share in the profits once it broke even. In 2012, a customer hiring a maid through Gauri could expect to pay around 7,150 rupees for someone to work for a 12-hour day. In 2015, the calculator estimated pay for an eight-hour day at 9,600 rupees—at that point it no longer offered the choice of a 12-hour day online. By this time the firm had recruited and trained a few hundred women. The company kept 10 per cent of salaries to pay for overheads that included rent, training and a nurse to provide first aid, or help a maid get tests or hospitalization when required, but nevertheless firmly operated in the red on capital provided by Gauri from a personal loan. Her customers, like those who rely on Mrs Sen, were well-off, but even so they told her that her salaries for basic cleaning pinched.

'At one point I thought, wow, maybe I'm being very unreasonable with my price points because I would get, "Ms Singh your prices are exorbitant." "Are you importing maids from overseas, from England?" and so on. The general going rate at one time for dish-washing was 300 rupees. That's ten bucks a day to wash some fifty dishes daily. That's ridiculous.'

The pushback confirmed something that Gauri had come to believe. If she, who could easily command the respect of her clients by the way she looked, dressed and spoke English, if she who was one of them, was facing so much resistance, then how could maids change the equation by themselves? In a household where they were far outnumbered by people from a different class, and with new women arriving in the city every day, eager to take their jobs, what chance did they have of convincing their employers to pay them more, allow them to use the toilet, or give them a weekly day off?

Instead, she decides class warfare needs to take place between members of the same class. People like us, she argues, won't change their behaviour unless they're likely to lose face in front of another member of their own social class, unless they come to believe what they are doing is not the norm for their social class, or the social class they aspire to join. 'They won't listen to a maid,' she tells me on another occasion, referring to her elite clients. 'They'll listen to someone like me.'

Many rights activists may be wary of the idea that workers—or members of any other group—lack the agency to win victories for themselves, that they need someone of a higher social status to lobby on their behalf. And certainly the struggles for independence in India; civil rights for African-Americans in the United States; against apartheid in South Africa; and for Dalit rights in independent India would have been severely delayed had people waited for buy-in from those they were struggling against, whether British, white, or upper-caste Indians. But the idea that in some kinds of struggles you need to enlist both entities in a power dynamic—and not rely only on the disempowered to change the status quo—makes sense to me. I still remember being baffled by the subtext of an 'anti-date rape' class at my Chicago public school in the late 1980s. While the girls were herded into a room to be taught how to fend off such an assault, the boys were sent off to play basketball. As girls, our awareness had to be raised to the possibility that a crime would be committed against us if we were not careful enough, but the boys were not required to undergo any kind of awareness-raising about the lines they should not cross.

More than two decades on, women's rights groups in many countries target their messages of equality to young men as well as women. Labour groups often try to work closely with companies to improve factory conditions around the world. In the US, Hand in Hand is a network of domestic employers that seeks to guide people who want to 'do the right thing' in their homes. Another major domestic rights group there has called on employers to sign a pledge to proceed ethically in their housekeeping practices.

As things stand, many maids, at least those new to the city, are loath to complain about the treatment meted out to them until it becomes unbearable. The mostly Bengali migrants I meet at The Maids' Company recruiting office when I visit in January 2014 share stories of past employers, and paint a sobering picture. During a discussion about the importance of learning Hindi, Seoli, a short, sturdy Bengali woman, describes a few episodes with a family she had worked for in the past. 'I did all her work but I couldn't understand everything she said, what to do? She told me to iron clothes and I just stood there quietly because I didn't understand what she said,' Seoli tells the others. 'Brother gave me such a tight slap and said, "Daughter, why can't you learn? Learn fast. We'll all like it if we can understand each other."'

'He slapped you?' asks Preeti Chauhan, the company's housekeeping trainer, who instils proper door-knocking etiquette and other skills in the recruits.

'Bhaiya was nice,' Seoli responds.

'He slapped you?' Preeti asks again.

'Those people were nice,' Seoli replies.

Now I try. 'But they were hitting you.'

'Just two three slaps. "Why can't you learn?" For that. But because they hit me I learned Hindi good, out of fear,' Seoli chuckles.

Preeti tells the women, if someone hits you, they can go to jail. It's a crime, she explains to them. It turns out that Seoli is not as accepting as her comments have led us to believe. She actually did end up calling the police on that employer. 'She used to slap me all the time, from when she woke up,' Seoli says, referring to the daughter-in-law of the household. Even when Seoli fell and fractured her hand on the stairs she continued working. 'If I hadn't served her tea on time, she'd give me a slap. So I got very angry. She said, "I won't give you your money. Get lost." She threw my stuff outside. I called the police.'

When the police arrived, the woman pulled a classic gambit so common as to be routine when a worker leaves—or tries to. She accused Seoli of stealing her smartphone. But Seoli was helped by two unexpected sources. A neighbour told the police that Seoli was a good person and that she had seen her being hit by her employers. And the employer's young son, not yet schooled in the notion that family and class solidarity must be absolute, burst into tears during the proceedings and told the police, 'Papa hits aunty a lot.' The police, not known for their sensitivity and clearly not conscious of the possible risk to the little boy of involving him further, asked the child if he had seen mummy's phone. The boy went and fetched it from under the pillow, where he had seen his mother put it.

'If madam makes even the slightest accusation of this kind, come to us right away. Don't accept it,' Preeti tells the women, her face serious. 'If someone slaps you, swears at you or accuses you of theft, don't swallow it. Come to us right away.

'Why should you do this? Today, they may accuse you of something small. If you don't make a fuss, tomorrow they may accuse you of something big.' Preeti also adds that if an accusation of theft of an item is brought against a maid, two employees of The Maids' Company will go search the house of the person against whom the accusation has been made. If the item is found, it's up to the employer to decide if she wants to file a police complaint.

This particular clause of The Maids' Company contract underscores the prickly negotiations inherent in trying to improve upon the status quo while at the same time trying to satisfy people who have rigid and highly hierarchical expectations. But if, at times, Gauri's contracts appear to bow to employers' sometimes invasive wishes, for the most part they try to venture where placement agencies rarely go, even though it is the maid brokers who opened this door by bringing written agreements for the first time into a sphere where, for the most part, everything is agreed upon verbally.

Because placement agencies take a large commission up front, a receipt and a rudimentary contract have become common between employers and the brokers. These contracts are for the most part very basic—laying out little more than the parties' names and addresses, the salary and fees, and the worker's start and end date. Placement agency contracts don't address work conditions, leaving that almost entirely to the employers. The Maids' Company contracts, by contrast, delve into minutiae that at first brush seem unusual to find in a work contract. Each clause, shaped by one or another of Gauri's experiences with clients, offers a unique lens into how employers behave when left to themselves.

Most people don't brook interference into their household matters, whether regarding their relations with their spouses, their upbringing of their children, or their relations with the help. But through the Trojan horse of the contract, which accompanies the much-desired maid and promises refunds and other protections attractive to the client, The Maids' Company clients are persuaded into laying bare their housekeeping to the scrutiny of Gauri and her colleagues and promising to hew to their standards.

In one of its clauses, for example, the contract stipulates that, 'The client shall treat the maid with dignity and provide a proper toilet, which the maid [will] use on a daily basis.' That was added in the earliest contract, after Gauri did a pilot experiment providing maids in Ludhiana, and many maids reported being barred from bathrooms in their employers' homes. Even in Gurgaon, she recalls one maid telling her that the couple that had hired her told her to go outside. 'Where the fuck is she supposed to go?' says Gauri. (Guards and drivers are often not given access to a bathroom either, which is why the wealthiest neighbourhoods, with the most domestic help, are as likely as a busy public road to afford the sight of men peeing against a wall.)

Another clause in the contract states, 'Drinking water must be made available to the maid.' This was added after maids said they were embarrassed to ask their new employers for water multiple times during a hot day and would often go without drinking any even as the temperature crossed into the forties. Helping yourself would be a no-no for a newly hired maid—it's not for nothing that refrigerators with locks are available for sale in India.

Maids on the longer shifts—eight hours or twelve hours—began reporting that employers were so eager to extract every last minute of work out of them, perhaps because they felt the service was expensive, that they were chivvied into more work when they tried to take a break or sat down to eat lunch. So another clause was added: 'The maid shall be provided 2 teas (mid-morning and mid-afternoon) with lunch in a 9/10 hour service. The maid shall be provided 1 tea (mid-morning) in a 4/5 hour service.'

The Maids' Company's household survey that new employers must fill out before a maid is placed with them goes into even greater detail, specifying that the tea breaks must not be less than fifteen minutes, while a forty-minute break should be allowed for lunch. If lunch isn't going to be provided, the maids should get an additional 1,000 rupees a month. The family is also asked to state whether the maid will have to cook her own lunch or if she will be eating from food prepared for the whole family, whether she should eat before the family or after them?

These are not minor questions, and not addressing them upfront means that every day a maid is tiptoeing across a minefield to figure out what she may and may not do in her workplace. One maid tells me that when her employer had not returned from a morning outing until quite late in the afternoon, and had not phoned with instructions on when she would return, she went ahead and ate lunch. When the employer returned to find that she had eaten already, she was apoplectic. 'Who do you think you are to eat before me?' she shouted. 'Am I the servant or are you?'

It is this kind of anger and rage that Gauri hopes to change most of all. She believes the relations between employers and the help, with the veneer of familial ties and a familiarity bred over months and years have been too intensely personal. The help—and their employers— would be better served by drawing sharper lines between the work and the person who does it, to separate the two in a way that Marxist thinkers might critique, but that Gauri thinks could liberate both the worker and her employer. 'There's no need to shout, scream and go nuts on her or feel insecure that, "If she goes, what will become of me?"' says Gauri. 'You should be focused on your domestic work, not your domestic worker, not on controlling and micromanaging her.'

This is a fairly uphill battle, something Gauri herself comes to feel some five years into the venture, when the prospect of scaling up to other cities is looking increasingly distant. Changes in Indian taxes that have driven up what she must charge employers haven't helped. But more than that, she says, 'I spend more time training the market than I do the labour.' In 2016, Gauri decided to take a different approach, all but shutting down The Maids' Company, and putting her efforts into a teaching app that serves as an intermediary between madams and maids. Like the platforms that allow professors to assign reading and students to access these instructions, the app, Dekho Seekho, allows employers to select recipes, assign tasks and pay salaries, and workers to receive these assignments and teach themselves housekeeping and pasta recipes from specially created videos in multiple languages. One video enlightens viewers on the three ways to make a bed and how to dust fragile glass ornaments with a sock. Another teaches the recipe for shepherd's pie. On the worker's app—but not on the employers'—there's a little animated video about the dignity of housekeeping jobs.

At one point, Gauri mulls over the idea that it might be possible to develop this further into an 'Uber' for maids, but decides that could only happen if both employers and help clear some kind of stringent security process; in other words, that stage is a long way away. I would have said at one point that the Uber model isn't adaptable to homes, people are still used to getting into vehicles driven by people they don't know. It's hard to imagine them leaving their homes in the hands of strangers. Then Airbnb went a step beyond Uber to show that people can be made comfortable cycling in and out of a stranger's home—or inviting strangers into their own homes. Is the ideal domestic work relationship of the future one where the worker has no contact with the employer, and vice versa, where work is done and payments made via an app without the overlay of a personal relationship?

The worst relationships are far too intense, it is true, driven both by the still-feudal attitudes that shape the relationship, but also by the stress of running an Indian household. The madams know that whether the maid comes or not, meals must be provided and the schedules of other family members must not be disrupted. Even in well-paying, kindly households, such sudden upheavals aren't uncommon, because upheavals in the life of women who work as maids aren't uncommon. The insecurity generated by not knowing what crisis a new day will bring leads many women who run their households with outside help to fixate on the women who work for them, for it is she who makes the lives they like possible, and so they boomerang between gratefulness and irritation, dependence and distancing. The maid becomes a metaphor for all the ways in which life in India is full of disappointing and exhausting encounters and on whom, in the privacy of one's home, it is acceptable to vent these frustrations.

For a worker, meanwhile, almost the only way she is able to improve her working conditions is by putting her life story before her employer and enlisting him or her as a kind of family elder. She needs to become a supplicant, deferential and help-seeking. And so many maids sometimes decide to read the scolding and slapping meted out to them not as unacceptable transgressions, but as markers that they truly are part of the family, and that therefore their well-being will eventually be looked after. After all, is this not the way many husbands discipline their wives, or parents the children whom they love and for whom they hold themselves responsible?

And yet, if the worst relationships suffer for being too intensely personal, that enmeshedness is also a hallmark of some of the best relationships that exist. You hire domestic help so that you don't have to think about housekeeping, so that you can run from the stream of things that constantly need fixing and attending to in a well-run Indian home, the many fresh meals that need to be provided, the never-ending cleaning, but it doesn't quite work out that way. Instead, what happens often is an exchange of responsibilities.

That is a realization that each generation of domestic employers often eventually comes to, as British women living in India during the raj did more than two centuries ago. In the early 1800s, Mary Martha Sherwood, a clergyman's daughter, asks another Englishwoman what happens to the children of Indian women who start nursing their employers' children. 'They commonly die,' says the woman, who appears to regard these deaths as the unavoidable collateral damage of the job. But Sherwood is aghast. 'This is murder,' she exclaims. The other woman responds, 'Whenever they nurse a white baby they cease to care for their own.' The only way to avoid this, she tells Sherwood, is if the English mother who has hired the wet nurse goes to 'the trouble of keeping the infant within her compound, and seeing it daily'. In other words, one woman cares for her ma'am's child, and in turn, memsahib looks after the other woman's infant.

When people from Jharkhand or West Bengal or Uttar Pradesh get placed in homes across Delhi through the interventions of a Mrs Sen or a Mr Srivastava, they roll the dice in a game that might place them, behind those walls, with one of the Indian families who pride themselves on being good employers, who understand that if you want

a good conscience when it comes to your domestic help, you cannot
seek a complete sloughing off of domestic duties. Or, that roll of dice
may land them on a less lucky square. Until they pass through those
gates to the interior of those mysterious walls, they have no way of
knowing what they will find.

PART III

The Sahibs

KHAN MARKET

LALA RAM NARAIN KHOSLA, THEN the manager of a sewing machine factory, came to Delhi sometime in the 1930s. Like many entrepreneurial Punjabis, he was beckoned to the city by the opportunities to be had from the building of a brand-new capital for the British Raj. His son founded a different business in the 1950s, supplying machinery for businesses. Eighty years later, his grandson, Deepak Khosla, together with his son, continues to run that business, manufacturing generators and compressed air machines. And all of them live in the Prithviraj Road bungalow that Ram Narain Khosla bought, around the corner from the city's popular Khan Market, which, despite its ramshackle inner lanes, grew from being a better-than-average neighbourhood market to a hub of bookshops, restaurants and bars popular with the city's elite. Now fancy personal care shops, like Kiehl's and L'Occitane have sprung up next to cloth shops and crowded groceries that have somehow managed to hang on.

We are sitting in Khosla's lawn on a pleasant February morning in 2014, in front of the bungalow where he lives with his wife, two sons, their wives and, at that time, two grandchildren. I have just asked the genial man in his sixties which of his dozen or so domestic helpers I may interview. Perhaps the slightly morose-looking man in a grey uniform who served us tea? 'We generally don't expose them to outsiders,' says Khosla, who is prone to fits of chuckling. He breaks into a chuckle now. 'Except for serving tea and coffee. But you can ask *me* anything.'

Had he perhaps not read my email? I thought I had been rather clear that I wished to interview both employers and their staff? I try to rephrase my request in a more palatable way, using more and more florid metaphors over our two meetings. 'Suppose I'm writing a book about a marriage and I only write the husband's side, won't you feel that—'

'This is a different thing, this is the Khosla family,' Khosla says. 'You can do this servant interview with other families. In this family it's been forbidden.'

'What if they would like to talk to me about their lives?' I persist.

'You can contact them in Khan Market,' Khosla responds.

'Khan Market?' I ask, the wheels slowly turning. Perhaps he sees on my face the shadow of a plan to stalk his cook. 'No, no, don't do that,' he chuckles. 'Don't do that.'

In meeting me, and arranging for me to speak with his daughters-in-law, Khosla is already pushing back the discomfort expressed by the joint family he lives in when they gathered in the evening to discuss my request, he tells me. Even though he's the patriarch, Khosla is just one vote among six adults since, as in most joint families, big decisions are decided by consensus and careful negotiation. I have only got this far because of personal connections: my mother's school friend is his cousin, and it turns out his schoolmate is my editor, although they haven't been in touch in years. Khosla spends large parts of our first interview trying to get me to get our mutual contacts on the phone—a bit of a weird time to catch-up, I think at first. Then it dawns on me: I am still being vetted.

In my time as a journalist in Delhi, I've rarely interviewed the wealthy, except for the occasional puff piece. In general, the people I've interviewed live in hovels, not mansions; from their grandfathers and father they have inherited a sliver of land, or debts, or nothing at all. Vital as it is to illuminate the contours of poverty in any country, journalists often turn to the poor and destitute as subjects for in-depth investigations for a less than noble reason—interviewing the poor is just *so* much easier. Whether it is the courtesy generally accorded a visitor just about anywhere in India, or the deference accorded to people recognizable as being 'sahib log', as journalists often are, when you turn up at the doorstep of a poor family and seek to ask about their lives, they don't tell you to get lost. They don't invoke notions of privacy. They don't insist that you must show them your quotes because, don't you know, journalists so often get it wrong. As a result, we have become rather spoiled by the generosity of the sorts of people we so often interview. Is it generosity or is it ignorance? Do they know, as the rich do, that if they tell us to go away there isn't a whole lot we can do about it?

Or perhaps it is us journalists who signal to some groups but not others, that they may not refuse us. When it comes to a family in a village or a low-income city slum, we think nothing of turning up on their doorsteps or barging into their hospital rooms as the case may be. When interviewing those higher up the food chain, though, we kow-tow, we beseech their handlers, we agree to terms and conditions, as I have, with many of the upper-class people I have interviewed.

In fact, the most difficult thing about interviewing the poor—apart from the crowd that inevitably gathers—is figuring out just how much generosity to accept. If you are there for a few minutes, a woman is dispatched to make you tea. Stay longer than a few minutes and many families insist that you stay for a meal, opening up a real conundrum. To decline an offer of food is a loaded decision in a country still riven with prejudices of caste and religion. On the other hand, if you accept, you might be taking food out of the mouths of people who can ill afford to spare it.

These questions never arise when turning up on the doorsteps of the affluent. The main reason for this is a logistical one: it is quite hard to actually reach the doorstep of a rich Indian family. Before the doorstep, comes the driveway, an obstacle course of Audis, BMWs and the like. And much before the driveway, there are the high walls, the gate and a guardhouse whose occupant's opening gambit is kryptonite to the intrepid journalist—'Appointment hai?'

At the very start of my reporting for this book, I had a naive vision of what my story would be. In that happy time between conception and action, when a piece of journalism is briefly the most perfect version of itself, I imagined finding the modern-day counterpart of a home like that of the immensely wealthy Tagores, the privileged Calcutta business family that produced the writer and poet Rabindranath Tagore and many other writers as well, including some of the first female editors of magazines in India. The Tagore family staff in the late 1800s numbered at least thirty people whose salaries totalled about 250 rupees. These included coachmen, wet nurses, two maids, French, Brahmin and Muslim cooks, and a variety of what could be called footmen—people who stood outside the doors of quarters of different

branches of the family to announce guests, call other servants and run
sundry errands. I fantasized telling the story not just of Rabindranath
Tagore, but of the man he remembers telling him stories and dunking
his head in water when he was naughty. But it was not to be. Indian
employers were exceedingly reluctant to let me interview their help,
and for that matter most workers I interviewed wanted me to have
nothing to do with their employers.

There were many reasons for this reticence. It's possible that many
employers I approached were unenthusiastic about being interviewed
because Delhi newspapers had increasingly begun reporting on the
abusive Indian employers of domestic help. Just as likely is the
possibility that employers were worried just how much their staff,
particularly long-time staff, knew about them. 'They are like the lizards
on the wall, always there, always listening,' one female employer told
me in an interview, not meaning it as unkindly as it might sound.
Outside of your family, who can know as much about you as this
person who sees you every day? Trying to imagine my own cook
being debriefed about me by a stranger, I felt mildly uneasy.

My cook—and the neighbourhood apartment-to-apartment
garbage collectors, it must be said—for instance, know when I get
my period. But, in addition to this, the cook alone knows how much
rent I pay, what I've purchased recently, and how I talk to my mother
when no one else (almost) is around. Not even my closest friends
have each of these pieces of information about me. But then, I know
quite a bit about her too, from the fact that she works occasionally
as a property broker to the fact that she keeps her main occupation a
secret from her family in Bengal, who themselves have many servants.
I know, too, that for a brief period, she hired someone approximating
a nanny to help her out when her daughter was young and she landed
a high-paying job at a farmhouse for an expat family. If I know all
this from less than three years of working together, Mr Khosla must
know a great deal more. I decide to take up Mr Khosla on his offer to
stand in for his servants. But it soon appears that Mr Khosla doesn't
seem to know all that much about his staff. Where does the son of
the staff member he feels closest to work? Some office. ('He is not
a domestic servant. Everybody is rising,' Mr Khosla adds.) What has
happened to the daughter of the other long-time indoor male staff

member? Married to some man in some company. Of course, he may know perfectly well which man and which company, and this might be an effort to protect their privacy (or make it difficult for them to be tracked down by a persistent journalist). But the haziness I suspect is more likely due to the fact that he has never been the main person responsible for dealing with them. In general, in India, that responsibility is a woman's, at least for staff who work inside the home. 'The lady of the house was my mother and now it's my wife and my two daughters-in-law,' he explains. His domain, and that of his sons, and probably one day his grandsons, is the office and the business his father started.

'We have no bar on women but they don't show any interest. Like Vani wants to do her beauty treatment [business], Ruchi wants to do her dental [clinic], they have no time for our business,' he insists. 'They are not interested and *we* are not interested. We prefer they are busy in their own lives. In the evening we meet as husband and wife.' At those times, they try not to bore one another with shop talk relating to one sphere or the other, and they certainly don't interfere with one another's spheres. 'It's a very clear demarcation. My wife won't decide what is the manager's salary in the office, I won't decide what is the cook's salary in the house,' says Khosla. 'But the drivers are part of the company so their salaries will be decided in the office. The drivers, the guards, the outside staff, that is not decided by my wife or my daughters-in-law.'

There are only a few workers for a household who, in India, are considered to be more properly the employees of the men of the family, such as drivers, and sometimes security guards. And this difference in status comes with tangible differences in pay and other work conditions. At the Khosla home, the cook earns about 12,000 rupees and doesn't have a regular day off (but can take leave when needed). The drivers earn 15,000 rupees to 20,000 rupees, and are entitled to overtime, and a fixed weekly off. 'They have lot of opportunities with offices and banks and foreigners. So it's more difficult to get a driver,' he says. 'Cooks don't keep leaving the job. Drivers leave as soon as they get a better job.'

In the case of the Khosla family, the drivers are actually company employees. Yet even in other families, including that of my parents, drivers are treated as if they are in formal jobs. The difference in attitude to jobs done by men is sometimes enshrined in public policy. In 2016, the Indian government decided security guards must be treated as 'skilled' workers, which meant a higher level of minimum wage is now due to them. No such determination has been made for cooks or nannies.

Many of the workers in this house were hired as young men by Khosla's mother, and several of them are in their late fifties. In some cases, the younger workers are their children or extended relatives. But in recent years, the placement agents have got a toehold even here, in the realm of the old retainer, supplying nannies for Khosla's grandchildren. And as some of the older workers retire, the family may well have to turn to the market to replace them as well.

Khosla tells me that one of his drivers is on the verge of retirement, while one of the men who does housekeeping work is also approaching that age. But fortunately, the driver's son, who in recent years has begun living at the Khosla residence, will remain in Delhi and is likely to take up the mantle. Khosla describes this man, who at the age of forty is set to inherit his father's job, as among the children of their help who is doing the best. The driver who is retiring has told Khosla that he is looking forward to spending more time with his wife, who has lived in a hillside village the entire time that the driver has been working in Delhi. 'He's been away forty-three years,' Khosla chuckles. 'He lives here in my house but he's never brought his wife.'

'She's never come for a visit?'

'Maybe,' says Khosla. 'I don't remember meeting her. They have farmland or something, she must be busy with that.'

'So you and she wouldn't recognize each other if you met?'

'I don't think so.'

Later, I find myself coming back to this detail, marvelling at the asymmetry encapsulated in it. The driver has spent more time over the past few decades with the Khoslas than with his own family, he knows what his employer's wife, children and even in-laws look like. But his own wife would be a stranger here, in his home away from home. Yet, there is nothing very surprising in this play of shadow and light in this relationship: on the one hand a person about whom every detail is knowable and must be known, on the other hand a cipher. In my own parents' home, one maid has a young son in the village whom I've never met and probably will never meet, though she has been part of my family's life for a decade and has easily met over a dozen of our extended family over this time, serving them tea and samosas on numerous occasions. It's an unevenness that can span generations.

My cousin and his wife were visiting from California not long before I met the Khoslas. An aunt and uncle of mine assigned one of their most trusted drivers to my cousin for the brief visit—someone who has been with them decades, a man I have seen at their home for as long as I can remember. My cousin and his wife sit in the back and I sit next to the driver so we get to chatting. He asks me about my sister, remembers when my grandmother lived in this part of town, across the road, and recounts to me the locations of all the different homes she and my grandfather owned in this city before his sudden death of a heart attack after a card game in a hotel in Civil Lines plunged her into financial distress and fire sales. I'm amazed. And ashamed. This man is a repository of my own family history. But, until I heard my cousin say it, I was not even a hundred per cent sure of his name.

MAYUR VIHAR

INDIA'S FORMER AMBASSADOR TO FINLAND is dancing. At least, as he shimmies one leg forward, and then back, and then does the same on the other side, it looks rather like that. Part moonwalk, part jitterbug, Om Prakash is demonstrating his technique for polishing to a high-gloss shine the tile floors of the apartment he and his wife share in a colony for retired diplomats in East Delhi's Mayur Vihar area. I have heard about them from my mother, who lives a few floors away in the same tower in the red-brick Indian Foreign Service flats, once located in a nothingness. Over the years, that transformed into a quiet, tree-lined residential lane surrounded by similar housing complexes, which was later widened to make way for the metro station that is now the backdrop for cycle-rickshaw drivers fighting for fares in front of the complex.

The reason my mother tells me about the Prakashes is that they have no servant. They are famous in the complex for having no servant. And this is not the 'no servant' of other families, who on further probing admit yes, well, they do have someone who comes in for a few hours each morning to do the sweeping and mopping and dusting, who doesn't? Not so for the Prakashes. Between the two of them, husband and wife in their sixties, they do the cleaning and cooking in their 1,200 square-foot flat, an apartment that seemed unbelievably spacious back in the 1980s to the young diplomats who scrimped and saved to buy flats in the complex.

The Prakashes did have help when they were stationed in Japan and Ethiopia, Italy and Finland. One of them was a man who hailed from the Prakashes' home state of Haryana and had worked with Om Prakash's father, perhaps on the farm in Haryana on which Mr Prakash grew up. But by the time the Prakashes returned to India, their man was settled abroad with no plans to come back anytime soon. On their return to Delhi, they had to start anew and they found it difficult to adjust to part-time help, most of whom in this part of town are South Indian and speak Tamil. The Prakashes missed the trust they had had with their old help; around here, they say, people sometimes go to the bathroom with purse and phone tucked under an arm when the maid is around. 'Both our servants were utterly honest. If you left gold coins lying around nothing would happen. Once you get used to these kinds of people you can't get used to anybody else,' said Mr Prakash.

The couple realized that they no longer needed to have someone around all the time as they did when their children were young or when they were working and hosting diplomatic dinners as was often required in their roles by the Ministry of External Affairs. Nor are they called upon to provide regular babysitting duty for their grandchildren. 'All our children are abroad,' he says. 'All my responsibilities are technically over.'

So began their experiment of not having any kind of help at all. There's a division of labour of sorts, with Om Prakash doing the cleaning while his wife Vanita does the cooking.

'He gets up at 5.30 or something. I keep sleeping,' says Mrs Prakash, who is wearing a white kurta with a green pattern, her shoulders draped with a green chunni on the warm September morning when we meet. 'He makes coffee for me and gives me the coffee.' 'Semi-espresso,' adds her husband. 'Not the paper filter. Pressure brewed.' Then they go out for a walk. At seven they go to meet their laughter club in the park downstairs. Later, they come back and make breakfast, usually something light like fruits and oatmeal. At some point in the morning, Mr Prakash will sweep and mop the floor, standing on two square pieces of towel and slip-sliding around the room. Kneeling with a cloth to mop the floor, the typical way, isn't very easy past your forties. After experimenting with different techniques, and different mops, this is the process he found that worked best for producing a streak-free shine.

'He doesn't let me do floor work because he feels he can do it well. Om feels good about doing a job well. He wants to give me more comfort. Say I want to make oatmeal. He'll cut fruits for me,' says Mrs Prakash. 'Suppose I'm out and I start chatting with a friend, he'll have made the rice.' 'I normally don't do kitchen, but I do the rice,' adds her husband.

A tall, slender man in his sixties, with only a little white in his hair, Mr Prakash looks like he could have been in the army. But instead, his roots are in a farming village—his concern with the purity and wholesomeness of the food they eat comes from that rural upbringing—he is the oldest of eight brothers and sisters. Until he was fourteen, he looked after his younger siblings, and helped around the house, as well as out in the fields, in addition to studying at a local school. 'My mother was asthmatic so she couldn't handle dust. I had to help her with cleaning. I had to help her with fodder for the cow and grinding wheat,' he says.

That changed when he was a teenager. His father, who had as long ago as the 1970s decided that there was no future in farming, dispatched him to Delhi so that he could attend a better government school and try to get into college. 'In ninth grade I moved...my father rented a small apartment for me,' he says. He remembers returning home to work on the farm as a college student and having the bad luck of having his exams scheduled for the period when he was in charge of irrigating his family's fields at night. Every family had a time slot when it was their turn to draw water, and if you didn't take the water you missed your chance for two weeks. The Prakash family's slot came between 11 p.m. and 1 a.m. the day before he had to sit for his electrodynamics paper. But he still passed the exam and did well.

He wasn't among the thousands and thousands of Indians who dream of entering the civil services from the time they are in school. For most Indians, the surest path to upward mobility is a government job, and among government jobs the Indian Administrative Service and the Indian Foreign Service the most coveted. After college, Mr Prakash began teaching at a university and was, for the most part, happy with his job. Slowly, however, he began to think he too should sit for the notoriously tough entrance exam. He was finally convinced when he saw the abiding regret of a fellow student who had been at the top of his class at college, whose doctoral thesis had been praised by all his professors, had had a shining path ahead of him in academia, but who kept lamenting, 'I should have sat for the exam.' At around that time, India raised the entrance age for the services, a step that was supposed to make the service more egalitarian by allowing people who had taken a longer time to finish school or college, possibly because of coming from a disadvantaged childhood, to apply.

'It got me thinking it's better to have appeared and failed than to have a remorse all your life,' he says. He first got into the police force, which Mrs Prakash says concerned everyone who knew him. 'He's not the kind of guy to go after guys with a stick,' she says, with a smile. Then he transferred into the Indian Foreign Service, earning about 600 rupees a month at first.

'I was happy in the IFS,' he says. 'You are removed from the day-to-day hassles of living here in India, which is a hassle whether you admit it or not. Even for the reasonably rich it's a struggle. There's no way to make money without being corrupt in India, which I'm incapable of. So for me the IFS was a very clean service...a good life.'

They lived in Addis Ababa and Tokyo and Milan. Now that they've been back in India for several years, they both say that household help have a different attitude to their jobs and employers than they did in the past. 'Before they wanted to keep employers happy, now they think the employers should keep them happy,' says Mrs Prakash, adding, 'She never is happy. No one ever says, "I gave this to my maid and she was happy."' 'And it's not just maids,' says her husband. 'Plumber, electrician, they just try to make half the job and finish it later. There's no pride in finishing the work. Before, there was loyalty. Humne unka namak khaya hai, we'll be with them until the end.'

The couple offers many examples of why it's better to do your own housework. 'Leafy vegetables, if you don't wash them eight or ten times, there are all kinds of worms in the environment they grow in India. No maid will do that,' Mr Prakash says. 'I fill a sink, leave them half an hour and then wash them several times. [The maid will] say, "I won't make that vegetable. Because it requires a lot of effort."'

The Prakashes spend a lot of time pre-processing vegetables for later use, the kind of thing that in other countries is done by food corporations. 'We freeze it in packs. We pack it like the way you get spinach outside,' he says, 'Semi-cooked.' Otherwise, even a simple dish like Japanese gomae, a spinach dish seasoned with sesame, a dish they must have had a million times in Japan, which is supposed to take no more than fifteen minutes to make, is laborious. By the time the spinach is prepared for washing, boiled and wrung out—as I found the one and only time I made it—an hour or more can easily go by.

The daily housework the couple describes must total up to the vicinity of three hours a day, not counting special efforts, like baking bread or making their own tofu. 'If you make tofu, that takes two hours,' says Mr Prakash. 'We do that once in a week. Once I bought tofu and I saw it wasn't tofu. So now we make our own.'

The Prakashes insist they have more free time than others in the complex who have servants. But they admit it's hardly a lifestyle that would be possible in a household with young children and two adults who are working full-time, or even for them for that matter, when they are older and less mobile. In their sixties, they are aware that if they live another decade or two, they may have to give up their independent ways. But Mr Prakash said he would find it difficult to adjust to the part-time help with fixed hours that is common in this complex, primarily because it doesn't have any housing facilities for domestic help. 'I think it was a miscalculation, people knew that you need help, you may need help later also, it was just the money,' he says. 'At that time three or four lakh rupees was a lot of money so they tried to save.' If they ever do need to return to hiring help, he hopes they find somebody willing to live in their apartment with them. Perhaps by converting part of the living room into an additional room, he and his wife could make space for full-time, live-in help.

'I want someone I can trust completely,' he says. 'And if I want someone to give me something at eleven at night, then I want someone to give me something at eleven at night.'

NEAR HUMAYUN'S TOMB

'IT IS A GREAT RESPONSIBILITY,' says the lawyer, telling me of the ethos he imbibed from his grandparents, with whom he spent a lot of time as a child in South India while his parents were away working in the Middle East. 'The fundamental principle was if the child of someone who worked for you was doing the same job [as their parent] and hadn't done something better, you had failed that person.'

For a couple in the income bracket of more than five lakh rupees a month, the lawyer and his wife live in a fairly modest two-bedroom house, not far from one of the city's most beloved Mughal monuments, Humayun's Tomb. He points to a large day bed covered with a blue bedspread, wedged against a wall in the living room near a dining table, 'That's our third bedroom.' There is no guard at the front door, and no flashily expensive car parked outside. Unlike some people with their kind of earning, they don't shell out thousands of rupees dining out, choosing instead to eat mostly at home. But this unostentatious life includes an extravagant quantity of domestic help compared to most other people they know in their thirties. 'I call it Gandhian living,' says the lawyer, 'but you need ten people to wash and starch and iron your khadi.'

A typical affluent Indian nuclear family in which both parents work, and there is a child or two, will have three people to help out: a housekeeper, a nanny and a driver. But in this home, there are no fewer than ten men and women who rotate the duties of cooking, cleaning and childcare, as well as some office duties at the lawyer's practice not far away. It's the kind of home that makes foreigners wonder how Indian families require so much help when they are able to manage with one person who does everything. Easily a lakh of their monthly income goes towards household help. And a significant quantity of time.

Their household is organized a bit like one of India's most popular craft clothing chains, Fabindia, where a job that could be done by one person is carefully divided among four: one man rings up your purchase, another packs up the items, a third hands it over to you when you present the bill, and a fourth at the door hands back the bags you checked when you walked in. The lawyer muses, 'Are there redundancies—not redundancies—are there people who are underemployed? Certainly. Am I underemployed? Certainly. I could work harder.'

The extra hands make it possible for people to take care of the children for parts of the day, so that the nanny, who is on call at night, can sleep. They also make it possible for a worker to travel even at short notice for a wedding, a festival or a death in the family, the latter by itself a category of leave that can appear in some cases to require a dozen days a year.

The large numbers of household help were a shock for the lawyer's wife, who doesn't recall having anyone other than a part-time cleaner for most of her childhood in Delhi. Her mother did all of the cooking and later, when extended family members moved in with them, a young sister-in-law took on the mantle. When they first started dating, her then-boyfriend already had about five employees even though he lived in a one-bedroom flat. 'There were six guys and me,' she remembers. 'And there was one bathroom.' When the children came, they hired a few more people. This time, perhaps at her urging, some of them were women.

Over the years, the lawyer has restricted his hiring to people with roots in Delhi, Rajasthan and Uttar Pradesh. He noticed that workers who came from further than an overnight train or bus ride away didn't stick around for long. If they had to go home to sow crops or deal with a crisis, they would go for months at a moment's notice and then come back and find a new job. He didn't like that; he wanted people who would work for him for the long haul, that he could, using the management speak he often uses when describing his household, 'invest in'. He distrusts the people sourced from far away by the placement agencies that have cropped up in much of Delhi and Gurgaon, where his wife's parents live. 'I'm shocked when I go to Gurgaon. I don't think I could ever live there,' he says. 'It is a mercenary culture where you don't know anything about the people who are coming in. They come in, they do their job, and they get out.'

The local dhobi, from Uttar Pradesh, is one of his most prolific recruiters. His most trusted employee, practically his lieutenant on the home front, with whom he is in constant touch via Google Calendar and other apps, is from Rajasthan, where men are more conservative. Initially, when the lawyer married, this man wouldn't look at the lawyer's wife—let alone take instructions from her. For a long time, she reciprocated the shyness, refraining from issuing him instructions directly, going through her husband instead. Since they got married, he says he finds himself at times mediating between his household staff and his wife, for whom in the beginning, he says, 'there was no difference between a waiter in a restaurant or the person who brought her morning tea...I'm her undersecretary. She will say this hasn't been done and I have to run around and find out why. I'd like her to take more responsibility,' he says. 'If someone has not done something or slighted her...she may not as yet be able to see things from my perspective. I have to place myself in that position and try to make her understand that there were reasons why it couldn't be done, and I have to explain to them that they had to do it, that it wasn't a suggestion.'

His housekeeping system combines many of the benefits of the informal work world with some of the perks and tech of the more formal work world—there's health insurance and smartphones for everyone, and the salaries are in line with the average South Delhi live-in wage in 2015, but higher for the nanny, who earns 25,000 rupees or about four times as much as the typical office assistant to a Minister of Parliament earns, according to the *Indian Express*. Housekeeping tasks are tracked over Google Calendar. My presence at lunch, for example, was added to the online calendar, so the cook knew to make more food than usual. The housekeeping lieutenant consults the to-do app on his phone regularly updated by the lawyer—this week it consists of items like 'clean cobwebs' and 'tape up window'—and checks off tasks when they've been been done by one worker or another. 'I treat them as a team trying to accomplish a particular task as I do in the office,' the lawyer says.

But as it often is in India, the highly modern facets of this household are an overlay masking a much older ethos, one where the employer is the 'mai-baap' for his workers—practically the state. They are there to make his life better, and he too is there to make their lives better, from finding them better cell phone plans to providing free legal services from time to time. Of course, those strands of feudalism are entwined with some of its more troubling ones—he freely acknowledges he's a shouter, both at home and in the office, and while he believes in offering swathes of time off during the year, he doesn't consider a regular weekly day off a must.

The lawyer's to-do list includes not only tasks vital to the well-being of his own family, but also the cook, the cook's wife, and the gardener. The week we meet, for example, the lawyer got a text message offering special long-distance rates on prepaid cell phones. Using an app, he added the plan to the phones of the workers who regularly call other Indian states. Another day, he realized that two men who mainly do office work and who live in a room at the office didn't have bed linen, so now one of the things he checks up on weekly is making sure that fresh bedsheets are dispatched to the office and brought back to the house to be washed. In addition to renewing insurance for his home, office, family and car, he must keep on top of renewals for the health insurance policies for his workers and their families. 'When you've got ten people, and you've got forty or fifty family members, the chances of one of them falling ill in a year is quite high, so this is for my benefit, not theirs,' he says. Otherwise, he says, 'if someone trips and falls, I'm out 50,000 rupees.'

Then there are the life crises. When one cleaning lady's husband secretly sold the home a previous employer had helped her purchase, the lawyer went about annulling the sale and securing the property for her. Another time, when the same woman's teenage daughter ran away with a boyfriend, he went to court and filed a habeas corpus petition to compel the police to look for the young woman. On other occasions, he has submitted bail applications (and paid the money) for family members of the help who were arrested. (The next best thing to having a doctor or lawyer in your family is being employed by one.)

Down the line, he expects to pay partly or fully for the weddings of the daughters of his workers. But even with the added responsibilities, the lawyer says he's coming out well ahead. 'As you've seen, I've not done anything other than talk since you've met me,' he says. 'And we have kids in the house.'

It's true that our more than two-hour conversation has taken place over a leisurely weekday lunch that includes freshly made buttermilk and about three different vegetable dishes prepared that morning. Neither the lawyer nor his wife get up at any point to fetch anything during the meal (although the lawyer says that, of late, he has begun clearing the table alongside the help because he's worried about the level of entitlement it will foster in his sons to see him just sitting there the entire time). The table was laid before we sat down and rotis keep appearing at Goldilocks intervals, not too fast, not too slow.

After lunch, a tray of filter coffee arrives. Then another one. One child is sleeping, watched over by the live-in nanny; the other alternates between jumping on the daybed, drawing with a crayon, and wandering off to another room to play with one of the many domestic help. But all this is eclipsed by what he tells me next. The lawyer says that not only did he not lose sleep when his children were born, he gained it. His normal schedule that entailed working late into the night and then grabbing five hours of sleep, left him tired and cranky once the children came along. Having a full house of help allowed him to rejig his schedule and now he sleeps more than he used to. 'If it wasn't for this lot, I wouldn't be able to sleep eight hours,' he says. 'I wouldn't be able to function at work.'

Both children depart to the park at some point, neither parent is quite sure exactly when, their relationships with most of their help are of long enough duration that they have the confidence to allow that to happen. But even in the midst of all this trust, there is, if not suspicion then at least the awareness that you cannot be—or cannot be perceived to be—too trusting. Even before the children were born the lawyer says he had video cameras installed in the house, which he can monitor anytime, from anywhere, on an iPad.

Despite the couple's efforts to bring their children up in a way that masks, at least for a while, the deep social divisions not just in society, but even in a progressively-run Indian home, they're both aware that they might have already failed. His wife tells me, 'A friend's child who came over…knew when to switch languages depending on whom he was speaking to.' Asked by his mother to present the toy he had brought as a gift, the young guest first turned to the oldest woman in the room and in Hindi asked her to wash the toy. 'Fir main aake doonga (Then I'll give it),' he said. Until then he had been speaking with everyone in English. 'At three years old he's able to assess a room and decide who's a servant and who's not, even people he hadn't met before, even though that person was sitting on a bench next to me,' says her husband. His children are younger than the friend's child, but it's only a matter of time—months maybe, not even years—before they too are able to make the most important assessments to be made in India when walking into a room: who works for whom, who has money and who doesn't, who is at home in English, and who isn't.

A tiny encounter like that underscores what the lawyer can't help but feel at times—that the edifice he has tried to create is just another set of the emperor's new clothes. He has devoted a lot of time to thinking about how to be a better employer, about fairness, about how to erase some of the hierarchy between himself and the men and women that work for him. And yet, he says, at times what he feels in his heart is that there is something artificial, even fraudulent, in his efforts. Perhaps the lines are fewer in this household than in others, but they exist nonetheless, their presence to be found in tiny details, like the extra-special chocolates in the fridge that everyone knows without being told are just for the family.

'I will clear up from the table, I will make my bed but it's clear that I don't do an ounce of the work that they do and yet pretend to be equal,' he says. 'It's being a hypocrite.'

MAGNOLIAS, GURGAON

AFTER CROSSING MANY JOURNALISTIC CONVENTIONS over the previous months, while working on this book—don't interview friends and family, don't pull a Thomas Friedman and quote your cab driver (or maid)—I'm breaking the most sacred one of all. Always identify yourself as a journalist. When I accompany Amit Kapoor, a customer service employee at The Maids' Company, to an appointment in 2015, I do not identify myself as a journalist. Instead, I'm there as Amit's colleague, to help a prospective client find the right maid.

At meetings like this, Amit, a clean-cut young man from Himachal Pradesh, with a bachelor's degree in business, takes notes about what a family wants in a maid, and then tries to find them a match. One November, I head with him to Gurgaon's prestigious Magnolias complex, where some floors in the towering white buildings of the complex are home to single apartments covering 6,000 square feet. At the entrance of the gated complex, where fretwork flower motifs conceal lift shafts, Amit and I sail through quickly, but the Bengali woman we have brought with us is checked a little more closely by a female guard.

Much of the time it is a woman Amit deals with when it comes to hiring maids, but this time we're here to see a man, an entrepreneur in his fifties who is just moving his family into a large new apartment. A man with stubble opens the door and asks us to wait in the foyer while he checks with his boss if we are expected. A few minutes later we are invited in. After depositing our shoes at the door as requested, we troop across a gleaming Italian marble floor to approach a seating area of white leather couches. Apart from these couches there is not a whole lot of furniture, nor art on the walls; clearly the place is still being set up. A man, dressed in white, is seated on one of the white couches. His feet are shod in socks and slippers. Italian marble can get chilly in winter.

Amit and I are asked to sit but Prarthna, who is under consideration as a potential maid, is not part of that invitation. A tall, thin woman who holds herself very erect, in a blue cotton sari and a cardigan, she remains standing next to the sofa. In the past, Amit's boss, Gauri Singh, has endeavoured to make sure maids being brought for consideration are invited to take a seat along with everyone else. On one occasion, when a client asked a maid to relocate herself to the floor, Singh interrupted and said she would have to do the same. But Amit is just in his twenties and less sure of himself than his boss and I am mildly intimidated by the feeling of being there on sufferance not to mention the vast gleaming emptiness of the apartment, so neither of us follows Singh's tactic of standing up in solidarity with Prarthna.

Amit starts to give the brief biography that he's been trained to offer, but he has hardly got a few words in when the client hushes him and begins speaking to Prarthna directly. What does she know how to do? How long has she been working? Why did she leave her last job? Once, when Amit tries to add something by way of further explanation, the man tells him brusquely, 'Don't interfere when I am talking with her. Your turn will come.' A short while later, Amit again tries to say something, and the client tells him, 'Quiet, quiet, boy.'

Amit has still not managed to get many words in when the businessman orders his stubble-faced assistant (who usually works at his office, but due to the blurred lines of working in a family-owned business is here to help with the hiring of the maid) to take Prarthna into the kitchen and conduct a test. Prarthna is supposed to look around the kitchen and point out things that are dirty and clean. I can't help be reminded of editing tests I have taken—if you don't do enough, you will be seen as timid and careless, but do too much, on a story that's already appeared in print and has been deceptively included, for instance, and you could come across as over-enthusiastic to the point of being offensive. Focused on trying to guess what's supposed to be the right answer, you second-guess yourself. Amit asks if he can go along with her to make her comfortable, but neither he nor I are allowed to accompany Prarthna to the kitchen, perhaps for fear we'll telegraph the right answers to her. It's the first time she has been in this man's home and she's likely nervous. Anybody would be nervous being asked to point out things that are dirty in someone else's home, even a friend's home. It feels uncomfortably like a trick question.

Prarthna comes back and in a very soft voice lists things that need cleaning. The man on the sofa tells her she hasn't spotted everything and sends her back twice more to the kitchen to look around. Once, when she is giving a slightly expansive answer to a question about what she saw in the kitchen that needed cleaning, he cuts her off and tells her, 'Just answer what is asked. No more than that.' The man tells us he is testing this woman's ability to follow a simple command of which, he adds, he's already very doubtful. But then, he says, it's a nationwide problem. 'Indians don't know how to listen. They hear. A sound enters their ear, that's all.' He makes a gesture in the vicinity of his own ear, to demonstrate, sort of like the trajectory of a whining mosquito spiralling towards the ear canal.

I think the man's hearing is none too great either. At one point he asks about the maid's police verification and Amit responds, 'Yes sir, verification and all those things we have done. Please don't be worried about all these things.'

The question has been answered but the man doesn't appear to have heard the answer. 'You see, Amit, you didn't listen to what I asked. You answered something else. I asked about verification.' He tells us how wonderful maids are in America. 'You leave the key with her and go out. Two hours later the entire house is shining.'

I know what I'm thinking and later it turns out Amit is thinking the same thing. In America, you don't get weekly dust storms. In America, your maid has a vacuum cleaner, a Swiffer, a steam mop, a dishwasher and all sorts of tools that attempt to make cleaning less drudge-like, because in America, as my sister once told a maid who was enquiring about her domestic arrangements overseas, she is the cook and her husband the jamadar. In America, you wouldn't ask your cleaning lady to leave her shoes at the door. In America, you wouldn't talk to your cleaner the way you are talking to this woman right now—unless, of course, you had imported her with you from India.

However, the interview is not yet over.

'How would you clean this floor?' he asks Prarthna. I can tell even before she opens her mouth that whatever she says is not going to be the right answer. He's made up his mind in advance about that. She says she would sweep it with a phuljharu—a soft grass broom. No, of course, that's not right. This marble is so soft, he tells her, that sweeping it will scratch it. You just have to wipe it, he says.

Then he asks another question, perhaps the unkindest one of all. 'Which is more important?' he asks. 'Food or cleanliness?'

Prarthna is from West Bengal. Many of the women in this part of Gurgaon have migrated from Malda, from villages like Colony, where Lovely's mother and younger siblings live. In the city, Lovely and her three sisters eat well—tomatoes and onions most days, okra, even chicken sometimes. In the village, trying to make the money Lovely sends go as far as possible, Lovely's mother and her youngest siblings didn't eat vegetables or fruit in the two days that I went to visit. Meals are rice and a small amount of potatoes. A little dal. While I visit, the meals are supplemented by extra carbohydrates from neighbours, for my benefit, although I clearly don't need the supplementation. This constant worry over food, even among people who in theory are above the poverty line, can be surprisingly abstract to us city dwellers, who can spend on a single, perfectly mundane meal in Khan Market an amount that would keep a family in Colony on rice for the month. So Prarthna only has to think for a moment to answer this question correctly. 'Food, sir,' she answers.

The man's response is swift and savage—though his tone is calm. 'Then you should leave this house. There is no place for you here if that is what you think.'

When we recount these proceedings to the supervisors later, they are irate. One of them says that The Maids' Company has women working in so many of the Magnolia apartments, and all those apartments are laid with Italian marble and all of those floors get swept. She knows perfectly well that if a maid were to skip that step, the employers would be on the phone at once alleging kamchori: work theft.

He must be new money, Amit's supervisor says, which is why he is so conscious of the splendour of this new home, and so petrified of marring it. He hasn't had a chance to get used to it yet, she guesses. The office staff carry out a spot of Facebook sleuthing and soon find the client's son online. On his Facebook page there are pictures of him standing in front of tulips in Holland during a work or study abroad trip. The family is involved in manufacturing; they are actually 'making in India', as Prime Minister Narendra Modi is exhorting Indian businesses (and foreign ones) to do. Another photograph shows the son standing next to a large tyre. In yet another, the son stands in front of an old-fashioned wooden door, the kind of door that opens into an apartment that is significantly less upscale than the one which the family is now moving onto. Some of the staff break into laughter. 'Look at where they've come from,' says one. The family has jumped from middle class to enormous wealth. That should be something to be celebrated. They, and their purchases of apartments, and their hiring of engineers, and their hiring of help, are all good for the economy, after all. But they don't make it easy to be happy for them.

Because of my status as an honorary employee, Amit's supervisor asks what I think they should do: drop this person as a potential client or pursue it further? I suggest giving him one more chance. Perhaps she, a middle-aged woman, should accompany him in her starched cotton sari as mediator. After all, it is exactly this kind of person whom they want to change surely. But the supervisor isn't so sure. She has taken that chance with other clients already, and so she knows from experience, there are some people you can neither please nor change.

A smiling woman peeps into the office of the president of the Noida Sector-50 Residents' Welfare Association (RWA), which governs a housing development to the east of Delhi, in the state of Uttar Pradesh, that conveys its authority partly by housing itself in a grey concrete-building inspired by Delhi's municipal architecture. 'Thank you so much for such a wonderful opportunity,' she says.

'Thank you for your hard work cleaning,' responds Vimal Sharma, whose black, quilted vest matches his mop of jet-black, dyed hair, which in turn matches a bushy moustache. It is 30 January, the day Mahatma Gandhi was assassinated in 1948, and in homage to the father of the nation, Sharma, president of the Sector-50 RWA, a neighbourhood association that covers some 40,000 residents, has organized a weeklong special event. The journey from Delhi to here requires traversing the city's bubbling river, a park filled with elephant statues built by a previous state leader, occasional swathes of still vacant land, and heavily congested commercial areas that are often shrouded in haze. But this neighbourhood is one of houses spread tidily around several parks, a multitude of private schools, and great deal of enthusiasm for events organized by the residents' association.

'We have gathered the residents, about 400 or 500 people, and we are doing a cleaning exercise because Gandhiji loved cleanliness,' Sharma tells me.

They make quite a procession with a small tractor pulling a wagon, pushcarts and a rubbish truck as they sweep through the neighbourhood's sextants: A, B, C, D, E and F. The RWA managed to rope in members of the local city administration—there were two engineers, and someone from the health department. City neighbourhoods are usually swept by municipal sweepers, usually women who are middle-aged or even elderly. The fervour with which

Sharma is being thanked leads me to think that perhaps the residents did their own sweeping and therefore are feeling particularly pleased with themselves. Sharma quickly disabuses me of that notion. 'No, no, we have a sweepers' team,' he says. 'So each resident will direct four sweepers and say, for example, "Go clean A-Block." Two ragpickers will go along behind them to hold the rubbish. This was to give all of Noida the message to make the residents aware about keeping cleanliness, so that we all remain healthy. The participation was very good, and we kept blasting cassettes playing hymns the whole time.'

The hymn that was most played was one of Gandhi's favourites, but despite the date and the choice of music, the exercise is more truthfully a homage to Prime Minister Narendra Modi, who on Gandhi's birthday a few months earlier, on 2 October 2014, launched a national cleanliness campaign—Swachh Bharat Abhiyan. He did so by sweeping up a neighbourhood where city street sweepers live and exhorting Indians to carry on with Gandhi's unfinished business. Many Indians loved the act, seeing in it a brave attempt to finally awaken a community conscience in a city where dust is scrupulously excised from homes, but whose residents think nothing of littering, urinating and desecrating spaces that aren't private. The home is a temple where one can exert control; to invest in public space in India is to invest in chaos, and to reap constant disappointment. The only public space that the capital's residents are able to bring themselves to care for are those they have grabbed for themselves and turned private: the park abutting a house, the spot in front of one's house lovingly cordoned off with potted plants.

For a while, political, business and entertainment leaders emulated Modi, and were photographed on the street, brooms in hand, next to neatly swept piles of dirt. Even though the woman or man who had actually done the sweeping often lurked outside the picture frame, the celebrity sweepers helped steal for Modi the thunder of another political party that had made the broom its political symbol two years earlier. In that instance, too, a group made up mainly of men did some sweeping of neighbourhood lanes—the same neighbourhood adopted later by the prime minister—to highlight their goal of ridding the country of the filth of corruption. Women may do most of the actual cleaning, on the street and at home, but in India, men have always dominated the public discourse—and performances—around dirt, both literal and metaphorical. And women thank them for it.

When Sharma isn't organizing cleaning performances or festivities around other national holidays, he and other RWA officials are the ambassadors of the owners of the approximately 10,000 apartments and homes in this area to the local administration. Often, they provide services that the local administration should be providing. It is the RWA that actually polices the neighbourhood, since beat policing is almost non-existent in this neighbourhood carved out of Uttar Pradesh farmland about fifteen years ago. Fees paid by residents each month defray the costs of a team of eighteen private security guards hired and managed by the RWA, Sharma tells me. 'They patrol in groups of three on motorcycles. If they have suspicions about anyone, they grab them and bring them to the guard room,' he says. 'We can't stop people from coming in, we don't have judicial powers. You also came. We don't have the power to just pick anyone up and imprison them. But, yes, we do take precautions on behalf of our residents.'

There is a phone call. From my eavesdropping, I glean that the man on the other end is complaining that poor children being taught by a woman in one of the local parks are ruining the plants. 'They pluck flowers or they pluck the entire plant?' asks Sharma. 'Send us a letter that, "Make sure the kids you are teaching in the park don't do things like this." We will depute two men.' The caller is somewhat but not entirely mollified, so Sharma makes some more soothing noises. 'I'll try to make sure there are guards there this evening. I understand your distress. Horticulture is very time-intensive,' he adds.

Being as large as it is, the Sector-50 RWA is better organized than many similar developments created through 'cooperative societies' to pool funding and apply for land at subsidized rates, and Sharma is a fount of knowledge about his neighbourhood. When I tell him I am investigating wrongdoing involving employers and their domestic help for my book, Sharma immediately offers several examples. First, he tells me of an incident that happened in 2007, after a woman moved into a large house in the neighbourhood. 'Without the least enquiry she hired a girl. For four hours that girl cleaned very hard, she did all the madam's work that was pending for months, here, there, cobwebs. Madam was very happy. Then she said, "Madam, I'd like to rest for an hour," says Sharma. Madam was also in a good mood and agreed. She must have fed her well, adding extra ghee and all. Instead of resting, in that one hour the maid cleaned the house of all the cash and jewellery that was in it and quietly left the way she came.'

Then there is the murder of a Chandni Chowk jeweller who had a home in this sector. 'The domestic servant did it,' he says. 'In the night, he must have been taking money or something, he was murdered.' Later, I find news reports on the murder in question. It turns out the servants went missing, raising police suspicion. But I can find no news reports that say whether the servants were ever arrested, let alone convicted of any crime. I can't help but think this could well be another one of those cases where the predilections of police to suspect the help turn out to be wrong.

In a famous case of misplaced suspicion, Noida police began circulating rumours that a dentist couples' daughter had been murdered by their live-in helper, only to find that the help had been murdered too, his body decomposing on the rooftop while police were busy building up a case against him. Such suspicion can be widespread, at least in the minds of those tasked with investigating crimes. At a police sensitivity training session that I once sat in on, a woman dressed in a bright purple pantsuit asked a classroom of mostly bored cops to respond 'yes' or 'no' to a series of written statements. One statement said, 'In case of theft at home/shop, the first suspect would be the servant'. Almost all the respondents circled 'yes'.

In the early years of Sector-50, though, servants were scarce and no one worried all that much about looking into the criminal tendencies of the cook if they were lucky enough to find one. When the RWA chief and his family moved here from Vasant Vihar, after renting out their home to an embassy, they brought along their old servants. But the servants were homesick in the still largely unoccupied area, and they soon went back to Delhi. Sharma ribs one of the other RWA officers who is present, joking that she would much rather her husband run away than her maid.

Eventually, alongside the large homes, India's best solution for affordable housing also developed: slums. Where there's a possibility of a job, people build for themselves, first with a bit of tarp and bricks, then later something more solid, recreating the relief camps they have sometimes fled. 'When all these colonies sprang up, these unauthorized colonies, then it became easy to get domestic servants,' said Sharma. The population of domestic help here is now nearly equal to the population of home-owners and their families, he claims.

Some 15,000 to 20,000 people work as live-in help, while another 20,000 part-timers come in every day through a specially designated gate, he says. As the number of servants grew, and reports of crimes allegedly committed by them percolated around the area, the residents' association came up with an idea: why not create a system of identification for domestic servants?

At the start of each financial year, 1 April, employers drop off a form with information about each of their help, a photocopy of IDs and two photographs. A copy of the information, photo attached, stays with the RWA, which issues passes to each worker. Another copy along with a photo, is sent to the local police station, with whom the association is often in touch. The information sought from the help includes their name, age and home address. They don't however collect information about their wages, days off or when a maid who hails from another state last went home. The RWA forms do ask them to state their religion. When I ask why, Sharma demurs. 'It's better if we don't talk about that.' (Later, though, he veers into an unprompted discussion of minorities, the ills of affirmative action and one Mughal emperor's patricide, rounding off the soliloquy with the statement, 'It's in their DNA.')

The exercise of registering help is repeated each year, around the same time. 'Each year they need to be renewed. We don't care if your servant is with you from twenty years,' he explains. 'That way if there's any incident, this could help the police.'

But what if someone hires a maid and doesn't bother to get a pass made for them? Would the RWA actually find out? Yes, its chief insists. 'In this sector, the gate that opens has CCTV cameras and there are six guards there. So whenever anyone enters, they have to be entered in the register and get a pass. So immediately someone would get to know, because we would call and say this servant Lakshmi wants to come to your house, what is her purpose?'

Strangely, my friend and I arrived here in his SUV and we were not required to register ourselves or be issued a pass. It transpires that this is because we did not come in by the gate designated for the use of the maids. As car drivers, we could come in by any gate we wanted. 'Come at 6.30. Then we can show you in what quantities girls and women are coming in here all at once, in what a crowd. You won't be able to stand,' he says. 'That's why we've designated Barola gate, Gate No. 1, for them since they come in by the thousands. They can't come in by any other gate.'

City authorities and the media often laud residents' associations as an exercise in municipal democracy, offering city residents a way to participate in the running of their neighbourhoods. They are an improvement on what came before, when municipal bodies, unaccountable to any specific neighbourhood, ran everything, and not very well. But it is a limited form of democracy. If the situation prior to the existence of RWAs was like colonial America—taxation without representation—what some cities have now is the sort of democracy that prevailed in the newly free eighteenth-century United States. The franchise is only open to men and women who own property. Those who live here but don't own—tenants and servants—do not get a say. So when RWAs undertake crime prevention, or other community interventions, their gaze is myopic, focused on protecting homeowners, not their help. You can treat someone as a potential threat to be policed, or as a potential victim in need of protection. It's quite difficult to do both.

IT IS A VARANASI CONFIDANT of politician Dhananjay Singh, the building contractor Kush Upadhyaya, who helps me secure an interview with the Minister of Parliament. I have turned up unexpectedly one June day at the builder's Uttar Pradesh home, which my enterprising taxi driver and I are able to find after four hours of asking directions from random people armed with little more than the directions 'behind the dhaba off the highway'. When we arrive on a June day, Upadhyaya is both hospitable and helpful, the armed guard at his gate notwithstanding. He speaks of Singh, who hails from the nearby Uttar Pradesh town of Jaunpur, with lavish praise and says he is known around here as the champion of the poor and that he treats everyone—Brahmin or Dalit—the same.

I have been seeking to interview Singh for months after he and his wife, Jagriti Singh, residents of the MP's zone in Lutyens' Delhi, were arrested by police in 2013 after the then Bahujan Samaj Party (BSP) lawmaker called the authorities to report the sudden death of one of his maids.

Being arrested is not new for Singh—he has easily been arrested (and usually acquitted) more than a dozen times since he was a young man involved in student politics in Uttar Pradesh, a fact that leads newspapers to frequently refer to him as 'dabaang' or strongman, much to his dislike. Until I met Upadhyay, my efforts to interview Singh were in vain. First, not long after the arrest, his personal secretary's phone was disconnected, according to Airtel. Later, when the secretary's phone was back on, he told me that Singh was unavailable because he had gone on pilgrimage after being released on bail. Clutching at straws by now, I tried to quiz the secretary on where the MP had gone to pray. 'Is he a devotee of Vishnu? Shiva?' I blurted. If the interview wasn't going to happen perhaps I could snatch a little bit of colour over the phone, maybe just enough to write something like 'the disgraced MP was folding his hands at a Shivling on the banks of the Ganga'. Or, for a foreign edition, 'The disgraced MP was folding his hands at a shrine to India's blue-skinned god of destruction'. But it was not to be. 'Mr Singh respects all faiths and gods,' the secretary replied, before hanging up on me.

When I finally sit down with Singh, it is a bright September day, ten months since he and his wife were first arrested—she on suspicion of murder, among other crimes, and he on suspicion of acting as an accessory and concealing evidence—but they have not yet been charged. He arrives fresh from a workout at the gym at the Constitution Club around the corner. He is wearing track pants and a bright yellow T-shirt and carrying an iPhone and headphones. This is a departure from his usual attire in court, where, dressed in impeccably ironed beige khakis and button-down shirt, he towers over most people there. A red string is tied around his right wrist. His clipped moustache and bland expression don't fit at all with what I expect a UP politician with a lengthy rap sheet to look like.

Singh tells me he became interested in politics early, as a teenager in the early 1990s, when what he describes as the 'Ram wave' was taking place. When Singh was fifteen, the Hindu nationalist L. K. Advani, of the Bharatiya Janata Party, led a procession across the country to rally Hindus around one of the party's key causes—the building of a Ram temple at the site of the Babri Masjid in Ayodhya. Singh went on to win the election as a state legislator for the first time in 2002 as an independent candidate. Six years later, he joined Mayawati's BSP, which was looking to field a parliamentary candidate from his constituency. He became a national lawmaker the following year, in 2009, when he was thirty-four. 'I thought being in government I can serve people better in my constituency,' he says, explaining his reasons for joining a party focused on the country's most downtrodden castes despite being an upper-caste Hindu himself.

Since his arrest, his party dropped him, and even though he ran as an independent in the national polls that took place a few months before we met, he was not re-elected. He will soon have to vacate this bungalow, and its living room full of knick-knacks. On a side table, gleaming white china horses gallop forth from a silvery wave. In a corner, a tribal woman made of bronze carries water vessels. The doors into the room are festooned with purple scalloped curtains edged with beads. In the corner is the dark aquarium in whose murky depths a fish or two lurks, and which has featured in the police report at the time of the arrest, with one of the Singhs' servants telling officers that one of the many beatings he incurred in this house occurred after he was blamed for damaging the pump cleaning the aquarium water.

The servant who described being beaten is none other than Ram Pal from Varanasi, who ended up working in this house when he stole away from his mother and sister in Chittopur for a job. Apart from him, Golbanu Bibi, also known as Rakhi, and another maid from West Bengal, ended up being placed here by a maid broker used by the MP's wife. Initially, only people from Mr Singh's home village worked here. But his wife began hiring people on her own via a Bengali placement agent from West Delhi. Perhaps she felt that the men hired by her husband—from whom she has become increasingly estranged—acknowledged his authority but not hers, or at least so some of the statements taken by the police suggest. 'She felt that since they are from my area, they'll listen to me more, this was on her mind,' Mr Singh says. By the time of the death of the maid around Diwali in 2013, he had filed for divorce from his wife and was living in a nearby bungalow he also used as an office, only coming here to see his son.

With his wife presently housed at the city jail (where she would remain until finally securing bail nearly two years later) Singh is back here temporarily, and the house, when I visit, is full of male staff who seemed to know Singh well, including the man who brings me a plate of burfi when I arrive. Singh says he isn't able to comment on the circumstances of his wife's arrest, and tells me he wasn't home at the time of the maid's death; he believes his arrest on suspicion of trying to cover up the crime is a political conspiracy against him. Generally, though, Singh says he blames the spate of reports of crimes against help both before and after his arrest on the maid brokers. 'I'll tell you the basic problem. Who does domestic violence happen to, why are incidents like this happening to servants?' he asks. 'All the agencies that are coming for getting work done, they bring untrained people to houses. People are coming from Bangladesh, from Jharkhand. They bring people from poor areas like Orissa. They bring people from areas

where there is a lot of poverty. They bring people on the agreement
of 2,000, 2,500 rupees,' he continues. 'Here they charge 7,000, 8,000,
6,000, these kinds of charges, okay? They don't train them that much.
They send them at the rate of 5,000. The guy who is paying 5,000,
those poor guys don't understand the language, they don't understand
what you are saying, ten times you have to explain a thing to them.
You understand? Then the man becomes irritated.'

Like many people in Delhi, he believes that some of the help have
illegally migrated from Bangladesh, something which he says should
be investigated, and says it's improper that one of the maids adopted
a Hindu name to use at work. He says he only hires people from
around his hometown, so that they have everything in common—
language, culture, food, faith, worldview—so that such irritating lapses
in communication will not occur. He can relate to them, and they to
him. 'Whenever a servant came to work for me, they were from my
area. My accent, my language, everything, they can understand,' he
says. 'We eat and drink the same things. These sorts of people used
to work for me. She couldn't get along with them, so she would
chase them all away.'

When I ask about salaries of the help in his house, Singh dismisses
the question. Salaries and working hours belong to a different kind
of ethos; these are his people from his town. It works differently, he
explains, and his explanation is not so different from what the lawyer
of the 'Gandhian living' style might give. 'The whole responsibility is
mine,' he says, 'my old people I have gotten them all government jobs
somewhere. Like this guy is working in my house, I'll put his daughter
in a school [as a teacher], in a girls' school. She'll get 13-14,000, 15,000
rupees. I made a house for him. I give more than 10-12,000 rupees a
month. Cash. Someone gets sick. There's rain, someone has to build
a roof. A shed. Someone has two children and they want to buy a
cow. Then I'll give 30,000 separately for that.'

He says people should treat their servants out of compassion—but
also out of a sense of self-preservation. 'The worst work, the one we
don't like to do, the domestic worker does that work. So we should
speak kindly to him, with love, so that he'll do his work with greater
enthusiasm. He wakes up before me, he goes to sleep after me. Am
I right or wrong?' he says. 'When you don't talk to them politely,

when you're physically abusive, at the end of day aren't they the ones cooking your meals? You must have seen there was a story about a woman who mixed urine in the food she prepared. It was on the Net. Aaj Tak, NDTV they all ran it. In her interview she said that her employer used to hit her. And this was her method of taking revenge.'

Mr Singh's words about treating his help well call to mind what his friend, Mr Upadhyaya, the Varanasi contractor, had told me about the politician. He said Mr Singh had remonstrated with him in the past if he ever scolded a servant in front of him, citing a karmic reason, one whose underpinnings were more than slightly at odds with the fact that he had once won a ticket from a party devoted to breaking apart the idea that a servile occupation was a sign of a bad cosmic credit history. 'If the servants had done something wrong, hadn't cleaned up properly, and we scolded them, then he would say this is wrong,' says Mr Upadhyaya. 'He would say if someone poor is working in the home of someone else, it means they are working off the sins of a past life.'

PART IV

Madam

CHAKKARPUR, GURGAON

PREETI CHAUHAN, A DIMINUTIVE JAT girl, has never known the luxury of having a maid. Her students sometimes bump into her as she wipes down her front steps, on her hands and knees, in her lower middle-class neighbourhood in a farming village called Chakkarpur that has been swallowed up by the urban sprawl of Gurgaon. Just twenty-three, Preeti graduated from a college in Haryana with a political science degree. She considered other jobs, in retail at local malls, but didn't find them appealing. In 2014, when we meet, she is responsible for assessing the table-laying and other skills of new recruits to The Maids' Company, and teaching them how to win over a new madam.

Chakkarpur's streets are dotted with sari and bartan shops and child care centres and nursery schools. At the 'convent' nursery school on one of its main streets, a group of men is often clustered just outside smoking hookahs. The neighbourhood's walls are dotted with 'to-let' signs. Here and there, snuggled between the taller tenements, large one and two-storey bungalows with gardens accommodate the landlords who put up those signs, and whose gates have nameplates that almost always bear the surname 'Yadav'. The Maids' Company runs its classes out of a house rented in the area, an easy walk from where many of their maids live.

At a morning session in January that I observed Preeti lead, a new recruit has just finished laying a table and it is almost entirely wrong. The plates are okay. They are in the centre of each tablemat, as they should be. But the spoon and fork have been placed at a rakish angle on the plates. The glasses are on the right, but in India, no matter your class, you eat rotis with your hands, so they should have been on the left, to be clasped with the clean hand, no matter what the Lonely Planet might tell travellers to India about hand taboos. This would not do.

The upper-middle-class Indian household, according to Preeti's warnings, appears to be presided over by a capricious and whimsical creature, prone to flying off the handle, known as ma'am, or sometimes madam. As Preeti proceeds with the course, asking her somewhat timid pupils how ma'am is likely to react to such-and-such faux pas, it begins to seem to me that madam is a close relative of the Queen of Hearts from Alice in Wonderland, but of a considerably weaker constitution.

'Is this how you used to lay the table in your previous home?' Preeti asks a quiet, slim woman named Ohabun, who is Bengali. She then shows the woman how she ought to have done it: the bowl for dal and a spoon should go to the right of the plate, while the fork and glass should be placed to the left. Indian food is oily, she points out, and if your employer picks up a glass with a greasy hand, she may break it. The implicit warning is that even if sir or madam drop the glass all by themselves, you will still be blamed for putting it in the wrong place.

Knives are only used at breakfast and are laid on the table with the sharp side facing in. All the forks should be the same, not from different sets, as should all the plates and glasses. Don't mix steel and glass glasses, she tells the women. Nor should a worker take four trips between the kitchen and the dining room when she can load everything onto a tray and bring it over to set the table at each mealtime. Such a lethargic approach will irritate madam, for sure. (Sahib, it is understood, has already left for office.) And, finally, never ever let your fingers touch the inside surface of the bowl or plate—always handle them from the outside—so madam, who is frail and much more prone to illness than you are, doesn't pick up your germs and fall ill.

The women, mostly Bengali and Bihari migrants to Chakkarpur, take this all in seriously and quietly. Their world is just one of many economically disparate worlds clustered around M. G. Road, the main thoroughfare along which the metro from Delhi to Gurgaon runs. There is a certain symmetry to the development of this part of Gurgaon, and lives of its residents. The men and women who have flocked here often work in and around the malls and gated communities built by India's biggest real estate developers—DLF, Unitech, Sahara. In the evening they go home to tenements built by the farmers who have lived here for centuries. The developers got their capital from loans and investors and down payments; the farmers got their capital by selling their farmland to the developers.

In the maids' own home—usually a room with an attached kitchen and bath—there will be neither dining table nor table-laying, because sitting and eating as a family at a table is a practice common only among a small group of Indians. When the maid goes home, after clearing the table and washing the dishes at the home of her employers, she will eat in a very different way. When the meal is cooked, she will serve her husband and he will sit on the floor or on a low bed, eating in silence. The children may have eaten earlier, or she might feed one on her lap after her husband is done, before finally feeding herself.

Preeti goes through these drills several times a week, she tells me. For her pupils, the homes they will work in are still dangerous mysteries, with their different rooms for different activities, specially designated places for things, multitudes of ornaments that have to be picked up and wiped and are likely to be both expensive and breakable. Underlying all of this is the sense that, while they are coming to these homes to clean, they are also possible purveyors of infection. 'Madam's house is always closed and when we touch anything of madam's, our germs spread,' says Preeti. 'If madam touches those things, she will get sick easily. But if we drink tap water, our stomachs don't even hurt.'

Preeti explains the necessity not only of being hygienic but of being seen to be hygienic. She suggests washing hands within eyeshot of ma'am and explains the importance of hand sanitizer in the modern Indian upper-class household. It's practically the new Ganga jal, offering talismanic protection from the dirt and impurity of India: just a few drops takes it all away. Before touching madam's things, the maids should wash their hands with antiseptic soap for ten seconds, or apply hand sanitizer. Some women have told the company they want the maid to apply hand sanitizer each time they put away their kids' toys, or touch anything belonging to the child.

'Now I'm going to assess you,' Preeti tells Ohabun. 'I'm thirsty, please fetch a glass of water.' Ohabun gets a glass, rinses, wipes it and fills it with bottled filtered water—not tap—and then presents it on a tray. Preeti scrutinizes the glass closely and is pleased to see there are no water droplets on the outside of the glass. That would look sloppy.

'It was all very good, but you made one mistake in the beginning,' she says. 'You went into the kitchen but you didn't wash your hands. You didn't, did you? That was a very big mistake.'

Then they proceed to examining her ironing skills. Ohabun sets the ironing board up against the wall and Chauhan corrects her. 'We pull the ironing table away from the wall, otherwise that's how you get scratches. And what will happen if you scratch something?'

'Madam will slap me?' says Ohabun, a little uncertainly.

'No, no,' says Chauhan hastily. 'But you'll definitely get an earful.'

Ohabun's bangles jingle as she irons. Another supervisor present comments that madams often don't like maids to wear bangles, irritated by the jingling and jangling that reminds them of an obtrusive presence in the house, even though that presence is there to help them. Chauhan agrees, saying that the bangles also hit against surfaces that are being dusted, sometimes leaving a mark. She advises against jingling anklets and low-cut tops as well, saying cleavage will show when squatting and mopping the floor. She tells the women to pull their hair tightly back in neat buns, with no loose strands at all, so there's less chance of it shedding or ending up on something. Wearing hair loose and open is for madams. In any case, it's best not to go to work looking so attractive both for the suspicions this may provoke at home, as well as the unwanted, even unsafe, attention it may attract on the way to or at work.

After Ohabun has cleaned the bedroom, Chauhan goes in to check her work and returns with a gotcha. There was a glass hidden behind the foot of one of the two beds, which Ohabun would have noticed if she swept or mopped thoroughly under the bed. 'You missed this,' she says, 'Madams sometimes do this to check your work. Leave things in places that you will only see if you clean thoroughly.' (Although the contemporary narrative holds that men are more relaxed and forgiving when it comes to housekeeping, it wasn't always that way. One reformer, Abby Morton, writing in the late 1800s about the epidemic of housework that was sending many anxious housewives to New England mental asylums, had this to say about the role of men in that anxiety. 'It is always what is not done that a man sees,' she wrote. 'If one chair-round escapes dusting, it is that chair-round which he particularly notices. In his mind then are two ideas; one is of the whole long day, the other of that infinitesimal undone duty. The remark visible on his countenance is this: "The whole day, and no time to dust a chair-round!"')

It is that kind of man that Preeti invokes when she tries to make madam seem somewhat relatable, just another woman under someone else's thumb like they are. She does that when trying to impress on the women why it's so important for them to arrive at the same time everyday, and the consequences for madam if they don't. 'If you don't go on time, she will have all the same problems that you have at home,' Preeti says, in a discussion on punctuality. 'You tell me: if your husband isn't able to leave for work on time, then doesn't he scold you? He scolds you a lot, right? In the same way, won't she get a scolding from her husband? She will.'

VASANT VIHAR

'DO YOU KNOW HOW MANY bored housewives have affairs with servants in this city?' asks Prabeen, an elegant woman in her mid-sixties who has worn her silver-streaked mane loose for decades before granny hair was ever a trend.

'No,' I answer. And I suspect, neither does she, despite recounting all sorts of exciting stories about nefarious servants, or the nefarious doings of memsahibs with their servants, all of which I sadly suspect are based on not a shred of evidence.

A dear friend of my mother's, my interview with Prabeen sometimes put me in mind of my efforts at finding eyewitnesses to a shoot-out in Delhi many years ago. At first, dozens of people were able to offer me remarkably vivid accounts of what had happened, and what they had seen with their own eyes. But it all fell apart when I asked, 'One last thing, sir. Could you show me where you were standing at the time?' Then the hemming and hawing would begin, and it turned out that not only were said 'eyewitnesses' not, in fact, eyewitnesses, but were often removed by many degrees of separation from the original source.

Still, Prabeen's spirit is not as easily squashed as the 'eyewitnesses' I'd interrogated and she continues blithely on, insisting her source on the torrid servant-housewife liaisons was a senior police official for South Delhi whom she had met in the course of work for a women's support group called Saheli that she had helped found in 1980, a period many grey-haired Delhi doyennes look back on fondly as the flowering of the women's movement, albeit mainly among a certain class. Prabeen often reminisces about her work at the centre, long since left behind, especially the outings to descend en masse on a police station with a victim of domestic violence. Once there, they would shout slogans and make a scene until police agreed to take down a formal complaint.

'When I was working in Saheli, I'd gone to [the Deputy Commissioner of Police]... And he had kept us waiting, we had taken an appointment, it was a particularly gruesome dowry case we had to talk to him about,' says Prabeen. 'Then this huge family came out, very Maru [Marwari] looking, very rich businessmen...and [the police official] said I'm sorry we kept you waiting but you know these people had this huge lakhs and lakhs worth of jewellery stolen and they had put in a case and now they've withdrawn the case. So we said "Why?" Because they realized the wife was having an affair with the servant. And it was the servant who stole it. And why are the wives having affairs? Because the husbands are out the whole day making money.'

She urges me to go question senior police officials on this topic to which I mutter evasive replies. I never end up directing such questions to a police officer but later, when I am idly Googling for reports of such cross-class relationships, I stumble instead across a trove of Indian erotica centred on the maid. The stories on the site, told by male narrators, are peppered with such a wealth of realistic details about class and poverty in India as to make for a kind of porn verité. One writer begins his sex fantasy this way, 'I kept a maid, who was a widow of one of our contractual worker who died due to excess alcohol.'

In another fantasy on the site, a man's maid returns in the evening for a little hanky-panky, but her employer-lover is dismayed to find her wearing the same rather sweaty sari she was wearing in the morning, when she came to clean his house. 'Sir,' she says, 'I had to go clean four or five houses and had no time to change.' The narrator apologizes for 'troubling her' about her clothing, and the story continues. In another story, the man persuades his paramour to use the house shower before they have relations. But in one story, perhaps the most transgressive of all the fictions on the website, the narrator's wife dies, and before her death blesses his remarriage to the beautiful maid with whom he has fallen in love. Prabeen's stories of transgression are more tantalizing, though, because there's a stronger whiff of authenticity to them— invariably due to the presence of a police officer.

But it is over the coffee tray that the conversation moves to her more heartfelt concerns with the help of today. She looks disconsolately at the tray that has been set before us on her plant-filled terrace on a warm February morning. Its offensiveness is not immediately obvious to me. The French press is filled with fragrant black coffee, and is chaperoned by two pale blue cups of a sort familiar to anyone who has shopped on Canal Street in New York's Chinatown. But to Prabeen, this tray, as with so many things in India, is one more example of how life has become less perfect than it used to be. In particular, how much less perfect servants are than they used to be.

She herself takes care to make sure that the things she does, she does perfectly. Her home is full of beautiful things, like the appliqué cloth from Turkmenistan displayed inside the glass-encased top of a dining table. Outside her living room with its glass sliding doors that let in masses of light a bougainvillea is being trained to grow along a ceiling. One day in the future little tendrils will curl downwards, hanging their flowers with tiny white stamens and pink papery leaves over the heads of her dinner party guests like an Indian pink version of mistletoe. She dresses in carefully tailored saris and suits of her own design made from antique silks and other rare fabrics, eschewing the practical synthetics that many Punjabi women start to adopt as they get older.

She runs a boutique catering service, supplying Middle Eastern feasts—boiled quail eggs, beet salad, mint seasoned lamb koftas—to rarefied gatherings. Sometimes she hosts cooking classes for visiting tourists who want to learn how to cook a proper curry. Very well versed in the finer points of the domestic arts, Prabeen knows exactly how a tray should be arranged, and explains all the things wrong with the one that is sitting before us.

A well-laid tray speaks. It will tell the careful observer the duties expected of host and guest, and the regard in which the guest is held. It will also minimize even the slightest unnecessary effort on the part of either. Our teaspoons should have been laid on the side of the saucer next to the handles of the little blue Chinese-patterned cups, not on the other side. The cup handles should have been positioned towards the right (it is still not a welcoming world for left-handed people). And, as she is the host, the black handle of the French press should be pointed towards her, not towards me: a guest does not pour her own coffee.

'This is a properly served tray,' she says, after making the necessary improvements. 'Tomorrow it might come totally wrong. There's a certain sloppiness which has come in. But you know, I'm more pernickety than most.'

This is true. A maid who works for her, and who took on some temp work at another house, remarked to a man she saw dusting an intricately carved piece of art with a few flicks of a duster, 'My madam would make you go over that with a paint brush.' (To which the man remarked, 'And I would walk out.')

Although I'm impressed that there are so many ways to get a tray wrong, I want to ask her: aren't we women hurting ourselves by amassing this knowledge, caring about it, and then insisting that others care too? Male Indian food writers sometimes lament the freshness and flavour lost in cooking now that women don't wake up before dawn to grind fresh spices for the day's cooking. Good riddance, I say. Surely we'll be better off once we dispense with the civilizational niceties—morning spice grinding and teaspoon placement rules—that always seem to fall to women? As a corollary to that, if we could forego upholding such standards—or insisting on having our proxies in the form of maids uphold them on our behalf—wouldn't housekeeping be much less fraught?

On a different channel, though, the little devil sitting on my shoulder has just made a suggestion. If other memsahibs are instructing their help on teaspoon placement, then wouldn't it be okay for me to ask my cleaner to return the fans back to the gentle tropical breeze setting I like when she departs? Invariably I come home to find them on her preferred setting, a gale reminiscent of a Blackhawk landing, perfect for drying freshly mopped floors. Then the winged apparition on my other shoulder wades into the fray, reminding me that it is a brief journey from exacting to crazy.

But Prabeen links what she sees as the lack of care in putting together this coffee tray to the disarray she also increasingly finds in the world outside her beautiful home, something increasingly on her mind as national elections approach that year. 'It's a malaise all over India—at every economic and professional social strata of life,' she says. 'My earlier people who used to work with me, they had a sense of pride in what they were doing; they also had a greater sense of loyalty that, yes, this person has been good to us, even if she does scold us once in a while.'

Employers often have an idealized idea or memory of the perfect servant, the sort of attendant they insist their parents had or someone they remember from their childhoods. These hallowed figures may not have been past purloining some small thing here or there or having quirks that wouldn't be acceptable today—and older employers don't seem to consider such purloining particularly egregious—but they were absolutely, 100 per cent loyal. In a memoir Prabeen later publishes, she reminisces about the transgender ayah hired for her cousins to replace an earlier caretaker who had been dosing the children with opium.

Servants did not use to have visions of ideal employers; they accepted what they got. Or, if they had some hopes of their employers, these were often voiced with folded hands, as supplications, not demands. But people going into domestic work today are no longer so accepting. Many younger workers, at least those raised in the city, have strong ideas about what makes a good or bad job and what makes a good or bad employer, and many think nothing of turning down an offer and salary that might seem like fantastically good luck to their mothers. Younger workers think that older people whose kids are grown and young working couples without kids are good—foreigners are the best. Housewives who are home all day are the worst. For employers, this new situation, where there are two sets of expectations to be met, not one, can be startling.

Some of them adapt: it can be liberating to have an employee who can take the onus of doing the right thing off of you by setting boundaries herself. Friends of mine told me they were flustered when a prospective, well-qualified nanny responded to their eager invitation to come for an interview with the flat reply that she didn't work for Indians. Rather than banging down the phone, as an aunt of mine in her fifties told me she had done when faced with a similar remark, the couple tried to win her over and speak to her fears. The husband quickly responded, 'We're not that kind of Indian.' She remains with them and they remain on their best behaviour, on occasion departing briefly from their own dinner parties to drive her home if it has become dark.

For employers of an older generation, though, it can be harder to adjust. Which is why, when we meet on a warm February morning,

Prabeen is in the middle of domestic rearrangements, which everyone who knows her says are a frequent occurrence. Because she has high standards, and because she feels, if she were to do it herself, it would be done perfectly, she doesn't feel she's doing anything wrong by chivvying her workers till they deliver to the right standards. As Chopin streams through her bright, sunny South Delhi apartment, she fills me in on the current state of play.

A former live-in cook who left her to work for an expat family years ago has come back, tentatively, if Prabeen is willing to pay her 16,000 rupees. But Prabeen says that after two years of feeding her American employers bland soup, the woman has forgotten all the elaborate recipes Prabeen had taught her. Most people blame foreigners for driving the salaries up; Prabeen doesn't have a problem with the salaries. She's willing to pay 16,000 or 18,000 rupees, which at this time is at the generous end for salaries for cooks and cleaners in Delhi. But what she does blame them for is importing the slovenly housekeeping of countries that don't have dust and, because of their undiscriminating palates, raised on processed food, ruining the recipes she's imparted to this cook. Recipes like the date cookies on the coffee tray before us. I had assumed they were store-bought, it turns out they are homemade, baked by the prodigal maid. Prabeen looks as disparagingly at the offering before us as she had at the coffee tray. 'I can't pay 16,000 for this pastry,' she says. It is dense, she says, when it should be light and airy; this doesn't stop me from having three.

Still, there are many good things about this cook, not least of all, her religion. Despite the fact that many in Hindu-majority India say they suspect churches of fostering a conspiracy to weaken India, many Indians also seem to be convinced that a belief in Jesus Christ leads to better housekeeping. In recent years, picking up on this preference, maid brokers have added words like 'Sister', 'Mariam' or 'Charity' to their agency names as a crafty form of marketing, leading Hindu employers to regard the church as the motherlode of maids. One Catholic Church in a South Delhi neighbourhood whose own priests refer to the [7 a.m.] Sunday Mass as the 'maids' service'—since the hymns will be over before sahib and memsahib wake up—is pretty fed up with this perception. In response to frequent enquiries, the church placed a gigantic wooden board at the entrance to its red brick-covered building with the admonition: 'Do not enquire about maids here.'

But religion notwithstanding, a few weeks later when I check in with Prabeen I hear things didn't work out with the lady of the sub-par pastry. But not because Prabeen fired her: quite the reverse, actually, to her astonishment. Matters came to a head soon after Prabeen asked the cook to meditate upon why her work standards had fallen so much after her time working with expats and what she could do to improve. The woman returned after spending the night in Panchsheel Park, where her sister works for foreigners, and told Prabeen she had a considered and informed answer to her question: 'She had spent the whole time thinking about why her cakes were falling flat and her biscuits were so hard,' a voluble Prabeen said over the phone. 'She says, "Once more I've started working for an Indian...my status has gone down." And she was so unhappy she just couldn't perform!' said Prabeen in conclusion.

After this, there was nothing more to be said, and the two women parted ways. Prabeen had paid the cook about 30,000 rupees for two months of work, which included several elaborate parties entirely cooked at home to celebrate her daughter's marriage to a high-school sweetheart, now a chef living in London. Thinking it over, Prabeen felt she'd been had. 'I hardly ever scolded her since I didn't want to come across like a harridan in front of my son-in-law,' she said.

Prabeen felt that the woman had never intended to stay more than two months, even though she came to her saying she was tired of working for foreigners, with all the coming and going and the uncertainty. She believed the woman already had a gig lined up with the family coming to replace her previous employers, the aficionados of chilli and bland soup. But because she wasn't getting paid during the gap between her departing employers and those who were coming next, she'd approached Prabeen. Prabeen asked, why couldn't the woman be honest and say she was just looking for temporary work? Why spin her an emotion-laden story about looking for long-term work and being sick of expats?

Of course, it is possible that had she said that she was only available for two months, Prabeen might not have hired her at all. Or perhaps she had sincerely intended to come back for a longer-term stint, but found Prabeen more exigent than she remembered after her more easy-going employers. Every few weeks I tried the now ex-employee's number hoping to hear her version of how she and Prabeen parted, but was met with the message that the phone was switched off.

LUTYENS' DELHI

ONE WARM JUNE AFTERNOON I arrive at the government bungalow that is home to the politician Mani Shankar Aiyar, a Congress Party politician known for his outspoken and acerbic views, and his wife, Suneet Mani Aiyar. A home like theirs has to juggle duties that are equal parts domestic and political, such as having a visiting Chinese delegation over for tea, shortly after hosting a working breakfast of omelettes and cornflakes, for example. The bungalow is around the corner from the prime minister's residence, as well as the one-time home of late Prime Minister Indira Gandhi, now a museum constantly surrounded by tour buses. The Aiyars' home is also not far from the government bungalows where I met the former MP Dhananjay Singh, although the décor here is quite different, composed of pedigreed works of art and sculpture that lend this home too the air of a museum. Mrs Aiyar has a reputation as a collector of Indian colonial antiques, running a crafts business in the Jangpura neighbourhood that finds and restores rare pieces. At the entrance to the home, a painted wooden sculpture of Ganesh on a palanquin greets visitors, his arms painted red in contrast to his green dhoti, supported by a base that is decorated with carved birds and other animals.

When I arrive, Mrs Aiyar, fresh in a crisp, pale-hued cotton sari, greets me and asks me what I'd like to have; when I suggest nimbu pani, she points out that this will take her a couple of minutes to prepare, which will delay the start of the interview, as she'll be squeezing lemons and diluting sugar. I wouldn't usually have made such a labour-intensive request but it's very hot, and in a house of this scale, there usually is someone hovering in the background, making it unlikely the hostess herself will be inconvenienced. She explains that since it is shortly before five, it's not quite the end of her help's rest hour. And in any case, most of her help is away and have been for several weeks. June is usually planting time in the villages, the start of the winter rice-sowing season, the period when the majority of the country's rice is grown. One has gone back to address a dispute with her in-laws over property.

I drop the lemonade idea and settle for water instead and we repair to the living room, where we sit side by side on a peach raw silk settee in front of a wooden table piled with books and curios. The home reminds me of embassy residences overseas, decorated with objects from across the country, and traditions, so as to convey to visitors: this is India. And, in fact, Mr Aiyar was a diplomat before entering politics.

Politicians' families often have help from their own states or districts, often for very long periods of time. Mr Aiyar, though now a member of the Upper House, previously represented a coastal Tamil district. However, the people working in the Aiyar home aren't from that part of the country. Most of them were hired in the last five years and are long-time residents of not just Delhi, but Lutyens' Delhi, even if they originally hailed from the hills to the north of Delhi or Uttar Pradesh.

One part-time worker, who cooks Western food and is also entrusted with the dusting of many of the delicate works of art around here—as well as knowing which ones not to dust—lives on Akbar Road, where her husband is driver to a friend of the Aiyars. This woman, who completed two years of high school, is clearly a favourite, teaching herself to cook Western food from recipes that Mrs Aiyar translated for her, and which she writes down in ornate Hindi. 'Ingredients, matlab, "samagri",' she writes. Then, "method" she writes as "vidhi". So I dictate it to her then she tries it.'

Actually, she's not quite the absolute favourite. That spot goes to the Nepali driver who has been with the Aiyars for more than fifteen years, and appears to be a man of many and various skills who won't stand on ceremony about what is or isn't his job. He mixes cocktails when required, ferries one of the cooks home to the bungalow around the corner, or pitches in any way he thinks will be most helpful. He lives in one of the city's largest informal neighbourhoods, home to many domestic workers, Sangam Vihar, from where he often cycles over, in order to lose weight as a doctor has advised him to do.

'One day I walked into the kitchen right in the beginning [of knowing him] and he was busy. I was like, "What are you doing in here?" "Puri bana raha hoon, guest aye hai" (I'm making puris, ma'am, you've got guests),' she recalls. 'I was like, "My God". That's before I really got to know all his capabilities.'

Her main cook, who lives on the premises and makes the classic North Indian favourites that must make an appearance at most official dinners, is an elderly, partially deaf man who previously worked for her daughter—a friend of mine who has helped arrange this interview—but is a much better fit here.

'He's a very old, old-world, Punjabi-style cook,' she says. 'And he was hard of hearing. Like if they would ring up and say, "We're just leaving the office, take the mutton chops out of the freezer and marinate them in white wine and Tabasco", he wouldn't be able to do that. But you tell him, "Make a rogan josh, meat curry, butter chicken", he'll do that.'

The other family that lives on the premises came to her through her gardener, a young Muslim man who lived in the servants' compound attached to the home of one of the country's most famous lawyers, who also lives on Akbar Road. 'So through him this lady turned up, she's a young woman, and what I liked about her, all her brothers were working in the neighbourhood, or at least living in the neighbourhood, so I could check they're not thieves, drunkards, or whatever,' she said. 'They seemed a decent lot and not a huge family. Because then again, with young boys, they may be on drugs...she looked pleasant enough, but she'd never worked before.'

The woman had previously been a security guard for a well-known fashion designer with a clothing studio in South Delhi, where her job was to prevent the women who worked there from departing with an especially nice bolt of fabric tucked into a handbag. Now she was raising an eleven-year-old son, after marrying her former brother-in-law upon her sister's death, as well as bringing up her nephew.

The workers at the Aiyars' house, like those working for my parents, are mostly in their thirties and forties, which Mrs Aiyar says is the ideal age group. For the most part their children are raised, even married, and they are settled in long-lasting marriages. For them, just as for Mrs Aiyar, the turbulence and exhaustion of having very small children to bring up is well in the past. Mrs Aiyar thinks that the women who come from Jharkhand are so young that it requires a greater responsibility on the part of the employer to look after them. But then, Mrs Aiyar is in her sixties, and like my mother, can command the respect of experienced workers who are middle-aged themselves. Women in their thirties or younger often prefer to hire people in their early twenties, feeling like an older woman may argue with or undermine them.

Despite the compounds of these government-owned bungalows having numerous servants' quarters, Mrs Aiyar hasn't filled them up. I'm surprised to see that although they entertain frequently, almost every day, the Aiyars have about the same number of workers as my parents, who entertain very little. One driver and three help in the house. The only addition is a watchman at the gate. Mrs Aiyar says she only wanted to give servants' quarters to families she really felt comfortable living with. The more families there are living in, the greater the numbers of extended relatives and friends coming and going or spending the night.

And the more families living on the compound, the greater the chance of rivalries, disputes, perceived slights and extramarital affairs. Just months after we meet, Indian newspapers report that the husband of a maid at the home of a politician has been found dead on the premises of the government-assigned residence, one avenue away. The police soon arrest a cook working for the politician, the then Minister of Poverty Alleviation, saying they suspect the cook of having an affair with the maid whose husband was killed. (Mrs Aiyar's previous workers, it turns out, were let go after they became involved in an extramarital relationship, she says.)

Because these kinds of quarters—set apart from the main house and therefore fairly independent—are increasingly uncommon and therefore highly sought after, many civil servants and politicians are able to pay very low salaries to workers in exchange for them. Or sometimes no salary at all, a practice that was very common in the 1980s and 1990s, and one that has not yet entirely died out. A housekeeper I met in 2015 working on the AIIMS residential campus, home to the country's most senior government doctors, said she had never asked for or received a salary in her almost two decades working there

for chiefs of the hospital departments. Mrs Aiyar's workers earn in
the range of 7,000 rupees a month, which is about what my parents
were paying at the time, and perhaps half or less than half what her
daughters pay their help. 'They don't even tell me because they say
you'll be so annoyed when you hear it,' she says.

Mrs Aiyar's responsibilities as a politician's wife require her to
undertake a lot more hospitality than in a regular home, sometimes
at very short notice. The day I met her, both a breakfast and a tea
meeting had taken place in the house. The morning had begun the way
it usually does. The elderly Punjabi cook woke up first, coming to the
kitchen to drink a cup of tea as he read a Hindi-language newspaper.
The Aiyars have a kettle in their own room. Mr Aiyar, as a politician,
keeps odd hours, waking early to catch a flight or catch up on work.
That morning he was up at 4.30 a.m. to work on a piece of writing.

'Then he came at 6.30 to sleep and then I had to wake him up at
8 o'clock. I had my hot water,' she says. 'Then we came back from
a walk and Mani wanted fourteen chairs inside and they put all the
chairs.' Meanwhile, someone else was dispatched to walk over to the
venerable members-only Gymkhana Club, a favourite haunt of retired
bureaucrats, to pick up sandwiches for the breakfast. At around eleven,
Mrs Aiyar looked over the dining room and kitchen but found that the
reminders she'd arrived with were unnecessary: the kettle had been set
to pre-boil, eggs and cereal had been set out on the counter ready for
requests from the dozen or so guests, napkins had been tucked into
glasses. For a breakfast with that many people, it would take at least
three to serve so that no one was kept waiting. Then, after washing
up and a hurried lunch for everyone, it was very nearly time to prep
for the tea at three, for which Mrs Aiyar sliced up cake and reserved
some sandwiches.

'Actually those people came at quarter to three. They were a
Chinese delegation, there were five of them. So Gagan and I made
the tea and we served it to them and kept the leftover sandwiches,
which are still leftover, for baby,' she says. Because, of course, as in
many homes, this is where her granddaughter and the nanny are to
be found, under her supervision, while her daughter is at work.

Most workers rely on their employers to employ their 'source
and force' powers on their behalf, and that is no different here. The

difference is, though, a phone call made on behalf of a servant connected to this household is likely to carry more weight than many other phone calls of the same nature. Being close to a politician, even one from a party that is out of power—a situation that can change in five years or less, and therefore is not worth being too concerned about—has its privileges. When the brother of the live-in housekeeper applies for a job, he asks his sister if her employers will put in a good word on his behalf. So she approaches her employers, perhaps a little nervously.

'Mani rang up that guy, and this fellow went for the interview, then he got the job,' says Mrs Aiyar, adding that the brother was well-spoken and well-dressed. 'He may have got it just on his own anyway…but everyone likes to have a reference. That is not so much that they're obliging Mani. Why should they? They get so many phone calls.'

Phone calls are also made when it comes to health, and the importance of having the networks to make such phone calls are equally vital to the rich and poor. Despite the proliferation of top-notch private hospitals and insurance plans, many believe that private doctors operate on commission, forcing treatments and surgeries that aren't always necessary if the patient is insured or can afford to pay. When my father is diagnosed with an ailment that may need surgery, my parents are unable to decide what to do until friends help arrange appointments for second opinions from government specialists whom they trust, because they have nothing to gain. 'Really, still, the best treatment is at AIIMS. And that's free. Only, you waste time,' says Mrs Aiyar.

In recent years, she's discovered a hospital run by a private trust. When a woman who works for her came down with dengue, and her assistant began making the most dire predictions—'People are dying, she's sure to die. Yes, madam, she'll surely die'—an alarmed Mrs Aiyar put in a call to the head of the charitable trust, requesting her to personally assess the gravity of the housekeeper's condition, and relay the information back to her.

Like the children of the help of the Varmas in Sunder Nagar, it seems likely that the children of some of the Aiyars' workers are headed towards, or have already entered, the world of white-collar work. Mrs Aiyar describes with pride the fact that her driver's son works at one of India's most respected businesses, Fabindia. He was such a prized employee that when he got an alternative job offer in Dubai, she says the company begged him to stay and offered him a pay raise. But despite a longstanding friendship with the family that founded Fabindia, the Aiyars never put in a phone call on behalf of the driver's son. In fact, Mrs Aiyar only found out the young man worked at one of their stores after bumping into him when shopping at the main store one day. 'He got the job through a labour contractor. And then he did so well they brought him to the main showroom in GK-I,' she says with considerable pride. 'He's so smart, if you met him you wouldn't imagine...he's not a highly educated man's child, you know?'

It's clear she would have been glad to make a phone call on her driver's behalf, but he never requested it. And one reason for that may have been that he didn't require it. Perhaps from many years of residence in Delhi, and particularly this part of Delhi, the Aiyars while still central to his life, have become just one of many connections in this man's personal networks. Although we want to believe in the possibility of social mobility, the odds against a family making a dramatic leap forward can appear so great that we are often quite astonished when presented with the evidence that it does sometimes happen. There couldn't be a truer sign of upward mobility than a man not needing to ask for a favour from someone he knows to be able and willing to give it, which, I suspect, is what prompts the admiration and pleasure with which Mrs Aiyar described her discovery to the founder of the enterprise, who had likely often met the driver when he ferried the Aiyars over for dinner, or vice versa.

'He's working in Fabindia and I didn't even have to speak to you,' she told her friend. 'That's really nice.'

DLF PHASE-I, GURGAON

THE PROSPECTIVE MAID, A SMALL, pretty woman, is from Haryana. A bout of illness led to her losing her previous job. By the time she was better, ma'am had hired a new maid. It's unusual to find local women in domestic work, since the livelihoods of many Haryanvi families rely on farming or the proceeds of farmland sold to real estate developers who raise condos on these former mustard fields in Gurgaon. On a crisp November day, Amit Kapoor, the client sales rep for The Maids' Company, and I take this woman to one of the older developments of standalone houses, when Gurgaon was still copying Delhi's bungalows, before it turned to building the gated condos more common now.

This Gurgaon neighbourhood, at walking distance from the tenements where many maids live, has been among the hardest for the company to break into. By renting an auto and a van to transport women to jobs at far-flung condos, The Maids' Company has been able to do well in gaining clients in the more remote condos, while also addressing the women workers' fears of harassment, or worse, that left many reluctant to commute to distant places. (Even here, the company's proprietor Gauri Singh complains about her clients' stinginess, with many at first reluctant to contribute 1,000 rupees or so a month to the van service, even as younger women workers reported being followed by men in SUVs to and from work.) Because of the fear of commuting, there is a lot more competition for jobs in neighbourhoods that women are unafraid to walk to, leading to many more options for employers like this one. Amit has dealt with this woman in the past—at the last moment she'll back out and say she's not sure about entering into a contract right now, he warns me.

When we reach the four-floor home, a guard stops us. But when we explain we have come to provide madam a maid, he allows us to

troop up a staircase paved in dark green marble, past two enormous
panting but placid dogs. The client, a plump woman in her forties,
wearing a blue-and-white kurta, is in a living room on the fourth
floor, seated on a sofa decorated with cushions upholstered in gold
fabric. She tells us there is already a cleaner taking care of two of
the home's floors and that she is looking for someone to clean the
other two floors and assist with winter work, like airing out woollen
clothes that have been in storage with mothballs.

We are at the second stage of the Maids' Company's matchmaking
process. If the client agrees, the worker we are introducing her to will
start work tomorrow. If the employer decides she wants to hire the
worker, she will pay 25,000 rupees, which includes two replacements
in case her maid has to quit for some reason before the contract is
up. If she doesn't like the woman, she can ask to be introduced to
two other workers during the trial period so she can find someone
she likes better.

The woman tells us to sit, and we shuffle over to the sofa opposite
the one she is sitting on. Kapoor sits, and then I do, but the woman
who is seeking the job remains standing next to me. In her 1998 book
on the culture of the chair, architect Galen Cranz wrote about the
fact that before the advent of industrialization and mass production,
the chair was a unique and uncommon perk in Europe, which is
why so many English words denoting leadership reference this piece
of furniture: chairman, chairwoman, department chair. In medieval
England, only the king sat on a chair, while others sat on stools or
benches; in India, a king might have had a throne or diwan, while
others sat on the floor.

Today the superiority of the chair may be coming to an end. On
the one hand, chairs are now cheap enough that they are no longer
so special, while on the other hand the dangers to health posed by the
chair economy are increasingly publicized. Even so, in India, where
floor-sitting and squatting coexist with chair culture, where and how
someone sits—or is invited to sit—can still be a loaded act. The plastic
chairs owned by a poor household in India are reserved for honoured
company while everyone else sits on the floor; in a rich household,
plastic chairs don't exist or would be reserved for domestic help not
allowed to sit on the fabric or leather-upholstered furniture.

In my own home, the maid isn't there long enough for the sitting question to arise. In my parents' home, though, we eat at a dining table, while the maids sit on low stools in the kitchen. We watch TV on a sofa, while the maids watch TV sitting on a rug. At a party I go to at around this time, when the politics and etiquette of sitting is on my mind, a woman who describes herself as the child of card-carrying Communist party members, speaks about her longstanding discomfort with the chairlessness of her parents' staff. They treat their staff well enough in other ways—decent wages, being polite—but it began to rankle in her that people who described themselves as devoted to equality did not mind that when they watched TV, family members sat on a sofa, while the maid sat on the floor. Eventually, as a result of her interventions, her parents upgraded the maid's seating. 'Now we sit on one sofa,' she says, 'and she sits on another sofa.'

What does the maid think about this upgrade? The woman I am speaking to doesn't know. In both of our cases, I suspect our focus on where the maids sit is driven as much by our vanity and our sense of ourselves as a certain kind of progressive person, as by concern for the comfort of the women themselves. If anything, the intervention might create greater discomfort for the worker by raising questions that didn't exist before—might she sit on her sofa when her employers are not sitting on theirs?

In my temporary role as sales agent, I decide I should at least occasionally try to follow the company founder's example of trying to encourage seating parity during interviews, one I didn't emulate when I accompanied Amit to the client meeting at Magnolias. Here, since we are all three in a row, it feels especially weird that two of us sit, while one stands. Perhaps too, at some level I feel able to impose my will in this matter at this meeting when I didn't at the other one, because here we are presided over by a woman, while at the other introduction, a man was in charge. As with the increased number of allegations of ill treatment brought by domestic workers against their female employers, I suspect that it's not so much—or not only—that women are more prone to being tyrants at home than men, but also that women are more likely to point out unfairness or bad behaviour in another woman because a woman's superior status is not accepted to the same degree as a man's. I gesture to the woman to sit down next to me; she looks uncertain, but does so. When she sits, a surprised expression crosses the client's face. But she doesn't say anything.

Instead, the woman asks the maid how many children she has and where she is from. Since many people in Delhi and Gurgaon express fears about migrant workers, and many also believe the Bengali workers are actually illegal immigrants from Bangladesh, the fact that this maid is a local, with roots here, ought to work in her favour. But it doesn't. The client frowns. Her husband runs a factory here and sometimes locals have beaten up and robbed the factory's migrant workers, she says. She says there are benefits to hiring workers who have no local ties, who, like the Bengali migrant workers, 'have been torn up by the roots'. Those who are from a place have 'networks', she says, imbuing the word with a sinister significance.

Also, she tells us, one of her previous maids was a local, and she stole. The conversation is conducted in English and I glance over at the prospective maid. Her expression hasn't changed during the woman's disquisition on the pros and cons of migrants and locals, and I'm not sure if this is because she hasn't understood what is being said or because, like many domestic workers, she's schooled in the art of not taking offence at behaviour that anybody else would be highly offended by. Still, we are all a bit surprised by the next question.

'What caste are you?' the client asks the maid.

'Valmik,' answers the woman. Valmiks are among the lowest castes, or rather out-of-caste, and they often do sanitation work. They would be unlikely to own land and this explains why the woman is in domestic work, and not a woman of leisure in a family living off rental proceeds. The client doesn't comment on this response or probe further. Later though, I wonder if it's the reason why, when she offers us sweets before we leave, she allows Amit and me to help ourselves directly from the plate, but doesn't do the same for the woman. At the moment of offering the plate to the prospective maid, she hesitates; instead, she takes a sweet from the plate and puts it in the maid's hand.

Amit tells the client that the company won't accommodate requests related to ethnicity or religion, something they've often had to grapple with, with many families saying they don't want to hire Muslim maids. A Kashmiri Pandit client was blunt, telling them that after her forced exodus from Kashmir, amid violence, she had come to hate Muslims.

She would quiz the workers who were sent to her on their practices of worship, sending back any maid who couldn't convince her she was Hindu. The client appears to accept this, and we get up to begin the tour of the areas that will need to be cleaned, among them a dark basement filled with glass furniture, including a glass bar and dozens of glass ornaments on every surface, which must require litres in glass cleaner every year to be kept free of dust and print marks.

At this point, the prospective client, who I suspect has been trying to bite her tongue, is unable to keep from speaking her mind regarding the unwelcome sight of the seated maid. More than money or work hours, it is around these things—where to sit, when to eat, which bathroom to use—that the sharpest lines are drawn. They're so commonplace that we don't even notice them, or know how important they are to our sense of propriety, until they are breached. She says to us, 'Amit, will she sit on my sofa every time she comes here?'

SUNDER NAGAR

NEERA VARMA CAN MEASURE HOW far she's come in life in closets. And, although she has always been part of India's privileged classes, she sometimes seems a little flummoxed at how much more she has now than in the past. Her family was never poor but like many Delhi clans, she can look back on struggles that might have led the previous generation of her family to feel it was teetering precariously on its particular rung of the class ladder. Her father fled to Delhi from what became Pakistan at Partition with five younger sisters whose weddings he had to see to, and studied as he worked, eventually landing a job in the Ministry of Home Affairs, in the office of Prime Minister Jawaharlal Nehru. When she was a child, Neera remembers having two pairs of shoes: one for home, and one for going out. Now everyone in her family can afford to buy shoes to match different outfits.

'When this house was built in 1954, there was only one cupboard in every room,' said Neera. 'Now we can't put all our clothes in one cupboard. Each person has to have at least two cupboards each.'

Her husband measures the distance he's come in cars. Three decades ago, Pavan's family of four had one car. 'Now we have eight members, we have eight cars in the house,' he said.

Chutki, their maid from the western part of Assam, who brings in a low straw stool from another room in order to sit and talk with me briefly on the Varmas' balcony, can measure the progress in her own life by the number of siblings who now want to have a close relationship with her. She was the youngest of six sisters and three brothers, in a tribal village of largely Christian Santhals. But when she began working as a maid in the West Bengal towns that bordered Assam when she was still a child, it was only her brother-in-law who came to look in on her every month or two. 'He came to make sure

I was okay,' she says. And to collect her wages.

But after a year working at the Varmas', when Chutki returned home with some 50,000 rupees saved up, everyone was so pleased to see her. She now has six siblings, after three passed away, most of whom need help in one way or another. Her oldest brother farms the little land her parents had to pass on. The wealth gap between Chutki and her oldest sister Pano, who had eked out a living selling kindling and working in other peoples' fields throughout her time in relief camps in Assam, is in its own way no less vast than the gap between Chutki and the Varmas. In a way, Chutki had her sister's husband, the collector of wages, since dead of tuberculosis, to thank for that. It was he who had first taken her over the state border from Assam to Kalimpong in West Bengal to work as a maid, when she was around eleven. Now he is buried behind his sister's house in another village, alongside his sister's children who have passed away.

One small problem with her new-found popularity, Chutki finds, is that it is all too easy to offend one or another of her now very loving relatives. If she gives a gift or money to one sibling, another comes to her crying. *It's not about the money. But do you care more for that sister than for me?* So, she says smiling her gap-toothed smile, she has to send money to each of them secretly.

She's happy spending her money on helping the family who put her out to work. Some years ago Pano returned from the relief camp to her own village, with her youngest children. Chutki helped her to build two rooms with solid earthen plinths and heavy mud walls plastered with cow dung. The roof remains black tarp, loaded down with sticks, but at some point, I don't doubt, Chutki's earnings will pay for a better house. All across these villages, other families also rely upon their Chutkis, girls who come home happy to hand over their wages to relatives who are practically strangers after so long. As the Varmas are to Chutki—a safety net—so are all these Chutkis to their families. On visits home, long-lost relatives urge these girls to marry one local boy or another. Perhaps they fear that if their girls marry Delhi boys, and start families in the city, the stream of financial aid will dry up.

On this visit home, though, Pano asked Chutki for something besides money. Pano's daughter, Mae, had been in Delhi for four years.

But in all that time, Pano hadn't seen as much money as her youngest sister appears to have earned in one. Not only that, but Mae hadn't come home even when her father died of tuberculosis, caught some time after the first big gondogol, the 1996 riots between tribal Bodo and Santhal factions, when the family had to flee their village for relief camps. Chutki returns to Delhi with the phone number of the home where Mae is working, and calls her niece, who is almost the same age as her.

'I asked what's her house number, where does she live. I asked what's the address, I'm in Delhi too. But she couldn't tell me, she was talking very fast. I called two or three times, she seemed very scared. She would only say Punjabi Bagh. I think she was afraid, maybe someone was standing nearby,' says Chutki. 'We were able to talk only a few times. Then I told madam, they're not letting me speak to her.'

Chutki asks ma'am for her help. Neera Varma agrees, not knowing that this effort would turn out to be much more intense than many of her other efforts to help people who have worked for her.

'My parents are now eighty-nine, ninety plus, and they are still educating two boys. One has got fixed now,' she said. 'One has become a chartered accountant and they have placed him as an intern somewhere. He's still living in my parents' house though my parents have moved from their house to my sister's place because they cannot live on their own now.'

Many families in India would be nervous of an arrangement like that, although they are not completely uncommon. In the neighbourhood I live in, my housekeeper's sister and her family live in an apartment built for them by her employer before he died. He also left instructions in writing to his children to not evict the housekeeper's family so long as his wife was still living in the old home. Court documents also show that some employers leave small bequests or instructions for ongoing pensions to long-time help, although it's hard to know how frequently this happens. But many employers are wary of being this helpful to the help, of initiating them into the world of documents and rights, proof and process, of providing copies of signatures, lest it be turned against them in some way, as some court cases attest. Even the Varmas know the stories. A man living on their very street went to the court with electricity bills, gas connections, a

passport, all bearing his name and the address of the Sunder Nagar
home he was living in. As far as the neighbourhood knew, he was
a caretaker at the bungalow. But that's not what he told the court.

'He says, "I am not a servant here",' said Pavan Varma, '"this is
my house."'

Now he and his purported employer are locked in a legal battle
over a home worth crores. Sometimes, versions of this story splash
across Indian newspapers, leading employers to turn a dyspeptic gaze
upon the meek-looking person bringing them a morning cup of tea to
accompany the paper. They are stories about old retainers who have
heard the phrase 'you're one of the family' so many times they seem
to have taken it to heart, at times writing new wills for the elderly
and lonely person in their care, wills that make entire properties over
to them. This is a crime employers fret about and yet cannot see
coming, and how could they? It can only be executed by the people
they have trusted the most.

The fear of the loyal servant who actually intends to usurp your
place is not of recent vintage, of course. Manucci, while working as a
physician in the court of the Mughal Emperor Aurangzeb over three
centuries ago, recorded in his four-volume memoirs a visit to a place
known as the Fort of the Servants, which got its name like this. Once,
the soldiers who lived in it went out hunting. When they came back,
they found themselves locked out, the slaves and the servants having
taken over the fort. They paraded, to the chagrin of their masters,
up and down the parapets and shouted raucous profanities at the
soldiers beseeching to be let in. Some departed briefly inside, raising
the soldiers' hopes that they would open the gates. Instead, when they
emerged again, they were dressed in the soldiers' fine garments. Despite
many entreaties, they refused to let the soldiers back in. It was not
until an elderly woman arrived, scoffing at the pleading soldiers, and
scolded and hectored the slaves, that they cowered and backed down.
The message of the fable, one that still surfaces today, is that you're
asking for trouble if you don't treat servants like servants.

But Pavan and Neera are not haunted by these spectres, whether
they surface in historical myth, in the newspapers or in whispers around
the neighbourhood.

'You've got to take chances,' says Neera, 'One is bad—'

'Doesn't mean everyone is bad,' Pavan intercedes. 'See, property values have gone up so much. These people also understand. They're living in the house, they understand—

'When we are talking,' says Neera.

'And what we are spending,' says Pavan.

'There is this one India we are seeing, we are affluent, you know, we are wearing clothes, nice clothes, nice bags and all that,' says Neera. 'At the same time they don't even have a square meal, that's also India.'

When someone from that other India gets a glimpse of her life, she imagines it propels them in one of two directions, and she is able and willing to help with one of those journeys. 'Either he's going to work very hard, break his back to reach here,' she says, 'or he's going to kill you and take your money.'

DEFENCE COLONY

DIWALI IS FAMOUSLY THE FESTIVAL of lights, but it could just as well be called the festival of housekeeping, when each house is swept clean by the soft golden strokes of a previously unused phuljharu. I once did this myself, when I moved into a two-room barsati in Delhi in 2006. It was small enough and I was feeling poor enough that for a few days I followed the example of a British colleague who, unlike many other expats or newly returned Indians, was reluctant to hire someone to do his cleaning.

The barsati came with wall-to-wall carpeting (an odd choice in a city this hot and dusty), a dun-coloured dust trap, which I promptly covered with grass matting sourced from the Tamil Nadu state emporium. As I swept its woven surface one muggy September evening after work, I saw that the freshly-dried grass strands of my new and tightly-bound broom were shedding little particles, creating a fresh layer of dust to replace what I had just corralled into a dustpan. If I swept too vigorously, larger bits of dried grass detached and strewed themselves about. Too big to be swept up, these had to be gathered up by hand and thrown away separately. A new jharu requires vigorous banging against a wall before its first use, but when I was a child, someone else was doing the cleaning, and I had never noticed that fact.

And so, although my apartment was a 275-square-foot studio subdivided by a thin partition, I threw in the towel (or rather, the pochha) and took up the landlady on her offer to avail of the services of her part-time maid, P., a dainty Rajasthani woman who liked maroon lipstick and graphic flower-printed saris, and who announced her daily arrival up the stairs with a tinkling of her silver anklets.

She told me that housekeeping was charged at 150 rupees a task in Defence Colony, a neighbourhood where plots on either side of a wide drain had been originally allotted, since the 1960s, to people who

had served in the armed forces. In the time I lived there it was notable
for its construction noise, as army families' descendants converted
their homes into buildings of several floors, suitable for renting to
foreigners and newly returned Indians. We shook hands on 500 rupees
for washing the breakfast dishes, daily sweeping and doing the laundry
a few times a week, as well as four days off a month.

Despite having a job where I was supposed to question why things
were a certain way, to wonder why there were so many children at
construction sites or about a property market that led millions to
squat despite the clear and present danger of eviction, these kinds of
questions were far from my mind when hiring a maid for the first
time in my life. I didn't analyse the forces that had shaped the pay
we arrived at, or wonder where she would go to the bathroom or
eat lunch during a work day that included cleaning several houses
from 7 a.m. until about 2 p.m., about an hour of which was spent
at my place. Like most people, I defaulted to a view of my home as
a place to escape the sometimes exhausting questions of conscience
that I often faced outside of it. Instead, it fell to P. herself, despite
the power dynamics being so clearly against her favour, to train me
to be a better employer.

Very early on in our relationship, I remember delivering a tirade to
her on her unpunctuality, a sin I ought to have been especially forgiving
of, given I am so frequently guilty of it myself. I can't remember now
why I was so very cross. Was it perhaps an ultra-hot day when episodes
of road rage and other kinds of rage bubbled up all over the city?
I don't remember those details but I do remember that she listened
calmly and when I kept interrupting her efforts to explain or placate
me fell silent as I repeated myself. Then, when I finally paused, she
said to me, 'Didi, if you're so upset, why don't you hit me?' And she
blandly raised up her blouse sleeve and presented her reed-thin arm to
me, as if it were the most natural thing in the world, a commonplace
way to soothe a hopped-up employer. At that, finally, I fell silent.

Is that the kind of person she thought I was? That I would hit
someone who worked for me—or anyone for that matter? Or, more
disturbing, had she seen something that I could not, a look on my
face or a tone perhaps that reminded her of the look or tone of
another woman employer who had hit her? Or the worst possibility

of all, was I actually on the verge of tipping over into doing what she was challenging me to do? Is this how it starts, when women, safe in the privacy of their own homes, pour their rage and frustration on someone so much less powerful than themselves? Maybe they arrive at that point after a seemingly mild predation, such as the threat to dock wages for a broken glass, a refusal to give a raise or stinginess when a festival rolls around. And when there is no censure, no pushback, next time there is a perceived transgression, a voice is raised. And when there is still no pushback, perhaps next time it goes even further. Perhaps not everybody has someone in their life, as I did, to hold up a mirror and warn them from going down this road.

Usually, though, P.'s prods were less shocking, as when she came to me a little over a year after she started working for me and observed, 'You do know you haven't given me a raise yet?' As P. tried gently to improve me, other forces worked sometimes with her, and sometimes against her. Not long after she began working for me, a friend from Kolkata, troubled by the 'market rates' so many of us took for granted, decided to calculate what it would mean to pay his part-time cleaner at the purchasing power equivalent of $10 an hour—what he might have paid for housekeeping in the US, where he had just moved from. He came up with a figure of 3,500 rupees a month, using 160 rupees an hour (the regular exchange rate at the time was about 45 rupees to the dollar). But when he and his roommate seated their maid on a sofa and raised the prospect of this salary to her, she respectfully declined, saying her husband would believe she was offering 'other' services if she were to return home with such an amount for cleaning.

When I calculated the hourly wage rate I was paying, I found to my horror it came to just 20 rupees an hour. While I didn't necessarily agree with the 160-rupee benchmark, the exercise was sobering. In real terms, the wage for domestic work appeared not to have expanded in more than a century. The British authors of a Raj-era housekeeping guide had advised pay of nine rupees a month for a live-in cook, which adjusted for inflation came to about 6,000 rupees in 2006; most Indian families I knew were typically paying around 5,000 rupees or so a month for full-time live-in help then.

Using a more contemporary comparison, I was paying P. less for an hour of work than I paid a male cleaner at the parking lot outside my office for spending a few minutes throwing water over my car, treating her time and effort as worth so much less than his. Slowly, I began raising P.'s wages, arriving eventually at around 100 rupees an hour, or about five times the capital's minimum wage, a noticeable enough improvement that she began sometimes referring to me in negotiations with her other madams, not always successfully.

When P. tried to get the woman across the road to raise her salary, which had stood for years at 700 rupees a month, she told her madam that I paid her four times more for far less work. This resulted in a phone call, because she hadn't believed P. 'Is that really what you pay her?' 'Yes,' I responded. She seemed a little unsure how to continue but then made an appeal to the importance of solidarity among madams. In an attempt to get me to recognize the maid's true character and therefore stop 'spoiling' her with my errant pay scale, she made this disclosure, 'You should be careful. I think she steals. One time I lost a lot of jewellery, you know.' 'And you know what else? That man she keeps calling her brother-in-law is her boyfriend.'

When our relationship was at its best, P. would eat part of the lunch that she had cooked for me, taking it out to the terrace to sit at the wrought-iron outdoor table, which was the only table in my home you could sit and eat at, while chatting and making flirtatious remarks to someone on her mobile phone. Possibly the aforementioned brother-in-law.

But our relationship did not have an unblemished upward trajectory, and that was my fault, not hers. At times, overwhelmed by work and by life, I would be short and irritable with her, although she had done nothing to merit it. Once, I complained how untidy she was making an outdoor cabinet by storing her makeup there—'It's becoming a kabaarkhana!'—even though the unit was literally that, a place we put old newspapers to await the kabaariwaala. Later I realized it was a mark of confidence that my home was the place she chose to freshen up at the end of her work day, but I didn't know how to make amends, and offer her back what I had snatched away.

In the end, when I moved house, we parted on good terms, although I didn't take her up on her offer to leave all her other madams and come work with me in my new, more distant neighbourhood. For her to sever her longstanding ties with all her other employers and put all her eggs in one basket—the basket of me—felt like too great a responsibility. Instead, I loaned her money for her daughters' wedding and attended the large evening reception P. hosted at a municipal park for her girls; they had a joint wedding after P. was lucky enough to find two grooms who were willing to get married at the same time. P. had invited all her Defence Colony madams, all her long-time employers, but I didn't see the others in the large crowd. At the wedding she assigned her brother-in-law, a handsome man with a charming, rakish smile and little hoop earrings, to make sure I ate enough and keep me company. P.'s husband, an elderly-looking and slightly nervous-looking gentleman, skulked around the edges of the occasion.

Even though, by the end of our relationship, I was paying P. far more generously than I had at the beginning of it, in some ways I felt I was doing worse by her. Perhaps this was because, as the years passed, I had a better sense of our respective economic standing, and of the oasis of privilege I represented in comparison to most people I encountered, including her, as a member of India's one per cent. Although I became part of that rarefied economic niche as soon as I moved back from New York, it took me a while to grasp my dizzying ascent, since the threshold for entry is far lower in India than in wealthier nations.

According to an analysis by economists Thomas Piketty and Abhijeet Banerjee, five years before my own entry to the one per cent, it was possible for an individual to join that select group of earners at 90,000 rupees annually (they don't provide figures for more recent years citing a dearth of detailed tax data). More recently, an Indian think-tank estimated that the one per cent in India consists of households earning 12 lakh rupees a year and above, or approximately $18,500, which comes to about 3 lakh rupees a year per person for a household of four.

When I moved back to India in 2005 and found a job as a wire journalist, I began earning about 40,000 rupees a month before taxes and deductions, then around $890, or about 29,000 rupees after deductions. That meant I was earning more than twenty times the average per capita annual income (the year before, in America, I had been earning perhaps 1.5 times the average per capita income.). At the absolute level, though, I was earning far less than I had been.

After taxes and deductions, I could count on 29,000 rupees a month.
The 500 rupees a month I paid P. in the first year I hired her, came
out of the 6,000 rupees I had left after paying rent, a car loan, petrol
and groceries, and sometimes less if an unexpected bill turned up.

But as I changed jobs, and my earnings increased, the gap between
what I spent on her wages and on myself widened. When I was paying
P. 20 rupees an hour, it had been the equivalent of an eighth of my
own hourly wage; in later years, the difference between her hourly wage
and mine was fourteen times and growing. As I started partaking to a
greater degree in the parts of the Indian economy that developed to
cater to earners like myself, frequenting its restaurants, multiplexes and
newly opened gyms, I found myself increasingly confused and jolted
by the strange values and pricing prevailing in the Indian economy,
and my own part in setting those prices.

Us one-percenters could spend as much on a dinner as the servers
of those dinners or workers in our homes earned in a month, and yet
we were much more likely to push back against a request for a raise
that seemed excessive than we were to argue with the purveyors of
our overpriced dinners and movie outings. Was this because we didn't
have any reference points for the 'right' price to pay for olive oil, wine,
restaurant outings or gym memberships because of their novelty in
this setting? Perhaps our price points for wine and gyms were shaped
by having consumed them somewhere else first, most likely paying
for them in dollars and pounds, as well as the idea that these prices
were 'fixed', while those for people were negotiable.

Our ideas about what to pay people were also shaped by the feeling,
even among the affluent, of having only recently escaped privation. My
parents, for instance, often recall running out of money well before
the end of the month in the 1970s, when they claim they lived on just
300 rupees a month. And despite now owning their own home, and
having savings, they still live in fear of running out of money, especially
now that they find themselves living far longer into retirement than
three of their four parents did.

I began mirroring the kind of mental conversions Indian travellers
often engage in obsessively, converting their purchases into Indian
rupees. But I converted the prices of things I consumed in one part of
the Indian economy into their equivalents in the part of the economy

represented by P., mostly with head-whirling results. My groceries, for example, became wild acts of profligacy when converted into units of P.'s salary. A packet of pasta was two hours of her work. A kilo of chicken from a fancy purveyor who claimed to raise them humanely was three. Two run-of-the-mill bottles of wine or olive oil could easily be what P. earned from all her madams in two weeks. A dinner at a nice restaurant with drinks was what she earned in a month.

I would like to say that this running accounting, like P.'s occasional prodding, made me a better person and a more caring employer, or spurred me to acts of philanthropy more generally. But that would not be true. Instead, my awareness of the discrepancy in our respective earnings and consumption manifested itself mainly in an ever-greater desire to hide from my maid the truth about how I spent money and how much of it I had compared to her. As the moment of P.'s arrival approached, that furtiveness kicked into high gear, prompting me to pick frantically at the 150-rupee price sticker on a packet of penne as I waited for coffee to percolate. And so, when I look back on our relationship what I remember most of all is the enormous relief I felt at being able to dispose of a tell-tale label by the time she trooped up the stairs, payals tinkling, to ring the doorbell.

PART V

TAKING CARE

THE CHILD NANNY

THE PLAY DATE—PARENTS MEETING OTHER parents whom they don't know particularly well just so their children can have fun—is only just beginning to catch on in India. The extremely professional adult nanny is also a fairly new convention. Until busybody anti-child labour groups began conducting rescue operations, sometimes seizing a girl from an employer's house based on a tip-off from a neighbour, many families found having a live-in playmate was the ideal solution to the sometimes tedious business of keeping children entertained when not at school. After all, who better to play with a child than another child?

When she was eleven, Lovely, the young woman from Malda who migrated with her family to Gurgaon, was hired through other helpers she met hanging out at local parks to be just such a companion. Her charges were a girl slightly younger than her, and a toddler. She was the junior caretaker, under the supervision of an adult woman hired through a placement agency from Jharkhand, who in turn was supervised by the children's grandmother from time to time. For this job, which she got around 2006, Lovely was paid 1,500 rupees a month. Lovely dressed the little boy, nagged his sister into eating breakfast, and walked her to the school bus. She and the girl were like best friends, she said, playing video games after the girl returned from school. Sometimes the two girls played a game called Fashion Show, dressing up and pretending to be on a catwalk. Or she would give Lovely a makeover. 'Sometimes she'd be the teacher, I'd be the pupil, or she'd be the doctor and I'd have to go to hospital,' said Lovely. 'We were such good friends.'

Around the time that Lovely began working for this family, India banned children under fourteen from working in people's homes as servants. Lovely remembers that there were billboards advertising the new law and police were conducting door-to-door drives informing people that they could go to jail for hiring children. Worried, Lovely's employer took her to the police to ask if she would get in trouble for having the eleven-year-old in her house. The police said at first she was too young and that Lovely's madam should not employ her. 'But my daughter is so attached to her,' her ma'am said, promising never to hit Lovely and to send her to school. The police said, 'Okay, then keep her.'

Lovely, eighteen when I first meet her in 2014, doesn't think the police advice was wrong. 'What work was I doing?' Lovely says, 'I was just with the children.' Ma'am didn't send her to school, as she had promised the police, but she was partly true to her word and didn't hit Lovely. And compared to how much ma'am shouted at the older maids in the house, it was clear to Lovely that her ma'am was fondest of her. 'She loved me the most because I was always with her children,' she says. Ma'am also liked the fact that Lovely, being little, didn't eat such vast quantities as the rest of her maids. 'If you keep three or four maids, they'll eat a lot won't they? I was small, so naturally I didn't eat as much as them,' says Lovely. 'When the other servants were eating, she would say, why are you guys gobbling your food like beggars? The other girls would get scared. She'd say, "How has so much rice got finished so fast?"'

In Lovely's opinion, ma'am behaved like this because she was 'crack'. 'She would get cross for tiny, tiny things and start yelling. Like, suppose without asking, I moved something,' remembers Lovely. Or she would give her children's clothes to the part-time sweeper, and then undo the donation with cutting remarks. 'She would say to her, "You guys are poor, you have nothing, but if I give you anything, you don't appreciate it." Being poor is not such a bad thing. You should have good manners. She drove the girls who came to work to tears. The ones who lived with her she would make them cry too. And if they talked to each other, she didn't like it.'

Ma'am could also be quite thin-skinned herself, taking stray comments to heart. Once, after one of the series of nannies reported back that a neighbour's maid had observed that ma'am was so fair, but unfortunately her son so dark, she forbade Lovely from taking her kids to the park to play outside in the sun. Lovely describes ma'am as very pretty and says sir, ma'am's husband, was very handsome. But he had a temper too. One day the driver turned up extremely drunk, and said something unflattering about madam, to boot. 'Sir fired the driver. But first he kicked him many times, and then he threw the money he still owed the man in his face,' Lovely remembers.

As Lovely began growing into a very pretty teenager, ma'am's attitude towards her acquired an edge, particularly regarding her appearance. If she left her hair open, as she preferred, the woman would say, 'There's no need to be so stylish.' But sometimes after shouting at Lovely the woman would burst into tears and come hug her. Then Lovely would again think, ma'am still treats me just as if she were my mother.

When Lovely had first joined, ma'am was working at a bank where she won an award for her work. But just a few months after Lovely started, ma'am left her job to spend more time with her children, particularly her daughter, after relatives complained her older child was going astray. Lovely privately thought her family spoiled the young girl, at least when it came to money. She routinely had as much as 5,000 rupees with her, at any time. And, as she grew older, she sometimes did things Lovely didn't approve of at all. A friend from school would come over and they would close the door and ask Lovely to leave. Once, she walked in and saw the two girls looking at a website with naked men and women kissing. 'You won't tell, will you?' the girl said to Lovely. Another time, at a cousin's house, Lovely suspects that the girl was kissing her cousin. At least, that's what the girl's aunt insisted, and she made Lovely come to the room where the two cousins were, saying her sister-in-law wouldn't believe her unless she had a witness.

Ma'am's son wasn't always so well-behaved either, but it doesn't seem that anyone was much bothered about that. When he was three, he said something rude to his new nanny from Nepal, who responded with a profanity. Then ma'am lost her temper, giving the nanny 'slap after slap' before locking her on the roof. 'I was watching and she saw I was frightened,' remembers Lovely. Seeing Lovely staring at her, eyes wide, ma'am tried to explain herself, telling her, "It's because she did something very wrong." But Lovely thought to herself, hadn't her son been rude to the nanny first? A few days later, Lovely quit. 'I thought I should leave this job because who knows what may happen to me tomorrow,' she says. 'She loved me a lot, but still.'

In her next job, at an 11-acre condo complex that advertises on its website that every home comes with a modular kitchen from England and a 'panic button', Lovely is again a companion, but this time rather than an honorary elder sibling, she's a surrogate child to a woman whose own children are getting music and fashion design degrees abroad. Lovely can't say enough nice things about this woman, and how well she treats her. She showers at her employer's house, they eat together, watch TV together. They discuss the state of the world and India, debating why the country is so unsafe for women after television channels are consumed by a horrific gang rape that occurs in December 2012.

Aunty fusses over Lovely, who breaks into fond giggles recalling how aunty and she gossip over paranthas. 'She'll make things for me, she'll make me juice or a sandwich. We're just the two of us eating together. And she won't give it to me on a different plate, we serve ourselves from the same plate,' she says. 'And if we share something, she'll give me a bigger piece than she gives herself, as if I were her daughter.' When she has broken things at work, Lovely has gone to aunty and offered to have her salary docked. But aunty says, 'Why do you talk about cutting money? Things break, it happens.'

Aunty cossets Lovely, but that's not the norm. The time they have spent in Gurgaon homes caring for boys and girls not much younger than themselves, has mostly been an education for Lovely and her younger sister Rina on what a very different entity childhood is for the affluent in India, and for everybody else. For the affluent, childhood is a hallowed and protected time; for everyone else, it's an apprenticeship for a long life of working. Lovely and Rina, around fourteen when she first began working, don't express sorrow for not having had childhoods like those of the children they have cared for. If anything, they're aware of how much more they have than others. Rina describes riding in a car with madam and her children, and feeling terribly sorry when a beggar taps on the window. But if madam doesn't give anything, she doesn't feel like she can. Lovely tries to help people in small ways, taking clothes to a nearby shrine where beggars congregate. 'They were so happy over a T-shirt,' she said. 'So why not give it away?' Her thoughts on giving are shaped by faith, by the idea in Islam that after you have enough to live on, you should give to others.

'If I earn 10 rupees, I can help someone with 5 rupees,' she says. 'Because I'll earn blessings from that, won't I?' When she has no money to give someone who has knocked on her door for money, she tries to offer a small kindness instead, a glass of water perhaps.

So Lovely and Rina don't grudge the children they look after their good fortune. But they can't help but be bemused by the children of the well-off, giggling at their oddities like the children they have barely stopped being.

'They're so fragile,' says Lovely. 'They're afraid of so many things.' One child Rina cared for was afraid of balloons, so much so that she had to be kept away from her brother's birthday party in the condo clubhouse. It wasn't the popping, but the balloons in and of themselves. The girl Rina cares for now is afraid of flowers and mosquitoes (a pretty practical fear, as these things go, most likely instilled by her parents). And sometimes they're afraid of work. At her first job, which involved picking up after a girl slightly older than herself and a boy who was perhaps twelve at the time, Rina remembers the daughter took care of some of her own chores. But the boy left everything for Rina to do. When his mother scolded him for allowing Rina to wait upon him, he told her, 'I like to be helped.' Later some of these frightened children will grow into adults with more pragmatic fears, of break-ins and robberies and of being taken advantage of by the servants, who will buy apartments with panic buttons.

Meanwhile Lovely's and Rina's younger sisters, ten and eleven, come home and do homework and wash their older sisters' clothes and clean the room and cook the evening meal, things they have done for years. The two younger girls are by themselves in their Gurgaon tenement until darkness falls and their sisters come home. Lovely doesn't get home until three or four, and when she changes her job in 2015, she starts coming home much later. Rina doesn't come home from her job until past eight o'clock. Most parents of girls in India would shudder at the thought of leaving daughters of that age alone without an adult—especially when neighbours know they are all by themselves. But what can Lovely and Rina do? More than a year has passed since their parents decided to return with the two youngest children to Malda, to the village where Lovely has bought some land, leaving a household of four girls, two of them not yet in their teens, behind in the city. Sometimes Lovely thinks about sloughing off the responsibilities she's taken on, sending her youngest sisters back home, and becoming a live-in maid, with neither rent nor groceries to worry about. But then she thinks of the school back in the village and the one her sisters go to here, where they study English. Lovely and Rina told their parents they would manage, and manage they must.

Lovely's dilemma is not unique. Most people who work as domestic help, often caring for other people's children, have to make compromises when it comes to the care of their own. One young South Indian woman I met who had been working at Prabeen Singh's house for a few weeks told me that most of the time she was able to leave her children with her mother. But at times, if her mother was down south, she would leave her son in charge of his baby sister, telling him to go to a neighbour if he needed any help. Her son was terrific, she told me. He would feed his little sister, play with her, and when the water came at the local municipal tap, would remember to attach a hose and fill the family's water canisters. 'I would not be able to work if not for my son,' she said. 'How old is he?' I asked. Six, she replied.

THE MOTHER'S NANNY

THE RELATIONS BETWEEN SAHIBS AND their cooks and cleaners don't run smoothly at the best of times. But those aren't as fraught as the relationship between parents and a nanny, or, most of the time, between a mother and nanny. When there's a child involved, it's a triangle, not a two-way relationship, after all. At its best, a mother feels her child is with someone who truly loves her, which may occasionally provoke pangs of jealousy she tries to suppress. At its worst, parents may feel fear and suspicion over how their child is being treated when they are not around, which they try to treat with layers of surveillance, both human, in the form of grandparents, and technological, in the form of CCTV cameras.

It is also a relationship where the rules that govern other kinds of domestic help are suspended or at least muted. With children, certainly with a first child, the parents are often themselves at sea, they have no tried-and-tested practices to impart. Fumbling your way towards a routine is part of the new parent experience. You might expect to be on the receiving end of 'advice' that is difficult to reject from some of the people around you—other mothers or, most commonly, your own mother. But if you have a nanny, and she is very experienced and you are not, she will also school you.

At least that is how it seemed to one Delhi college professor, when she became a mother for the first time in her thirties, and found herself under the tutelage of a highly-regarded japa, an infant nanny who is usually hired before the delivery and stays for the first month of the newborn's life. A japa is someone who might have once been called a wet nurse; now, a new mother would as soon as hire a woman to feed her child as she would hire a woman to sleep with her husband. Instead, she is sort of a mothering coach to Indian women whose teenage years and twenties have been marked by studying and work, rather than caring for a slew of younger siblings. Many affluent Indian women are coming to motherhood later than ever before, like women in other parts of the world. And when they do, they find mothering doesn't come as naturally as they were somehow led to believe it would.

If mothers are older, then grandmothers too aren't as young and energetic as they used to be. Once a grandmother could be as young as forty-five and still tending to a child or two under ten herself, but now she is likely to be a lot closer to sixty. I've seen it in my own family. My mother's mother was not yet fifty when my older sister was born; my mother was sixty when my first niece was born, and sixty-six by the time her second grandchild came along. So the japa is there to help a slightly shell-shocked woman learn to breastfeed, to interpret her baby's coos and cries, to gently massage the newborn. She's there to stay up nights with the baby so the frazzled mother can sleep and, most of all, she's there to handhold a new mother in ways that other women in her life may no longer be able or willing to. And yet, when a japa imparts her knowledge and experience, a new mother can find to her surprise that the generous tenderness and affection shown by the nanny to her child is not always extended to her. The professor remembers one moment in particular, when she and the nanny were by themselves at home, in a government flat situated behind one of the older malls in South Delhi, and she was pumping breast milk for her newborn, just a few weeks old. Everyone else was out at work. After several minutes, the woman took a look and exclaimed, 'Is that all? It's hardly anything.'

The professor was stunned and hurt. Perhaps it was not meant as an insult, but it felt that way. It was not even two weeks since she had come from the hospital in Delhi where she had given birth to her daughter pre-term. The doctors had told her that she would have to work harder at breastfeeding, because a preemie isn't as strong, and it's harder for her to latch on. The woman had been pumping, trying to boost her milk supply, so her baby would have an easier time feeding. Everyone today knows how important breastfeeding is, and most mothers who have done it rave about the bond it creates with your baby. But breastfeeding doesn't always go smoothly, and the effort to make it happen can make the first weeks very stressful.

Mothers who aren't able to nurse, even for very good reasons, don't make peace with it easily. Perhaps that's why the remark about her milk is one of the first that comes to mind when the woman talks to me about her relationship with that nanny, a woman of about her own age or perhaps slightly older. 'It was extremely disheartening,' the woman remembers. 'I felt very inadequate.'

Maybe, she thinks, their relationship would have been different if she had been the one to hire the nanny. Her present nanny, a soothing, soft-spoken woman, who has lived with her for two years now, and whom she interviewed herself, she speaks of with great affection. Now that her daughter is older and in playschool, the nanny spends time at stitching classes and is learning tailoring on a sewing machine she and her husband have bought for her. But the professor had been quite uninvolved in the hiring of the infant nanny. She hadn't planned on having a nanny as soon as the baby was born. She knew her husband would be very hands on, and her parents were around; she hadn't foreseen needing help right away.

But that plan changed soon after she came home from the hospital, when family members noticed that she was listless and detached, not her usual engaged, energetic self. It was only later that the woman realized why she had been so out of it in those early days, that she was suffering an episode of depression. 'That made me very diffident. That is why I went with the first person who was sent to me,' she tells me over the phone, on a day when she is at home with her daughter, now three, who is sick with a fever. 'I was hardly able to ask any questions. I was so very out of it.'

In the end it was her father who hired the japa, using the services of veteran maid broker Sunita Sen, who describes the japa she sent to this family as one of her most sought-after infant nannies. The woman's father found out that the woman had also cared for the grandchild of one of his friends; they recommended her enthusiastically. Certainly, there was nothing in her care for the baby that could be faulted, the professor herself concedes that. 'She was extremely competent and very good [with my baby],' she says.

But then, a nanny isn't there for the child alone. The woman remembers feeling that, when it was just the two of them, she was seeing a different side of the japa, a personality that was a more

manipulative and controlling one—and that no one else seemed aware
of. Yet, at this point in her life, this was the woman she was most
dependent on and grateful to, even as the nanny's words and actions
again and again poked at all the insecurities she already had about being
a mother. 'She had seen all these things before—this is her work—so
she used to sort of talk down to me all the time,' the woman tells me.

One time she remembers coming out of the bathroom wearing
the sort of clothes you do when you're tired and overwhelmed and
not planning on leaving the house and the japa scanned her up and
down and said, 'Aren't you going to wear a bra?' Another time the
nanny ridiculed the way she put a diaper on her baby. The woman
couldn't help thinking, here she was, someone with a PhD, who had
had scores of students come to her for advice over the years, being
chastised at every turn. Sometimes she wanted to turn around to her
nanny and say to her, 'Who the hell are you?' But then she would
look at her baby, thriving and happy in the woman's care, and bite her
tongue. Could she possibly trust herself to take as good care of her
baby as this woman, who was so capable and confident? Keep quiet,
she would say, not to the woman she wanted to shush, but to herself.

'PhDs and other degrees…are no use in these matters,' she says.
'You suddenly feel very disempowered, you're stuck at home, you
don't know what to do.'

It might have been the depression talking—that is likely what her
family members thought when she raised with them her discomfort
with the nanny only to find her mother and husband dismissing her
as overly sensitive and unappreciative of how lucky she was to be
able to count on such a caregiver. Before they had children, she and
her husband had pretty much agreed about everything including the
proper relations to have with the help. They had shared the same keen
awareness that many people treated their nannies awfully. When they
would go to restaurants and see a nanny standing over a child the
entire time that her employers were sitting and eating and drinking,
they would say to each other, please, let's not ever be like that.

Yet now, when she complained about this nanny, she couldn't help
feel that they were no longer in agreement about this, that perhaps,
ever so slightly, he was seeing in her shades of Indian women who
make a hobby of complaining about the help. 'She's only trying to

help,' he would say. No one said it but she felt the people closest to her were thinking that perhaps she was to blame for the prickly relations she was having with the nanny. 'Get over yourself,' she felt they were thinking.

Most of the time, it's the help who is subject to eagle-eyed scrutiny, and to impatient corrections. But if you have an experienced japa, every one of your fumbles is being witnessed and judged by an expert, whose expertise relieves them sometimes from having to show the usual deference shown by other house help. It isn't an easy art to teach or guide someone without belittling them—certainly employers in India don't demonstrate it very often, whether to their 'juniors' in the office or at home. Rather than becoming at ease with the baby as weeks passed, the mother felt wary and cautious around the nanny, conscious of being evaluated and somehow not passing.

'Nobody will feel sorry for you because at the end of the day you are an elite middle-class person in a South Delhi house and you've got somebody coming and helping you out,' said the woman. 'But the fact is you are part of a very unhappy relationship at that point in time.'

While some infant nannies become full-time nannies, many typically stay only for short stints, leaving once the new mother has gained confidence and skills. In this case, the professor's nanny was required elsewhere and she left. Her departure occurred around the time that her employer began dealing with her depression. With the nanny gone, she found herself doing a lot more for her baby than she had been doing until then, and it was good for her. Her lighter mood found a reflection outside herself—it was January, and the sun was starting to break through the smog that had kept Delhi skies grey for several months.

She took her daughter to nearby parks, changed her diaper, bathed her and gradually became less fearful about everything she might do wrong, stopped enumerating in her head all the different ways her baby might come to harm, and imagining all the different ways she might fall foul of the nanny. She realized that, up until then, she had been almost reluctant to handle her baby too much in the presence of the nanny. 'I was actually afraid that she'd tell me off.'

THE TRIBAL NANNY

IN 2008, NEETU AND SACHIN VERMA had their first child, a boy. Six, at the time of our meeting in their home, he hops about the room, at one point immersing his hands in my glass of water, and at other times flailing his arms about wildly and uttering little screeches when he wants attention. Neetu says that when he didn't pick up basic words like other kids his age, didn't even say 'papa' and 'mummy', she didn't worry too much about it at first. Boys develop later, she told herself. But, over time, his lack of words and obsessive quirks began to trouble her. 'If he liked the smell of a bar of soap then he would just keep sniffing that soap the entire day,' she remembers.

When he was two, she took him to be evaluated. Working at a hospital—she was lucky enough to land a staff job in 2004 as a nurse at AIIMS—and having public health insurance gave her access to the best doctors. Her son had all sorts of tests, including an MRI, which involves lying still in a claustrophobic cylinder, a difficult test for a hyperactive child. After extensive observation, the doctors diagnosed him with autism. For two years she took him for therapy, where nice men and women asked him to do things like separate different kinds of lentils into different piles.

She tried putting him into kindergarten at a nearby private school, hoping that being around other kids would help. Sometimes, after school, she would notice that his clothes were dishevelled and that he was more than usually distressed. Eventually, teachers told Sachin and Neetu that they suspected kids from older grades were bullying him, possibly even hitting him. They withdrew him from the school. 'We couldn't take a chance,' says Neetu. 'He can't even tell us if someone is doing something to him.'

Things just seemed to get harder and harder from then on. Sachin, who had worked for a while in sales for Nestlé, took care of their boy during the day. Neetu left for work at 7 a.m. after cooking lunch, and only got back at 4 p.m. After a cup of tea, she would proceed to cook dinner for the family. In 2010, the couple had another child, a boy. Not long after, Neetu was diagnosed with Hodgkin's lymphoma. She was exhausted from her radiation and chemotherapy, and from trying to return to work in between sessions; Sachin was exhausted from taking care of their hyperactive older son and an infant. But despite how difficult things were, Neetu didn't want to give up her job, as many women do when responsibilities pile up. 'I never considered that,' she tells me. 'What is life if not a struggle?' She was one of four daughters who had grown up in what was essentially a Delhi slum, and her father, who had also worked in a hospital, had worked extraordinarily hard to educate his five children, four girls and a boy. It was her father who, with the help of a hospital contact, got her enrolled in a nurse training course. None of her sisters are housewives like their mother was, says Neetu. So the Vermas thought of another idea.

Every day ads in the paper advertised twenty-four-hour help. Although their Uttam Nagar home was tiny—the live-in maid would have to sleep on the floor somewhere—they decided to hire one of the women being advertised in these flyers, as Om Prakash Verma, Sachin's father, recounted in an earlier chapter. She would clean the house and take care of their younger, more pliable son. That would leave Sachin free to focus on their older son; they didn't trust anyone else after the school experience.

Not long after they called, a man from a company called A. K. Enterprises brought a young woman from Jharkhand to their home in February in 2011. But in a matter of days, the woman told them she had been pressured into coming to Delhi and that she wanted to go home as her marriage had been arranged. The couple was upset. They had already paid more than 30,000 rupees towards recruiting her: 20,000 as the broker's fee and 12,000 rupees as six months' salary in advance. The recruiter the Vermas dealt with didn't want to take the maid back at first, telling them that the young woman would soon settle down with them, but Om Prakash Verma, who lived on the ground floor of the three-storey home, insisted. 'We said give our money back. If you're not getting a girl, then leave it. But he wouldn't give our money back. He sent the other girl,' says Om Prakash, who'd had plenty of experience in dealing with difficult characters from his time in real estate.

In a couple of days, the man from A. K. Enterprises turned up again, this time with Sunita, whom he had sourced through another maid broker. In just a few days, she too started saying over and over she wanted to go home to Jharkhand, and that she didn't like it in Delhi. She hadn't wanted to come to Delhi to work, she later said; she came because her mother forced her to leave her village and get work. The Vermas called the recruiter again. 'These guys push them into coming, or they buy them, I don't know how they bring them here,' said Om Prakash Verma.

This time the broker said he truly had no one else to send them, and to try to make it work with this maid as long as possible while he looked around. Then he stopped answering their calls. When they called, they found the broker's phone was switched off. They had heard from neighbours that this happened with placement agents: as soon as they get the commission, the girl departs. And if the broker gets the sense that he might be asked for a refund, he disappears. In the meantime, Sunita wouldn't stop asking to go home. Once, she alarmed the Vermas by threatening to jump off the roof. She could not have expressed her desire to leave in any stronger terms or made it clearer to the family that they were keeping her against her will, and against the law. I tell the Vermas I don't understand why they would not let her leave. Even if for no other reason, why would you want to leave your children in the care of someone who has no wish to be with them?

Om Prakash Verma says they wanted to send Sunita back home. It's not like they were happy sharing a house with her, either, he insists. Sunita came from a part of the country where Oraon, a tribal language, was common, which the Vermas didn't know a word of. So they spoke to her in Hindi, which for the first time in her life she had to communicate in all day, every day. It didn't make for the smoothest communications. The Vermas complained that she was a terrible caregiver. She diluted the children's milk with water and drank it herself, and she hit the children, they say. But this was a girl who had never before left her village and he said they were all afraid of being blamed for what might befall her if they were to let her depart on her own. Maid brokers often impress upon clients the necessity of 'handing back' the maid to the recruiter so they can arrange for someone to ferry her home. This is why the Vermas kept trying to contact the maid broker and leave her with him. 'We called so many times,' said Mr Verma. On one occasion, Sachin and Neetu took Sunita to the address written on the receipt the maid recruiter had left with them during office hours, hoping to hand the increasingly miserable teenager back to him. But the place was locked.

Om Prakash Verma says the family was afraid of facing accusations from the agent—perhaps even a police complaint—if eventually the broker should turn up to fetch Sunita and find her gone. They could be accused of selling her on or some other kind of crime. 'They would ask us, "Where's our girl?" They would lodge an FIR that our girl has disappeared. If a mishap happened to her, what would we have done?' says Mr Verma. 'I said to her, "Just wait, let us call him, then you can go from here."' He adds, 'If I take a thing from someone, I have to give back that thing, don't I?'

The Vermas weren't wrong to believe the agent would look askance at them if Sunita vanished, and it wouldn't be paranoia to expect a police investigation to commence. A couple in a neighbourhood not far from where the Vermas live also hired a maid from a Jharkhand agent a few years earlier. When the broker turned up later to ferry her back to her village, the employers told him she was already gone but the suspicious and worried man did not believe them. The girl was related to him and he could not possibly go back home to her village and tell her family that he had no idea where she was now. So, he went to the police. His complaint resulted in an anti-trafficking prosecution that eventually put a half dozen people behind bars after police discovered that the couple had sold the young woman as a bride to a man in Haryana for triple the commission they had paid to hire her as a maid.

But in Sunita's case, months dragged by without either the agent or a family member coming to take her home. Relations between the Vermas and the maid deteriorated sharply. A relative of the Vermas alleges that Neetu was hitting Sunita, which the family denies. Soon Sunita took matters into her own hands. Perhaps she became suspicious of the Vermas' promises to track the agent down and send her home with him. Perhaps she came to believe they intended to make her serve out her contract despite her pleas to be allowed to go home. Perhaps she came to believe that even after the contract period elapsed, she would be kept in the Verma home, under their control. After all, they could have taken her to the police, or to a local church with a congregation filled with people from her own state, or to an organization that helps domestic workers to help her get home. At the end of August of the year she was hired, Sunita went out to fetch milk and did not come back.

A day or so later, Neetu and her husband got a phone call from the local police station chief. A cycle-rickshaw driver had found Sunita wandering around and took her to a woman who was in contact with a rights group for domestic workers. A photograph of Sunita in the file kept by this non-profit, run out of the basement of the city's Catholic archdiocese, shows a young woman with a black eye, a scar under her left clavicle, and other bruises.

At the station, the two women from the group proposed that the Vermas pay Sunita 50,000 rupees in compensation for the abuse she says she had suffered as well as the work she had done for them. The Vermas saw this as blackmail. Neither side could reach a compromise and Sunita registered a police complaint. She accused Sachin and Neetu of hitting her with a rolling pin and burning her with an iron, of biting her. When I asked the Vermas about these accusations, and about the black eye in the photograph, Neetu Verma told me the maid had a skin disease. She said she was too weak and ill from her cancer to hit anyone, and that in any case, it was not in her nature. 'Ask anyone at the hospital,' she told me. 'They all know my character.'

The Vermas insist Sunita was made to file a complaint by the rights group in order to get money. Like many people, they believe that non-profits make money off settlements brokered by them. The non-profit in this case runs off grants, in exchange for which the group's social workers spend large swathes of time in the church's basement filling out logs about their activities for the year. But the Vermas, not knowing any of this, appear to believe the worst of the outfit. 'They'd made a parrot out of her,' says Om Prakash Verma. 'What does a village girl know about an iron? If she was saying "press" that would be one thing. But if she's using the word "iron", it's obvious she was tutored.'

Neetu was eventually charged with alleged assault at the nearby Tis Hazari Courts. The woman who helped Sunita file the complaint moved back to Jharkhand. When I call her to see if she can help me find Sunita, she tells me what she told the court: she has moved back to Jharkhand and could they please not call her for future hearings. The Delhi non-profit has also fallen out of touch with her, as well as lost track of the progress of the case they successfully brought. Years later, hearings continue to take place every few months, and are usually adjourned as one or another witness fails to answer summons. It might seem as if life could never go back to normal after being charged with a crime like this. But by the time I meet the Vermas, the case has gone from being a story deemed scandalous enough to be carried on several TV stations, since the alleged maid abuser is herself a professional caregiver employed at the country's largest hospital, to a minor nuisance that requires the Vermas to go to the courthouse every now and again. With no one answering court summons to give evidence, an acquittal looks very likely.

In 2013, Neetu was promoted to senior nurse at the hospital's trauma centre in charge of patient care, a job she says she finds very fulfilling despite the grim state of most of her patients: people who've been run over, people who've fallen on railway tracks, and people who've 'fallen from a great height' (possibly suicides, but they can't admit that to the doctor, because suicide is a criminal offence in India, so their accidents are often categorized as falls). 'It's very hectic,' she says. 'We are just trying to save as many people as we can.'

The Vermas say they don't plan to ever have a live-in maid to care for their children again, and that is now Sachin's domain. In the morning, as usual, Neetu wakes up and cooks lunch before leaving for her 7.30 a.m. shift. Her husband gives the children breakfast and takes the younger son to a playschool for a bit. A part-time maid comes in for a bit and cleans and washes dishes. Later in the day, Sachin goes down to see if his parents need help, or want anything when he goes grocery shopping.

During the day, Sachin takes care of both the boys, as well as checking in on his parents, and doing grocery runs for both households.

He's now self-employed, supplementing the family income by working with a local lender, making small loans to the neighbourhood's vegetable sellers and other informal entrepreneurs with tactics borrowed from India's microcredit industry. In the evenings he makes the rounds of his debtors, collecting 50 rupees here and 100 rupees there on the outstanding amounts. 'Before I know it, the day is gone,' he says.

His father wants to add something. 'He's the one who takes care of them, he's the one who cleans their bottoms, he's the one who feeds them,' says Om Prakash, who probably never did any of these things for his own two sons. 'That's how it is around here.'

THE EXPAT NANNY

SANTA TAMANG WAS ON THE bus heading to an interview with a Japanese couple at a home near Khan Market when her phone rang. Her friends had been urging her to leave the Indian family she worked for and find a position with the higher pay and much shorter working hours they enjoyed. When the nannies gathered at different homes on play dates, the two little girls Santa brought along were the only Indians present—apart from the nannies, of course. In 2008, Santa decided to follow their advice. First, she found a woman to fill in for her while she went home to her village in Darjeeling. Soon, the temporary nanny was calling to tell her she would be very happy to stay on if Santa was able to find a new job, which was kind of what Santa had hoped for. But Santa kept getting calls from her ma'am asking her when she would be back. She began ignoring the calls because she didn't trust herself not to succumb to her ma'am's entreaties. But on the bus heading to her interview with her prospective new employers she absent-mindedly answered a call from her old employer.

'By mistake I received her call on the bus. I didn't know what to do so I cut. Again she called, I didn't know what to do, I was really nervous,' says Santa, a slim woman in her late thirties with long, reddish hair that falls nearly to her waist. 'She said, "Don't worry, Santa. Don't worry, I won't call you back. Wherever you want to live, live, but at least receive my calls." And I said, "Okay, sorry madam."'

Santa did not feel good about ignoring ma'am's calls or disconnecting them, but she didn't know how else to pursue her dream of working for foreigners. If she answered the phone, ma'am would tell her how much she missed her. And then the two little girls she had taken care of for the past two years would get on the phone and plead with her too. Three and two years old, they would say things like, 'Santa didi, why you not coming? We waiting for you, we love you.'

What could she say to them? She could explain to their mother that she would earn so much more working for expats, an amount she didn't expect her employer to match because she could already see how her employer's efforts to improve Santa's conditions by reducing her work hours and giving her regular days off, were sitting poorly with the rest of the help. Santa's employer, who was pregnant with her second child when Santa was hired through a placement agency in Chirag Delhi, was not an expat. In her home, servants got better salaries than they would have in Pitampura, Dwarka, Mayur Vihar or many other parts of the city. But they were very definitely paid on an Indian scale and worked hours typical for an Indian home: 8 a.m. to 3 p.m. or so and then 5 p.m. to 10 p.m. It was quite by accident that Santa realized that there were people all around her, doing exactly what she did—doing less than she did, in fact—but being paid on a different scale, double or triple her wages. These people—some of whom became her friends—lived in India but might as well have emigrated abroad already. She set her sights on becoming one of them.

Ma'am had become friends with many foreigners living in Delhi through children's reading events she organized. Sometimes these mothers or their nannies would come over to their house, and other times Santa and the girls she looked after would go to their friends' homes, circulating in a tiny pocket of the city's most well-heeled areas: Prithviraj Road, Jor Bagh, Amrita Shergill Marg. At first, Santa found going to these other homes deeply embarrassing, especially if, as happened a few times, the gathering was of mothers and their children, not nannies. When the nannies compared notes about their employers, and their salaries, that was even more embarrassing.

When she brought these differences to the attention of her ma'am, ma'am was not affronted. She tried to make some changes. But Santa's shorter working hours and weekly Sundays off didn't go unnoticed by the other servants. Then ma'am agreed that the other servants should take Saturday off, turn by turn. But this did not end the jealousy, the snide remarks and the needling from the other workers. If, on top of this, ma'am were to try to match the salary Santa could earn working for an expat, the household would be in an uproar. Corporations might be able to get away with having employees on totally different scales—a foreigners' pay scale and a local one—in the same branch office, but in a household wages can't be kept secret and such disparity is a recipe for disaster. And while ma'am might be able to justify doubling or tripling Santa's salary to herself and her husband, she likely couldn't or wouldn't do the same for the rest of the help. So ma'am could very well understand why Santa would seek a new situation. But how do you explain all this to toddlers?

Santa had come into the family when ma'am's older daughter was one and when the younger one was still months away from being born. Apart from their mother, no one had spent as much time with the little girls as she did. She even had her own nickname for the younger daughter. 'You are my lucky champ', Santa used to tell the new arrival. Before her second daughter was born ma'am was stressed and irritable. 'Ma'am was little bit rude...shouting with everyone,' she remembers. But after the arrival of Lucky Champ, 'she became so nice, talking to everybody so nicely and everything'.

All these recollections came flooding back when she spoke with her ma'am on the bus ride. She told the Japanese couple she wasn't available after all and returned to Jor Bagh. She was happy to see everyone but also a little disappointed in herself. 'I wanted to do with foreigner people once, for experience. Because all my friends were doing, they're getting lots of salary, bonus...Saturday, Sunday off,' she said, 'I was at that time getting only 4,000 salary.' When she went back, ma'am raised her salary to 5,000 rupees a month.

Even though the wages were smaller and hours were longer than those of her friends, Santa was very fond of the family for whom she worked. She was impressed by how much her ma'am seemed to know about everything and her high standards. She learned how to wash and sterilize baby bottles and then put them carefully away with plastic tongs so that there was not a smudge or fingerprint on the glass or plastic. She learned how to reason with a little girl who wanted to climb onto the lap she saw her newborn sister sitting on and how to console the children when sir and ma'am went to work or to a party. Sometimes she would explain, 'How will we eat if they don't go to office and make money?' Sometimes she would pretend to be despondent herself, so that one or the other little girl would come to hug her and cheer her up.

Most of the time, though, she took care of the children alongside ma'am, accompanying them to the reading room, or to ballet class, or on impromptu adventures. One morning, when they were trying to entertain the two little girls, they ended up driving to Connaught Place in their nightgowns, where they all had breakfast. Sir was nice too but not so closely involved. If ma'am ever asked him to fetch her a glass of water, he would ask, 'Where do we keep the water glasses?' Or if he was ordered to change a diaper by his wife, he would come to Santa and in a wheedling tone, that a child might use to try to get out of a chore, ask her to do it instead.

Santa lavishes the kind of affection on the children she cares for that she never received from her own parents. She says her parents are the reason that for most of her life, she hasn't wanted to get married or have children, although now that she is in her late thirties and has a steady boyfriend who works for the Delhi office of an international non-profit, she might reconsider. Her father, a policeman, married five times, she says, mostly to cheat women out of money. He didn't send her to school and often hit her. Her mother abandoned her when she was a child and remarried too. She was brought up by one of her father's subsequent wives, a woman who had always wanted a daughter, and whom Santa describes as her 'real' mother. When her adopted mother died suddenly in 2000, Santa decided there was nothing to keep her in Darjeeling, where she had been working at a clothing stall in a border town bazaar. An aunty—that is, a woman who had once lived next door to her in Darjeeling—told her there was work in the Faridabad home where she cooked and cleaned. So she moved to the satellite town to the southeast of Delhi. She was twenty-one and it was her first time working in a home.

The family was very rich and Santa says she has never seen such a big house since. Unlike Santa, they were strict vegetarians—eggs and even onions were banned. Her salary was 2,500 rupees a month, an amount she never ended up spending because her employers and their guests routinely gave her tips that equalled her salary. Her job consisted entirely of answering the door and serving beverages to the various tutors who came to the house to perfect the children. 'Some time coming German teacher, some time coming science teacher, some time coming piano teacher,' she says. 'I had to inform kids, "Oh Raman, Ramya, German teacher here."'

An unkindly older woman often figures in Santa's anecdotes about her life, as in the stories of many maids. But in Santa's stories, the unkind woman is generally not madam, but a fellow maid who, with her own lot set in life, tries to destroy Santa's attempts to better herself. At the house in Faridabad, the aunty who had encouraged her to come work there admonished her for trying to read from the children's schoolbooks and told her not to practise speaking English in front of or with her employers. 'Shame, shame,' she told Santa. 'They are very big and educated people.' Nor did she ever let Santa go off and explore Delhi. When Santa found herself free, and would attempt an excursion, aunty would find new things for her to do, like teaching her dusting, though it was not her job. 'No, no, not like that,' she would say, when Santa would flick at furniture furiously and vigorously with a rag, sending dust flying onto the paintings.

But her Jor Bagh ma'am was different, always praising and encouraging her. She asked Santa to speak in English with her children, something many ma'ams discourage because they think it will stop their kids from speaking 'proper' English. She brought home books for Santa to study from—although here, too, an older woman who predated Santa began mocking her for trying to learn to read when she was 'so old'. She was twenty-nine at the time. Despite the snide remarks, she tried to improve her reading because she didn't want to disappoint Lucky Champ when she climbed into her lap and said, 'Santa didi, read me a story'. Ma'am also admired the stylish outfits that Santa wore, bringing with her the flair and the less buttoned-up sensibilities of northeastern India. Once, when a woman from Jharkhand came to work at the home, ma'am begged Santa to take the new maid to Sarojini Nagar and outfit her in her own image, in pants and shirts and skirts, rather than the 'boring' Indian salwar suits the woman was always wearing.

In 2010, Santa decided to try again to make it into the expat circle. The girls were older now and she hoped ma'am would understand that this would be a big step forward for her. She moved in with a friend who rented a room in a Muslim neighbourhood, next to a Sufi shrine, opposite Jor Bagh. The friend's sister, an at-home beautician, went to the homes of well-heeled Indians and expats, and so had built a large network of friends and acquaintances at all points of the

class system. Like Masterji, the tailor who helped bring Chutki and
Neera Varma together, she was well-placed to matchmake, and to
plug a vacancy mentioned to her casually as she buffed and polished
a woman's toenails. After years of Santa wanting it, and fearing it
wouldn't happen, it happened fast—an Australian journalist called her
up and asked her to come for an interview. After they spoke for a
long time, she asked Santa if she could start the next day.

And so Santa moved from Jor Bagh to Prithviraj Road, into a
quarter with 'AC, geyser, heater, *everything*'. She began working for
the Australian couple for 6,000 rupees a month for a half day of
work; in addition to Sunday, she had Saturdays off. The following year
she went to an eight-hour day at 9,000 rupees. When her employer
became pregnant and had her first baby, Santa returned to a six-day
week but saw a pay bump to 20,000 rupees to match her new nanny
responsibilities. If she worked more hours than that, she got overtime
pay. If they travelled outside of Delhi, she might get a stipend of an
extra 500 rupees a day or more.

Finally, she was among India's most elite ranks of domestic
workers. Despite sniffy complaints by some Indians that foreigners
are not all that great as employers of domestic help—they are very
demanding in their own way, or display racism in their selection of
which communities of Indians they will or won't employ as domestic
staff—it is rare to hear such complaints from the men and women
actually hired by expats. They know that there are extremely few Indian
households that will match both their wages and hours—even when in
an equivalent income bracket as the expat families. Santa earns more
than three times as much as a cook I met who had attended a year
of college and worked for a Delhi business family far wealthier than
the Australians that employed Santa.

In fact, her earnings would evoke envy in everyone from MP's
personal assistants to researchers at the city's elite cultural institutions.
At the end of 2014, the *Indian Express* reported that secretaries for
about a third of lawmakers earned less than the minimum wage for
their skill level, with salaries of several people hovering around 7,000
or 8,000 rupees a month rather than the minimum of 10,500 rupees
required for a college graduate who can operate a computer. At the
end of 2015, a performing arts centre named after a former prime

minister was offering someone with a master's degree and three years of archival research experience 30,000 rupees a month while a vacancy at a state-funded library for someone with a library science diploma was paying 10,000 rupees a month.

But then, as Santa says, childcare is not easy. It is a job that requires a knowledge of *everything*, and 100 per cent attentiveness all the time. You cannot tune out or surf Facebook or head out for lunch with your colleagues when you are caring for someone. You have to be ready to sing, act, play the clown at a moment's notice. And then, 'it's very risky', she says. If, God forbid, some accident should happen while the parents are away, the responsibility is yours. You have to keep an eye on the child at all times and explain any little bumps or cuts she may get, as she had to the other day, when another little boy bit the toddler she looks after on the cheek. You have to be reassuring but not cavalier, when you explain to a mother who bursts into tears hours later upon seeing the bite that her little girl has forgotten about that it's common for teething toddlers to do this sometimes. Expat employers may not be as distrustful as Indian ones—most Indian families will not leave their children in the care of their nanny without a grandparent present—but even so, you cannot count on them to always acquiesce to your advice and know-how.

Every mother feels she knows what's best for her child, says Santa, no matter how little experience she has or how much you have. Nor can you always transpose your know-how from one job to another. When she became a nanny for expats, she had to learn an entirely new food regime, where many things given to the Indian children she took care of as affection-expressing treats were verboten or strictly limited—fruit juice, sugary snacks, cookies.

There have been times when she feels she does need to tell a parent that maybe what they're doing isn't right for their child. It bothers her tremendously to see parents lose track of all the snacks their kids graze upon during the day, and then, perturbed by their picky eating at a meal, insist the child at least get a bottle of milk because she must be starving. Then, when the child throws up, more worry and chaos ensue. Sometimes she has to bite her tongue when her employer disagrees with something she's advocating, something she's seen work time and again, and tries to have the last word with this unassailable if somewhat hurtful logic. 'You don't know. You're not a mother.'

'Yes, I'm not a mother. But at least I have done lots of nannying, part-time also, lots of jobs I did, so I have experience,' she says. 'At least I can—in a few areas—I *can* tell you.'

PART VI

Scene of the Crime

THE CRIME BEAT

THERE ARE CERTAIN CATEGORIES OF news stories that are the McDonald's fries of a newspaper. They are, barring the names of the entities involved, pretty much the same everywhere, and generally to be found on the business pages. The stock market goes up and it goes down. The central bank cuts rates and it raises them. Companies buy chunks of one another. Other kinds of news stories, generally about politics and parties, are a bit more like McAloo tikki burgers, firmly related to similar offerings in other countries, but highly locally adapted. But to truly gauge a nation's personality, to imbibe the full, pungent flavour of its state of being (and also its particular dysfunctions and rot), you have to step away from McDonald's altogether and sample the street food of the news business: crime stories. At around the time I began working as a journalist in Delhi, in 2005, there were three kinds of crime stories that began recurring with greater and greater frequency, each of them a little peephole into the inner workings of this city.

There was the mobile gang rape story, one in which a group of men assault a young woman in a car that the men take turns driving around the empty streets of Delhi. Before I moved to the city these stories had appeared often enough on the front pages of newspapers that, in the months leading up to my arrival, I would experience panic attacks, imagining myself driving down a desolate road where I would experience a tyre puncture, allowing rapists to pop out from behind dark buildings and descend on my car. The dream or vision was an inverted version of the newspaper stories. In the newspaper stories, the car or van always belongs to the rapists, not the victim; the victim is invariably a pedestrian, out at a time or place that she shouldn't have been. Even in my dreams, my subconscious tried to reassure me by reminding me that I was protected, privileged. I would not be sauntering on the street late at night. I would be barrelling past, protected by a full metal jacket.

Then there was the story of road rage—or water rage, or electricity rage or just rage rage—a crime story about a minor irritant that results in a death. The crime would be unintelligible to someone who had not lived in Delhi. But for any Delhi resident, the stories about the boy clubbed to death for nudging a motorcycle with his car, the middle-aged woman bludgeoned over whose turn it was to take water from a shared pipeline, the man lynched for jumping a queue, are read only partially as warnings to tread carefully. The people in these stories—the enraged perpetrators and not their victims—also embody the fulfilment of a collective fantasy that we both fear and wish for.

We may have proven Malthus short-sighted and cheated death with our technological advances but that doesn't mean we don't feel the numbers. Delhi was a city of a million, then ten million, now twenty million. In the lifetimes of all of you reading this it will reach thirty million, maybe even forty. But as the contestants multiply, the spoils remain the same or increase only very slowly. So, most parts of a Delhi residents' day, even the privileged ones, involve a fight for something, from water to road space to parking to spots in a nursery school. Being privileged doesn't make you immune to this scarcity but you *can* hire someone to enter the fray wearing your colours: a driver, a guard, more guards, a personal security officer. In calmer moments, ensconced in the relative order of our homes, we joke about how these daily conflicts leave us on edge, wishing we had tanks to ram into the SUV that overtook us dangerously from the wrong side, or how the only solution for such scoundrels is one tight slap. We can joke because, in the moment, we were able to master our anger. But between the pages of the newspaper, without the fear of repercussions, we savour how delicious it must feel to succumb completely to the rage every Delhi resident carries around like a tumour, right there, in the middle of one's chest.

The third kind of crime story began to appear in a trickle at first, and then in increasing numbers from 2010 onwards, stories with headlines like 'Delhi Firemen Rescue Jharkhand Maid Locked in by Holidaying Doctor Couple' and 'Maid Rescued from Delhi Businessman's Closet'. Sometimes journalists reported that a maid had escaped by turning her sari into a rope that she climbed down to appear dramatically on the balcony of a neighbour living on the floor below. Sometimes, while going to fetch milk she would disappear, and later make her way to a church or police station. Sometimes a neighbour's maid would make a discreet call to an anti-trafficking rescue organization, a kind of non-profit whose numbers are growing. Sometimes it was an employer who broke ranks and called the crime in to the authorities.

All of these crime stories follow their own rhythm, peaking at different times of the year. If incidents of rage soar in the summer months as temperatures whizz past 40 degrees, then the rescues and runaways appear to intensify with the off-white smog that marks the city's winter months thanks to a surge in cars and motorbikes, the torching of crops in villages, and the burning of waste in cities by security guards and taxi drivers trying to keep warm through the night. They are tied subtly to the passing of Dussehra and Eid and the approach of Diwali.

The whole year is a battle against dust and Diwali marks the apex of this battle. Housekeeping websites offer advice on how far ahead to start cleaning the house, although like the IKEA furniture catalogue published for Saudi Arabia that Photoshopped women out, the world they evoke isn't quite true to life, since they offer advice as if madam were actually going to do the cleaning herself. The rest of the year, it is merely a husband, a parent or parents-in-law who might find fault with a woman's housekeeping or cooking. But at Diwali, the goddess Lakshmi and the god Ganesh are invited in to bless the house, and it is well-known that the goddess of wealth, and her son, the elephant-headed deity who oversees new endeavours and successful beginnings, don't like visiting a house that is dirty or dark. Perhaps dust gets up the trunk of Ganesh and causes a fit of the sneezes, compounding allergies that are anyway worsened at this time of year because of the gunpowder from fireworks and air pollution. And Lakshmi has twenty fingers at the end of her four arms, all the better to wipe along a wooden surface and come away with a little layer of grime that speaks loudly of slovenly dusting.

And so it is often in the orgy of cleaning that leads up to Diwali that the tensions running through a household can come to a head,

piercing through the shroud of secrecy that usually hangs over the
relations between a maid and her employer and laying bare the inner
workings of a household to the scrutiny and judgement of the outside
world, through the blaring and not wholly accurate accounts of cable
news, through words written down in police boilerplate and through
those dictated by a jocular magistrate to a court stenographer. Other
countries also experience these ebbs and flows. For example, in Saudi
Arabia, Dubai and other parts of the Middle East, domestic worker
groups note a surge of runaways—despite the risk of deportation—
around Ramadan, when hours are erratic and tempers short due to
fasting.

At first, it seemed to me that through these stories of rescues,
journalists were forcing the capital's middle and upper classes to
confront the rather large gap between the values they claim to hold
and the values demonstrated by their actions. It was certainly a gap
I often had to confront in my own behaviour. I thought I believed in
the fundamental equality of people, regardless of their occupation or
status, but when it came down to it, I had often treated the first maid
I hired in Delhi as if she were entitled to less from her work than I
from mine. In a society fraught with inequality, it is impossible for
there not to be a vast chasm between what one believes—or rather,
what one would like to believe one believes—and what one's actions
show one believes.

But over time I've come to think that, rather than forcing us to
look at our collective blind spots, the rescue story reinforces the very
ill it purports to be against, in the same way that a great deal of
Indian reporting on rape speaks volumes of a readership that revels
in salacious details rather than one that is soberly grappling with a
horrible crime. Some of the sexual violence reporting in Indian papers
(and in other countries too) almost salivates over the huge number of
attackers or the variety of wounds wrought on the bodies of women.
The maid rescue narratives too are a catalogue, carefully detailing all
the many ways, and all the many types of houseware—iron, rolling pin,
broom—used upon the unfortunate domestic help by her employers.

By focusing on the violence of some employers, and especially
the women among them, these narratives make our own predations,
particularly those of the men among us, seem positively tame. So what

if we pay much less than we could afford to, don't give regular days off, or our voices rise to a peculiarly sharp pitch while calling out to our maids? So what if an invisible Lakshman rekha makes it amply clear to the maid that she is never to pollute any of our furniture by sitting on it? At least, we've never taken an iron or a pair of decorative deer antlers to her. At least, we've never locked her in the closet, we think a little smugly. The maid rescue stories rather than persuading us that something is very wrong with all of us, set a bar that we comfortably can hurdle.

HABEAS CORPUS

WHAT HAPPENED TO MAKE THE rescuing of maids being kept against their will a more common narrative in newspapers? The uptick in rescues, and their increased coverage in the media, can be traced back, in great part, to a court decision issued on Christmas Eve in 2010. And that particular court decision, in turn, can be traced back to events that happened a decade earlier, events that, perhaps fittingly, centred around one of the city's original maid brokers: Sunita Sen.

It is now almost a quarter-century ago that a Bengali woman called Kalpana Pandit moved to New Delhi and soon found work as a live-in nanny through Mrs Sen's network. When, a few years later, Mrs Pandit fell ill and couldn't work, it was Mrs Sen she turned to for help. With little money for medicines and a six-year-old boy to take care of, she asked Mrs Sen to temporarily employ her daughter, Jharna Pandit, then aged thirteen or fourteen. After a month, she recovered and went to Mrs Sen's home to take Jharna home. But her daughter was no longer there.

Instead, Jharna was working at the home of a Kashmiri Hindu couple in Noida, friends of the Sens, where she was a companion to their child, who was a little bit younger than Jharna's own brother. 'Just play around with him and all,' is how Mrs Sen described the job in an interview. Jharna's employer was the India distributor of high-end Japanese car audio systems that ranged in price up to 20,000 rupees. Jharna was hired at wages of 1,000 rupees a month, the 'market rate' at the time. Mrs Pandit said later she was only able to get the employers' number after asking Mrs Sen several times. When she called up the house where Jharna was working, though, the employers wouldn't allow her to talk to her daughter. Mrs Pandit went in person to the address in Noida that Mrs Sen had given her, but was unable to meet her daughter. A couple of times she hung around outside the Noida house hoping for a glimpse of her daughter, but she didn't manage to see her.

She gave up going to Noida. By the time she went there and back by bus, it was half a day, and back then—and even today—most employers don't like their maids to take regular days off. Instead, she would check in with Mrs Sen from time to time for news of her daughter. Almost two years had gone by since Jharna began working in Noida when Mrs Sen gave her some very upsetting information. Jharna had vanished. A security guard had seen Jharna leaving in an autorickshaw 'at the vague hour', as Mrs Sen put it, of around 5 a.m. He asked Jharna where she was going and she told him, 'Home'. Around the same time, a driver who had been working briefly for the Noida family disappeared. This happened in August of 2000. Mrs Pandit heard about the disappearance from the maid broker the following February.

It wasn't the first time that a girl left with Mrs Sen for work had vanished. In September 2000, less than a month after Jharna had gone missing, a woman filed a police complaint of kidnapping. This woman said Mrs Sen had placed her niece with a family in South Delhi. When she called the employer's home to speak with her niece, the employer told her it hadn't worked out and she had dropped the girl back at Mrs Sen's. The aunt went there but the girl was not at Mrs Sen's. Finally, after several calls and visits, Mrs Sen told the aunt that the teenager had taken her luggage and departed soon after returning from the employer. 'Why was I not intimated?' asked the aunty from Orissa in her police report, complaining that 'Sunita Sen does not talk properly on this matter.'

Like the woman from Orissa, Mrs Pandit also felt that Mrs Sen had been less than sympathetic to her worries over her missing daughter, and might be in some way to blame. In February 2001, Mrs Pandit too registered a case of kidnapping with her local police station.

Mrs Sen, though, says things didn't happen the way Mrs Pandit says, and that she told the police as much. She says Jharna's mother consented to her daughter being sent to work in Noida; she also says Mrs Pandit often spoke to her daughter over the phone on different occasions and met her as well. Jharna's employer, Veer Kaul, didn't respond to an email request for an interview.

'She worked very nicely over there, she was very happy,' said

Mrs Sen, who maintains that neither she nor the Kashmiri couple were in any way responsible for Jharna's disappearance. The police and the courts agreed with her: no criminal proceedings were ever instituted against Mrs Sen in connection with the missing girl or the employers. In May the following year, 2002, the police told Kalpana that her daughter's case was closed. They probably thought the girl had run away with a boyfriend. No doubt she would come back home when she was ready.

When the children of poor parents go missing, the police rarely take an interest. Also in Noida, Bengali migrants in the neighbourhood of Nithari reported to police for years that children were vanishing, but the police didn't investigate. It was only after sacks of cut-up body parts were discovered in a ditch that parents found out what was happening to their children. By the time the police closed Jharna's case, it was nearly two years since the teenager had vanished. Many impoverished parents, used to inattention from the authorities, would have given up. But Mrs Pandit wouldn't let it lie. Somehow, she made her way to a non-profit in Green Park, that in turn put her in touch with a tall, serious lawyer in her early thirties with a jet-black, bushy mane of hair, who often represented rape victims, acid attack survivors and missing children. In years to come, her work would lead to rape crisis centres being set up across Delhi and to acid attacks being prosecuted more seriously. It was a long shot, but the young lawyer, Aparna Bhat, decided to file a habeas corpus petition asking city authorities and the maid broker, Mrs Sen, to produce Jharna. In the summer of 2002, a police officer rang the doorbell of the Chhattarpur flat from where Mrs Sen ran her domestic help empire and delivered a summons calling Mrs Sen to appear before the Delhi High Court.

At the same time, the court ordered the Delhi Police anti-trafficking unit to search for Jharna, and to report back to the bench monthly on its efforts. The unit sent officers to Noida to interview members of the household. The missing driver, Manoj, the most promising lead, was a dead end. The Kauls said he had been a company driver, paid for by Mr Kaul's Hong Kong-based employer. They couldn't provide any details about him or where he was from because, they said, all company records had been consigned to storage at the head office in Hong Kong.

The police faced another hurdle: the photograph Mrs Pandit had provided of her daughter was old and faded. The police asked the Kaul family, which had by then moved to England, if they had a photograph. The Kauls said they would check their family albums. When the police asked again, they said they hadn't found any photos; they would ask family members in Sudan to check in their photo albums. The police, using their photo-editing skills, tried to update an old photo of Jharna's and circulate it. When they showed the result to the head of the state-run channel, and asked him to broadcast the photo, he demurred. Nevertheless, the police sent it out to stations across the country. It's not surprising the photograph didn't produce any leads: a copy of it shows a face that looks more Muppet than human.

So the police looked for Jharna as you would a needle in a haystack, visiting all the places a young and vulnerable girl in Delhi might end up, and finding many such girls. They showed Mrs Sen pictures of Nepali girls they had rescued from Delhi's red light areas—Mrs Pandit often couldn't be reached—but none of them were Jharna. They looked at records of unidentified bodies consigned to a city crematorium, but no unidentified girls matching Jharna's description had been cremated. They examined unclaimed corpses of women that turned up at times in different parts of Delhi. Dutifully, they filed monthly reports with the court as instructed. Month after month, the reports ended, 'no clue came to light'.

Their search rippled out in wider and wider circles, becoming almost anthropological in its nature. They checked red-light districts in Mumbai. They spent a great deal of time among the Bedia, whose hereditary caste occupation, they told the court, was buying and selling girls. They searched ashrams around the holy city of Haridwar, because religion is sometimes a refuge for young women seeking to leave their past lives and family expectations behind. Perhaps a holy man had taken a new disciple. They continued to file monthly reports with the court, signing off, as always, 'no clue came to light'.

The police complained that Mrs Pandit was sometimes inconsistent in the aid she provided to the investigation of her missing daughter. Her address changed more than once and the addresses she provided, as with most of the addresses that the police are provided by any city dweller, gave them headaches. 'Check with the fishmonger' went one

forwarding address. But this is not surprising. Her life was one full of
uncertainty, ups and downs, mostly the latter. She had come to Delhi
from West Bengal with two small children—her son was just a baby at
the time—and split from her husband soon after. A few years later, she
became involved with a Nepali man she met in Delhi—a man Jharna
was afraid of, the teenage girl's employers told police at one point.

Mrs Pandit worked in fits and starts, falling ill for long spells,
losing jobs. By the time the court began supervising the search for
her daughter, her son no longer lived with her. He was living in the
home of a retired colonel in the wealthy South Delhi neighbourhood
of Vasant Vihar in circumstances that were unclear, but most likely
as a servant. One police status report said the boy was working as
a domestic help, another said his mother had left him to be looked
after by the former army officer.

Mrs Pandit's lawyers tried to explain to the court their client's
situation, why she could not be found where she said she would be,
why she could not be reached where she actually was. She didn't even
always manage to keep appointments with Bhat, the lawyer who had
first brought the petition, and who was doing her best to help recover
Jharna. 'The petitioner being a domestic help is not in a position to
be contacted by the police at her employer's residence for obvious
reasons,' Mrs Pandit's lawyers told the court at one point. 'If the
police visit her at her workplace she might lose her job.'

Slowly, the court's curiosity began to extend beyond Jharna's
possible whereabouts to a different question: how many Jharnas were
there? Mrs Pandit had already brought them one example, the woman
from Orissa whose niece had gone missing. Were there more, they
asked? Yes, the answer came back, oh yes.

Butterflies, the organization that had put Mrs Pandit in touch with
the lawyer, pored through its own files and submitted a collection of
grim reading for the judges. That list briefly details the cases of thirty
children rescued from domestic work in Delhi in the early years of
the new millennium. The two youngest children were seven years old.

The detailed case studies of some of the children made for
even more sobering reading for the judges. In one case, a young girl
was rescued from the home of a police constable, residing in police
quarters. All her neighbours were police too. One tiny silver lining:

it was probably one of them who called Butterflies with the tip-off. Another child was rescued from an army officer's home. Yet another, a boy with a limp, was being beaten nearly every day at the home in which he worked, in one of the bungalows in the heart of Lutyens' Delhi that houses elected Indian lawmakers. It was not a neighbour who called it in, but one of the residents of the servants' quarters who had held his (or her) peace until he feared for the child's life.

The court asked Ms Bhat to submit suggestions for halting the epidemic of missing children. At a meeting in April 2004, members of some of the most prominent domestic workers' and children's rights groups in the city began coming up with ideas. Just sending rescued kids back home wasn't a good idea, many of them warned, as they would just be sent back as servants or sent to work in places from which it might be even more difficult to extract them. As Ms Bhat and her team pored over statutes from all over India—a Karnataka direction banning child labour under the age of fourteen and laws covering interstate migrant workers, among them—looking for guidance to provide the court on how to help these children, two petitions similar to Jharna's came before the court.

In May 2007, some 150 families who had banded together after finding they all faced the same dilemma approached a West Bengal non-profit to seek help finding wives and sisters, and sons and daughters taken by placement agents to work. Some reported that the recruiters threatened them with harm when they persisted in asking for information about their family members. Well-intentioned agents with close ties in the village, who were unhappy at what they had observed in the offices of the city recruiters they had worked for, also came forward. They said they had heard of cases of workers made to continue working for a family even when they wanted to quit. Agents said they were told that unless they brought yet more people from the village, the ones currently in the city would not be allowed to leave.

Separately, in January 2009, a man called Hembahadur approached the child rights' organization Bachpan Bachao Andolan, because his teenaged sister and sister-in-law, placed in homes with the help of a Nepali man, had gone missing. Bachpan Bachao Andolan, whose founder Kailash Satyarthi won a Nobel Peace Prize in 2014 for his work on behalf of children, also filed a habeas corpus petition. This case led to raids on rooms rented by placement agencies in which twenty-six children under the age of fourteen were rescued. Like Ms Pandit, Hembahadur wasn't always the most cooperative client. One day he went out for a haircut and didn't return. But like Ms Bhat, Bachpan Bachao Andolan continued with the case.

All three cases eventually became part of the same hearings since they asked the same questions: Why are so many children going missing? What should be done with a child who is found? And who will rein in the placement agents? More than eight years after Kalpana Pandit first went to court, a two-judge bench provided some answers.

'Thousands of Indians are trafficked every day to some destination or the other and are forced to lead lives of slavery', said the bench in its 24 December 2010 ruling, describing the troubled landscape that had come to its attention. 'They are forced to survive in brothels, factories, guesthouses, dance bars, farms and even in the homes of well-off Indians, with no control over their bodies and lives.'

The court adopted many of the suggestions made by Ms Bhat and the rights groups. The bench told the city to draft rules that would improve working conditions and make it possible to keep tabs on who exactly the agents were bringing to the city and where they were ending up. Children suspected of being missing from their families, or under the legal age for work ought to go before child welfare committees, set up under a recently reformed juvenile protection act. And, when a determination had been made that a child had been made to work as a servant, the boy or girl should be awarded back wages pegged to the minimum monthly wage before being reunited with their families.

In September 2014, the government of Delhi finally issued rules for the city's maid brokers after many delays and a great deal of nudging by rights groups and the court. The rules were surprisingly robust. Agencies were to only recruit and place people eighteen and older and workers had to be issued a sort of passport, which, along with a photograph, would have the name and address of their employer, as well as details of salary, contract length and pay schedule, which could not be less often than once a month. It ordered all agencies to provide the labour department information on the names and ages of women they had placed, to be vetted by child and women's welfare agencies. And, almost as an aside, it said that wages agreed upon needed to be above minimum wage.

If maids placed by brokers are required to be paid minimum wage, then it can't be long until free-agent maids, who deal directly with employers, insist on that too (higher-skilled domestic workers already get above the minimum wage, but it's not the norm). What would it mean, in Delhi, for a maid to earn the minimum wage?

In 2016, the minimum wage stipulated by the capital's government for the lowest-paid level of worker was around 9,050 rupees a month, premised on a nine-hour day and a day off each week, counting a small deduction for food and lodging. However, most live-in domestic workers work at least twelve hours a day, and many get no more than two days a month off, or none. That comes to about ten additional days, meaning people in Delhi should probably be paying live-in help working typical hours about 13,000 rupees a month. And more, in fact, if employers were to hew to the terms of Indian labour law that deems any worker who operates a machine for any part of the day—surely microwaves and washing machines qualify—a semi-skilled or skilled worker. In 2017, Delhi raised the minimum wage dramatically for an unskilled worker to above 13,000 rupees.

The placement agency order was meant to be a temporary measure that would be replaced by law. It just so happened, at the time the regulation finally went into effect, the Indian capital was rudderless. The upstart political party, the Aam Aadmi Party (AAP), who came in second in the Delhi elections in December 2013 and ended up forming a minority government, quit in less than two months. A political appointee administered the city for all of 2014, the year the labour department order on placement agencies was issued. Fresh elections took place in 2015, and this time, AAP won by a landslide. But the party that selected a broom as its election symbol, and that campaigned by sweeping the streets where the city's sanitation workers live, has yet to turn the executive order into a full-fledged law, or properly enforce it.

Still, while many parts of the regulation remain to be implemented, there has already been a great difference. Since 2011, child welfare committees in Delhi have been awarding back pay at minimum wage to children under eighteen found doing domestic work, with dozens of hearings every year and individual awards sometimes totalling two or three lakh rupees, a fortune for many families. The children who receive these monies will never know it, but the fact that India's capital has an enlarged sense of its duties towards them is because for almost a decade Kalpana Pandit kept trying to find her child. Her child, though, has never been found. No clue has come to light.

PUNJABI BAGH

GODDESSES OF MANY ARMS ARE rarely depicted holding the weaponry that normal, two-armed Indian women clutch when engaged in class warfare (or the daily battle against dust). The rolling pins, irons, brooms and mops that feature so often in news reports of crimes by madams are nowhere to be found in Hindu iconography. Durga, who is one of the most popular embodiments of Shakti—female cosmic energy—is usually shown holding a sword, a trident, arrows and a sharp-toothed spinning discus. No housework for this one. She is also invariably portrayed as a fair-skinned beauty, complete with a full, high bosom, sharp nose, long almond-shaped eyes and rosy cheeks. Shakti Vahini, one of the city's best-known rescue groups, and increasingly active in the wake of rulings like the one in 2010 to prevent the trafficking of children to the city for domestic work, is named after this cosmic female force. Despite the celestial vision from which it derives its name, the Shakti Brigade has an unlikely set of founders: three burly, moustachioed brothers.

They journeyed in the opposite direction of Sunita Sen and her bureaucrat father, who left Bengal for northern India. The Kant children, three brothers and a sister originally from Uttar Pradesh, grew up in West Bengal, where their father was posted as a bureaucrat in the human resources department of a state-run coal mining company. Ravi Kant, the oldest of the three brothers, and now the president of the anti-trafficking organization, was born just a year after the 1967 peasant uprising in Naxalbari. By the time he was ten years old, Naxalites, who said they were fighting on behalf of landless peasants and sharecroppers, numbered in the thousands. This was a time of infectious idealism and utopian socialist visions, from the Naxals, but also from politicians who called for politics without parties, and urged those with wealth to consider these monies as something they were holding in trust for all Indians, not just for their own children.

Even so, the Kant parents were surprised when their oldest son announced he was abandoning his studies for the civil services, a sure-fire path to affluence, to script street plays that explain how AIDS is contracted. They were, one suspects, frankly aghast when their two younger sons, Rishi and Nishi, joined him. And yet, somewhere, their parents must have approved. When their father retired in 1998, he gave his three sons his life savings: 45 lakh rupees. 'We did not purchase a house, we did not purchase anything,' says Ravi. Instead, they poured the money into their work, and into the organization they had started in 2001 to deliver HIV treatment to women working in brothels in Delhi's red-light zone.

In 2004, they won a grant from India's AIDS control organization, and other grants followed from other government agencies, as well as overseas aid agencies. But slowly, starting the same year, their focus shifted from providing medicines to extracting young women from brothels and sending them back to their families, when possible. The move was controversial, because the brothers began working closely with police, even accompanying them on raids, eroding the trust health workers had worked hard to win from brothel owners. But they didn't only raid brothels. By this time, the effects of India's skewed sex ratios were beginning to be felt, and one of their first rescues was of a girl in Haryana who had been sold into marriage. The following year, in 2005, they traced a girl from Assam who had gone missing and sent her back home.

Over time, working out of an office in the city's Kingsway Camp area, close to where British rulers of India held periodic durbars, Shakti Vahini's anti-trafficking efforts have grown to include a third arena: the homes of middle and upper-class Indians. A trafficking victim, they argue, is just as likely to be found on her hands and knees, scrubbing a floor, as on her back. Now, in any given year, they set forth from their office in the Kingsway Camp area in the north of Delhi to conduct several hundred rescues, many of maids, as do a growing number of rights groups, including Bachpan Bachao Andolan. But Shakti Vahini, a partner of the Delhi Police's anti-trafficking unit, appears to do more than most, at least if you measure their activity in inches of newsprint.

A rescue, when it plays out on cable channels, seems dramatic.

But one of the most necessary requirements for a successful rescue is patience and a penchant for paperwork. A rescue requires spending hours at a police station, shoving barefoot parents who have come from Jharkhand or another remote state in front of police officers of varying degrees of dedication and integrity. The parents, often looking very bewildered, tell the police a tale they have no doubt heard many times by now. Their daughter left home one year, perhaps around age fifteen, promising to come back the following Christmas. Or sometimes she leaves without telling them. She calls occasionally. One Christmas comes and goes, then two. Then the phone calls cease. Without the intervention of non-profits, without friends in newspapers and at cable news channels, the police might tell the parents to wait a little longer for her to turn up. Privately, they may believe the girl is older than her parents claim and that she is living with a boyfriend in Delhi, which means revealing her whereabouts could put a young couple in danger. Parents who report missing daughters to the police may have these young women's best interests at heart; they also may not.

Once the police have been persuaded to offer their help, the Kant brothers will pack into jeeps and cars with anti-trafficking officers from faraway states and swoop down on particular houses or establishments, sometimes in the dead of the night. Often, when I speak with their spokesman, Rishi, he tells me he is exhausted after an all-night police search-and-rescue for trafficked girls. This makes me imagine the brothers are bachelors, because how would it be possible to balance marriage and children with jobs like this?

The men manage by living together, it transpires, as they did when they were children, in a joint family in a single Faridabad home with their wives, commuting to Delhi every day from Haryana. Two of the brothers—Ravi and Nishi—have children. Two of their wives work in professions with either fixed hours or ones that allow you to make your own hours—as a teacher and an insurance agent. The third is a lawyer. Together, the wives manage to hold down the fort with the help of two additional people who include Chacha, a man from West Bengal, who has worked for them for perhaps two decades. About ten years ago, the Kants hired a part-time worker so that Chacha could confine himself to managing the kitchen. Chacha has a big house in West Bengal, one of the Kants tells me, and comes and goes as he pleases. The brothers say they are not against people having domestic help—they are against the vanishing of women and children from remote villages to be servants against their will.

So when Chutki comes home to Sunder Nagar from her village in the summer of 2012 and asks her ma'am for help finding her niece, Neera Varma turns to Shakti Vahini, a name she recognizes on the list provided to her by directory assistance. The Kants promise at once to help look for Mae. With the help of anti-trafficking police, Shakti Vahini traces the phone numbers that Neera provided to a large two-floor home in West Delhi's bastion of new money, Punjabi Bagh. The home is in the 'Punjabi baroque' style that became popular in the 1980s: it has large arches supported by Roman pillars and other touches inspired by Italy. This is where the maid broker who brought Mae from Assam helped place her as a live-in maid in 2009, for a salary of 1,400 rupees a month. It is early October, perhaps a month after she first called Shakti Vahini, when Neera speaks with one of the Kant brothers again. 'We have found that girl,' he tells her.

Mae's employers, like many in this neighbourhood of Partition refugees, are a business family. Out of offices in Old Delhi, these families sold sanitary fittings, kitchen taps, wedding cards, cardboard sweet boxes, and undergarments—the unglamorous but necessary goods through which many of them restored lost fortunes and rebuilt their lives. In recent years, a few have moved away from the businesses started by their fathers and grandfathers and branched into more contemporary ventures: cable news, medical research, software development, gyms. Mae's employer was among the latter group, setting up a biotech business in 2002 that provided biological materials derived from mice and cows for clinical testing to the country's growing pharmaceutical industry, including many labs affiliated with the government. The business's website advertises the high quality of its cultures—'6,000 strains of mice model of gold standard of genetic purity'—as an image of a mouse and a wedge of cheese appears and disappears.

After discovering where Mae was, a Shakti Vahini worker, a young woman who had just graduated with a social work degree a few months earlier, submitted a letter to the Punjabi Bagh police chief asking for help in what would be her first rescue effort. 'Her family is worried about her,' wrote the social worker, adding that Mae's employers 'did not allow her to go home even when her father passed away'. The police chief assigned an officer to go to the house with the group of young people. When they got to the house, Mae herself opened the door. Only her employer's elderly mother and another maid, about the same age, were at home. With her employer's mother in earshot, Mae told the unexpected visitors that she was doing fine, and that she expected to go home in March. She also told them she was sixteen, according to the report Shakti Vahini turned in to the child welfare committee and a police statement taken that day. After hearing this, the police officer who was with them told the group that the employer wasn't breaking the law. They started arguing.

In India, it is not a crime under child labour laws to have a sixteen-year-old servant. But a law passed in 2000, tasked mainly with protecting minors who commit offences, offers some key protections to young workers. Under that law, someone who is a minor, and who is suspected of being a victim of sex abuse, violence or work exploitation, should be brought before child welfare officials for a determination. Rules to enable the law to be fully implemented were only finalized by the central government around 2007, which may be why some police officers were still unfamiliar with it at that time. It wasn't until a senior employee at Shakti Vahini spoke to a high-ranking police official that the group was able to escort Pano's daughter from the premises to the police station and then to the child welfare committee, which sent her to a state-run shelter. It was here, in a large compound with vast green lawns where peacocks strut and fan their tails, that Mae met her mother for the first time in three years.

Unable to speak Hindi, and with an ill husband and four other children to take care of, it had been unthinkable for Pano to spend the few thousand rupees a trip to Delhi would have required. But now that Mae had been found, Neera and Chutki sent Pano money to come to Delhi. That money vanished quickly on food for herself and the children. Pano pawned three-fourths of an acre of land to pay for the trip, including the expenses of a former schoolteacher who could speak Hindi and would accompany her. They stayed in Sunder Nagar with Chutki.

At the shelter, Pano said to Mae, 'Daughter, you were working in a home. How did you come to be in this place?'

'That man where I worked used me,' Mae told her mother.

Once out of the house, Mae made a startling revelation. She alleged, first to Shakti Vahini workers and then before child welfare agency officials, that in her third year of work, the head of the family, Rajan Sahni, began to rape her when other family members were out. It had happened perhaps five times so far, she told them, according to official documents associated with the case. Sometimes, in the days after an assault, he made her consume a tablet of some kind, she said. She had told the other maid, with whom she shared a room, what had happened, she said. But she didn't tell anyone else because she was afraid of being disbelieved. More than that, she was afraid of being banished from the Sahni house to another unknown home. Police opened an investigation but when they went to arrest Mr Sahni he couldn't be found.

At the meeting with her mother, Mae cried a lot and said she wanted to go back to Assam with her. But the shelter officials said that wasn't possible now. The legal process must take its course. A day or two later, Pano went back to Assam. But the visit with her mother, and the news of the pawning of the land, had reminded Mae of her responsibilities. When Mae appeared again before the child welfare committee, she told them she was worried about what would happen to her family now that she was not working. The money she had sent over the previous three years had meant so much to them, even though most of it had gone to a lost cause: trying to cure her father, who was now dead.

The head of the committee was moved by her worry for her family. During a hearing two weeks later, the committee ruled that the Sahni family must pay Mae about 1,94,000 rupees in back wages and compensation. They arrived at the calculation like this: she should have been earning minimum wage the entire time she was working, which would amount to well over 2 lakh rupees for the three years she had worked; the committee also tacked on 50,000 rupees for 'loss of childhood'. The salary the Sahnis were paying, including raises, came to 1 lakh for three years of work, but she hadn't received even that amount, she said. Mae told the committee she had sent 46,000 rupees to her family through the broker since she arrived (Pano reports

receiving about half of that). The committee subtracted the amount
Mae said she had already sent from the total it had arrived at, and
ordered the Sahni family to pay the rest.

The family resisted the order. Meenakshi Lekhi, a prominent lawyer
and spokesperson for India's ruling Bharatiya Janata Party (BJP), which
was at the time in the Opposition, represented the Sahni family at the
back-pay hearing. Mr Sahni's wife decided to appeal the ruling in court.
No court had found the family guilty of wrongdoing of any kind at
the time of the committee's wage ruling, she argued. In fact, a trial
had not even begun yet. And though the child welfare committee had
set Mae's age at eighteen the month she was rescued, as the juvenile
protection law allows them to do in cases of uncertainty, Mae's status
as a minor during her employment was in question.

A different lawyer for the Sahnis turned up a school certificate
for Mae that showed her to be born in June 1992, some four years
before the violence that forced her family to flee their village. That
would have made Mae over the age of eighteen for almost all of the
time she worked for the Sahnis, strengthening their appeal against
the child committee's orders. The child committee has no say over
wages for adult domestic workers, who are only covered by minimum
wage laws in half a dozen or so Indian states. In early November, the
police officer leading the investigation of Mr Sahni went to Assam to
investigate the authenticity of the school certificate. The detective went
to the school in Mae's uncle's village that had issued the certificate.
On his return, he reported that the certificate was genuine, verified
by a schoolmaster.

In the meantime, police continued to look for Mae's employer.
The Child Welfare Committee, which had asked several times for him
to be present at their hearings on Mae, was told by a family member
that he was travelling. On 9 November, more than a month after the
police took down Mae's allegation of rape against him, Rajan Sahni
appeared before the Delhi High Court asking for 'anticipatory' bail,
so that if he were arrested he would not be taken into custody. Ms
Lekhi represented him at that hearing, arguing that Mr Sahni was
innocent, and that he was being framed and extorted by his maid and
the non-profit that had helped her. The court declined the request.
On 21 November 2012, a week after Diwali, Mr Sahni was arrested.

Meanwhile, Mae was still in the care of the state, waiting for her former employer's trial to begin, when the city erupted. Just weeks after Mr Sahni's arrest, the city was horrified by the news that a young woman had been raped by five men and a teenage boy on a bus as it drove in a loop near the airport and the capital's diplomatic residences. Her frenzied attackers had caused such severe internal injuries that the doctors who treated her were shaken, saying they had never seen anything like it in years of practice. She died days later. After years of shuddering and then turning the page on news stories about rapes of young women by gangs of men in cars, something snapped. On 22 December, young women and men protested the assault and confronted the policemen who manned barricades to stop them from getting too close to Parliament. Not far away, on the same day, in a room in West Delhi's Tis Hazari courts, officers recommended to a metropolitan magistrate that Mr Sahni be tried on charges of rape.

Things moved quickly after that, at least by Indian legal standards. In the wake of the anger over what came to be known in the media as the Nirbhaya case, the city heeded the advice of prosecutors and women's rights activists who had warned for years that lengthy trials wear out a victim and give a defendant time to put pressure on her and her family, and set up special 'fast-track' courts for rape cases. Mr Sahni's trial was transferred to a fast-track judge on 9 January. Then a surprising thing happened. The very next day, Mae dictated a letter to a counsellor at the women's shelter to be sent to the fast-track judge, a copy of which was obtained by Shakti Vahini from the shelter using transparency laws. 'I lied about being raped,' she said in the letter. 'Rajan Sahni treated me like a daughter,' she wrote, 'I would like to go back and work in his home.' She also said that she had remembered her birth date, which earlier she had told welfare officials she didn't know. She wrote that she was born in June 1992, on the date in the school certificate produced by the defence lawyer. Please give me my compensation, she added.

Despite Mae's letter, a public prosecutor argued that the trial on the charge of rape should proceed, and the fast-track judge agreed. At the end of January 2013, the state began calling its witnesses, and Mae was the first in the line-up. For months Mae had given the same account, that Mr Sahni had raped her on different occasions, beginning a year earlier, when everyone else was at a party and he asked her to fetch him a glass of water. She told this account to the child committee. She told it to the police. And she told it to two different magistrates who recorded her testimony. But when the judge called her to testify on 29 January 2013, that was not what she testified.

Instead, Mae told the judge that on the day of the rescue, when she went to fetch a scarf from her room to accompany the group from Shakti Vahini to the police station, the young woman leading the team followed her up to her room. In those few moments, Mae says, the young woman whispered to her that she would get lots of money if she made a rape allegation against her employer. According to Mae, that's why she told the child officials that she had been assaulted. She said she continued to lie before the magistrates—when no one else was present—and even weeks later, out of fear of the young woman.

When the Shakti Vahini social worker was called to the stand two weeks later, she denied telling Mae to commit perjury, and tried to show the protocol she had followed in conducting the rescue. She had brought documents with her from Shakti Vahini's file on Mae to show the judge. But under cross-questioning by Mr Sahni's legal team she performed much more poorly than Mae, who had been unshakeable in her account, and burst into tears. She contradicted herself numerous times, confessed ignorance about the laws that gave Shakti Vahini the authority to carry out rescues and inflamed rather than allayed the judge's suspicions that here was a blameless employer being framed by a scheming maid.

In a scathing verdict, three weeks later, the judge acquitted Mr Sahni. And while Mr Sahni's acquittal was accompanied by twists and turns that were more dramatic than usual, it would have been surprising if the case had ended in any other way. In 2013, the year of Mr Sahni's trial, over three-quarters of rape trials decided that year ended in acquittals. Sometimes they ended that way because the alleged victim and the alleged assailant told the judge they were in love, and that the rape complaint had been filed by the woman's parents in order to separate them. Sometimes they ended that way because a woman close to a man had been persuaded to bring an allegation against a rival of his, and now thought better of it. Sometimes they ended that way because of the tiniest of discrepancies in statements

made by the victim: an Indian rape conviction requires that a woman
who has never been drilled in the art of remembering so much as
a multiplication table be able to recite in court, without the least
variation, the statements she made at the time she reported the crime.
And sometimes they ended that way because, like Mae, the alleged
victim recanted her story for reasons known only to herself.

The verdict was carried in an Indian daily the next day, and must
have occasioned a great deal of schadenfreude among employers of
maids rescued by Shakti Vahini. Imagine: the organization that had
dragged them to court based on nothing more than their maids'
statements was now being dragged through the mud on the say-so
of a maid. Overnight, the stories so often circulated by people accused
of harming their maids—everybody knows 'these people' lie, this is
nothing but an attempt at extortion—gained new credibility. All the
more so, because the judge didn't just acquit Mr Sahni, she also ordered
that Shakti Vahini and its employees be investigated for perjury, and that
perjury charges attracting jail time of six months be brought against
Mae. 'The interest taken by this NGO in the present case appears to
be more than normal,' wrote Judge Nivedita Anil Sharma, suggesting
there was an 'underlying motive'.

The police duly investigated Shakti Vahini. Chutki and Neera both
confirmed they had sought the organization's help, backing Shakti
Vahini's account of why the non-profit embarked upon the rescue.
But Mae also stuck to her story, that she had made the whole thing
up. She also told the High Court that she was happy in the shelter,
and didn't want to go home with her mother. At this hearing, where
Neera Varma accompanied her, Pano tried to touch and talk to her
daughter outside the court, still unable to believe that Mae didn't want
to come with her, but a shelter official swatted her away. On the basis
of Mae's account, and the fact that she had never mentioned being
sexually assaulted during the few phone calls she had had with her
aunt Chutki, police brought back a recommendation to Judge Sharma
that three Shakti Vahini employees be tried for suborning perjury. The
docket remains before the judge, waiting for her decision to move
forward with a trial or dismiss the recommendation.

In her ruling, the judge also reiterated a warning about what she
saw as an epidemic of rape allegations being brought by domestic

workers against their employers. In 2013, less than 10 of the nearly 600 rape verdicts handed down in Delhi fell into this category. But perhaps it seemed like an avalanche to this judge because most of these trials dealt with incidents in Punjabi Bagh, the neighbourhood that maid broker Mr Srivastava described as being one he hates to deal with, and so they came before her.

Even then, of the sixty rape trials that Judge Sharma decided in 2013, just five involved allegations brought by maids against their employers, while a couple of others were brought by women against maid brokers, all of which ended in acquittals. That year, just two trials involving allegations brought by maids led to convictions, in both cases against fellow servants, and in neither case before Judge Sharma. Despite these numbers, the judge was alarmed enough by what she was seeing that she held forth on it in her rulings on more than one occasion.

'A recent trend is surfacing where either a domestic worker is being underpaid or where she has been detained by the employer for an unusually long period or where her work is unsatisfactory that such a domestic worker has unfortunately resorted to invoke the laws relating to sexual abuse for achieving her goal,' wrote the judge. 'A spurt of cases are being registered on the false allegations made by domestic workers, migrant as well as local, regarding rape and physical abuse by the employers...this trend requires to be nipped in the bud.'

In some of the rape trials she presided over, there was perhaps enough information to form the opinion that the allegations weren't credible. In one case, a woman brought allegations of assault against two different men, claiming one or the other was the father of her child. Yet a DNA test cleared both men of paternity and pointed to a third man. False accusations of sexual assault do occur and do cause harm. In another case before this judge, the alleged accused was an extremely elderly man. While attending hearings in the case against MP Dhananjay and his wife, Jagriti Singh, in the death of their maid, I sometimes witnessed hearings in a rape case that often fell on the same dates, and in which the allegation had come from a maid working as a caretaker to an elderly man. I had seen this man at some of the proceedings, brought in in a wheelchair, visibly confused and at times, as the judge noted, sleeping through the hearings. Peering over the shoulder of a lawyer reading a brief for the case, I saw one of the allegations against the old man included the claim that he promised to make over his home to his caretaker if she would have relations with him. I approached his daughter, who had flown home from overseas for a hearing, but she declined to talk about the proceedings, saying it was too painful.

At the same time, in at least some of the cases before Judge Sharma, there was also enough information to suspect that employers had mistreated their help. The non-payment of a few thousand rupees may seem a trivial matter from the perspective of some Indians, for others the sum equals a month of food back in the village. As for being 'detained against your will for an unusually long time', what is that if not a violation of your most fundamental rights? As I read the judge's warnings, I couldn't help but wonder, while singling out one serious concern, faced by one class of people, why she didn't also call for these acts, against another class and equally serious, to be nipped in the bud? I approached Judge Sharma, who said she was willing to discuss this trial if the Delhi High Court authorized her to do so. The Delhi High Court declined to make Judge Sharma available for an interview.

In recent years, groups organized around men's rights, and in particular for the reform of dowry laws, argue that women are abusing the law, alleging dowry harassment where none has occurred. Meanwhile, divorce lawyers privately admit they sometimes advise a woman to file such cases to improve her chances of keeping custody or seeking child maintenance. Lawyers willing to be indiscreet can probably provide dozens of examples of steering clients, both men and women, to provisions of the law they are not actually entitled to use, when the laws and social sanctions that should govern the actual harm they have suffered aren't robust. When it comes to forced labour or wage theft, Indian laws don't really make it clear how a police officer should decide an employer has crossed the line from a reasonable request to a worker to take their village leave at a more convenient time to detaining someone against their will, nor how police should investigate and distinguish between an employer who is holding wages for his maid at her request versus one who is withholding them. As a result, such cases rarely make it to a court of law.

In Mae's case, for example, the fact that she had received just 46,000 rupees over three years of work didn't give rise to any criminal charges. In a country so poor, a job of almost any kind is seen by both workers and the upholders of the law as something to be grabbed tightly with both hands, not sharply scrutinized and picked over. Figures put together by non-profits suggest that millions of people work in conditions that qualify as criminal, in violation of Indian laws against indentured servitude. And yet, in 2015, law enforcement recorded just 426 victims of forced labour, resulting in 88 cases being registered across the entire country, according to the National Crime Records Bureau. The Indian criminal justice system doesn't spring easily into action on allegations made by workers against employers. Not so long ago, it didn't even spring into action on allegations of sexual assault. But in recent years, the chances have increased that if police act on nothing else, they will at least investigate an accusation of rape.

IN NOVEMBER 2012, A MONTH after Shakti Vahini rescued Mae, though I didn't know it at the time, I have my own first experience of a rescue—or rather an attempted one. It is just a few days before Diwali, on a sunny Friday, when I take a metro ride to Noida with a Catholic church-affiliated rights organizer working for the same organization that helped a maid bring a complaint against the Verma family in Uttam Nagar. On the way, she tells me that her activism is sometimes an embarrassing task for her. She has met maids who earn as much as 12,000 or 15,000 rupees a month. As a rights worker, she is earning less than 10,000 rupees, she says. She can't help but think, who is she to tell them how to organize for better pay?

After this somewhat despondent conversation, we alight at the very last stop of the Noida line and meet Nirmala Bakla, who goes by Irma. A small woman in a nylon sari with orange flowers, Irma came to Delhi's main Catholic church in January to ask for help finding her daughter, gone for almost seven years. Irma had at first tried to reclaim her daughter several years ago on her own. When she approached the family for whom her daughter worked, they said it was not possible to part with her at the time, as the employer's father had just passed away. Another time Irma's brother went, but he too was unsuccessful at bringing his niece back. Possibly, at the time, the employer's mother was ill.

The most recent time Irma went to seek her daughter, the family was no longer living at the house. No forwarding address or phone number had been passed on via the broker to Irma in the village or left with a neighbour. So in January 2012, Irma made her way to the Domestic Workers Forum, located in the basement of the church opposite the red-brick building that houses the city's most prestigious Catholic boys' school, incidentally my father's alma mater. There, the case was assigned to Nilima, a plump, round-faced woman from Jharkhand responsible for organizing workers in Noida. It is Nilima who found out in April, with the help of Delhi Police, that the employers had moved across state borders to the Noida suburb known as Sector 50. Together they go to meet the employers in Noida in April, and the head of the family says he will part with Irma's daughter in July. In July, he asks them to come back in November. Perhaps the third time will be the charm.

With us today is Irma's relative, Ursela, a woman who has a bad eye and a pronounced limp. Irma has been staying with her. From the metro station we squeeze into an auto part of the way, until we reach the landmark we're looking for, a large private school whose gates are covered with inspirational quotes like, 'If you can't fly then run, if you can't run then walk...whatever you do, you have to keep moving forward'.

The employer lives in a row of houses around the corner from the school; once we're there Nilima rings the doorbell. Neeta Arora, the lady of the house, opens the door, smiles at us in a friendly fashion and invites us in. She gestures for us to sit down on two white plastic chairs in the living room. She then chivvies two girls who appear to be teenagers—one of whom is Irma's daughter—to fetch two more white plastic chairs. The room is dark, with curtains drawn. In the corner there is a little prayer area, with a picture of the god Krishna as an infant, next to which there is a picture of a chubby little boy, as well as little figurines of Ganesh and the goddess Lakshmi. In the back part of the room there's a dining table and where we are seated, at the front of the room, there are three plush-upholstered brown sofas arranged around a coffee table. Mrs Arora catches me looking at the sofas and says, 'The sofas have just been dry-cleaned, they're all wet.'

She calls her husband Bharat Bhushan Arora to talk to Nilima, and he comes and parks himself on a sofa. His wife doesn't warn him the sofa is wet, nor he does he jump back up with a sodden bottom. It hadn't occurred to me to wonder why chairs are being brought into a room full of places to sit. With that, the penny drops. It would be a violation of the social order for the mother and aunt of her servant to sit on these sofas.

Bharat Bhushan Arora, a short man with a florid face and very dark

circles under his eyes, asks who I am. Nilima and I have agreed that
we will not say that I'm a journalist, as she wants to negotiate with
him, and the presence of a journalist may not be conducive to that. I
suggest we tell him I'm researching their organization and her work,
which is not so far from the truth. But perhaps I've miscommunicated
and Nilima tells him I'm there to check up on her work. I don't correct
her and from then on he treats me as an authority figure, from time
to time going over Nilima's head and turning to me with appeals,
such as 'Don't I look like an honest man?' or '*You* must understand
my position'. I guess he has pegged me as a sister in arms, a fellow
employer of maids.

Nilima is trying to negotiate not just for Irma to leave with her
daughter, but for back wages, since Irma says she hasn't ever received
any money since her daughter first came to Delhi to work in around
2003; nor has her daughter ever come home, not once. The Aroras
tell Nilima they paid the first two years' salary—at the rate of 500
rupees a month—directly to the agent (for comparison, in 2003, the
minimum monthly unskilled worker wage in Delhi was 2,800 rupees).
As the conversation unfolds and they discuss the number of years'
earnings that are owed to Irma's daughter, it becomes clear that she
hasn't received wages for nearly a decade.

Nilima is torn about what to do. On the one hand, she thinks
they should take Irma's daughter away as soon as possible. On the
other hand, she knows the family needs the money and she thinks that
leaving Irma's daughter there gives them leverage to get the money
their girl is owed. All this time Irma's daughter has been out of sight,
so Nilima asks to speak with her. Bharat Bhushan Arora calls out her
name, his voice rising sharply on the final vowel. The young woman
appears and shakes each of us by the hand, murmuring, 'Gesu.'

'Ah, that's how you say hello, is it?' Bharat Bhushan Arora says
genially. Has she never met anyone from her home while living here?

When we shake hands, I see that the young woman's hands are
beyond callused. Little grey flakes of skin are peeling off her palms.
On one palm, there is a large raised callus of yellowish skin. 'How
did this happen?' I ask when her employers momentarily step out
of the room. She looks away, out the door, and says, 'Pata nahin (I
don't know).'

There seems such an enormous age difference between her and her white-haired mother, Irma, that they can hardly be mother and daughter. But the high planes of their cheekbones convey at least shared membership in the same tribal community. Irma doesn't say much in the nearly three hours we are there. She speaks broken Hindi, despite a year spent living in Maharani Bagh as a house cleaner for 1,000 rupees a month in around 2005, around the time she had gone to ask for her daughter by herself. In her own language, Oraon, she might have been able to plead, cajole, argue. In Hindi, she repeats the same brief sentence. 'Today, we'll take my daughter,' she says, from time to time, and then nothing more, despite Nilima having urged her to show her emotions, and to not hold back.

Irma's relative, more comfortable in Hindi from her years working in Noida, is more emphatic. She tells her niece again and again, 'Get your shoes. We're going from here.' But Irma's daughter says nothing in response. She doesn't go to get her shoes. At one point she goes upstairs and returns with a cheap set of sheets wrapped in plastic. She offers this to her mother and aunt.

Bharat Bhushan Arora says, 'She's gathering her things.' He says he's not ready to let her go right now because they don't have anyone else. But he also says he has to make 'preparations', that he wants to send her home like a bride going to her wedding, with lots of gifts. 'There won't be one suitcase. There'll be suitcases,' he promises. 'She wants to buy a sari for her mother, let us do all these things.' But, he says, just let them keep her till February, until they find a servant to replace her.

There is another girl we've glimpsed who looks to be in her early teens. But the Aroras say they plan to send her back. She is too little and isn't able to handle all the work, they complain. Then they hastily add that she isn't really working here, she's come to see Delhi, without explaining how she ended up here, in this house in Noida. The two maids are dressed the same, in long T-shirts over short leggings, and no shoes or slippers, although at this time of year the gleaming cream-coloured marble floor, which they likely swabbed down together this morning, must be cold. We arrived around 3 p.m. and Nilima tells me later she asked them surreptitiously if they had had lunch yet. They told her they hadn't.

Mrs Arora echoes her husband, saying the new girl isn't up to all the housework. 'Hire someone older,' says Irma's relative. At this, Mrs Arora is outraged. 'Will you vouch for her character?' she says. 'Don't talk of all this.' Both the Aroras bewail the difficulty of finding 'decent' girls these days. In an unconscious black mark against their parenting skills, Bharat Bhushan Arora's wife says, 'I have a young man in the house. I can't take the tension of having the wrong kind of young woman in the house.

'The girls these days have mobile phones, they have a tongue on them,' she says.

As the discussion continues, with Nilima saying that Irma has already been very patient, voices sharpen. At one point, Mrs Arora shouts at Ursela, as she tries to contradict Bharat Bhushan Arora, 'Shut your mouth when a gent is talking.' She says Irma should be more appreciative of the care they have taken of her daughter. They could easily have thrown her out, or dumped her at an orphanage, all these years that Irma didn't turn up. 'Do you know what happens to girls in orphanages? Do you even know?' she shouts.

It is Mrs Arora who is raising her voice. And yet, Bharat Bhushan Arora tells Ursela, 'I'm getting scared of your voice. Look at your voice. Look at my voice, how politely I'm talking. That's the difference between us and you people.' He tells his wife to fetch Diwali sweets for Ursela to 'sweeten her voice'.

Both sides urge the young woman at the centre of this debate to speak freely—does she want to stay or does she want to go—but she remains silent, not meeting anyone's gaze, clearly deeply uncomfortable. Can this really be the right way to do this? Softly she pleads with no one in particular, eyes fixed on the ceiling, 'Just wait two months.'

Nilima motions me to step outside with her and then she asks me: what should I do? I am aghast. And then suddenly, unfairly, I am angry with her. I thought you knew what you were doing, I think. And if you don't know, you should leave this to someone who does, someone who knows the law and understands how to use it. Later, I try to remember that she is doing her best, that she and some of her co-workers have worked as maids previously, that many of them hail from the same villages and districts as the live-in maids they are trying to help, and can quickly form a rapport with the woman they are trying to help. Someone better versed in the law, from a different class and community, might not be able to win trust in the same way. But without the law, without the knowledge of how to put pressure on unwilling police officers, they approach this couple, and in particular the man, in the way women in India are most comfortable doing: they supplicate, they request. And that deference can scarcely go unnoticed by the audience to whom it most matters: the person they are trying to rescue.

If they knew the law, they could demand, not request. The law says withholding the earnings of a minor worker is subject to a three-year prison term. Of course, Irma's daughter may not be a minor despite her young face and slender frame. In that case, the law says that withholding the wages of an adult worker, or restraining their ability to leave employment, is a form of crime known as bonded labour that should be brought to the attention of a local magistrate. But this is not what happens. What happens is that after hours of talking and negotiating, Nilima agrees they will come back in February to take Irma's daughter. She tries to get the couple to agree that next time, when they let their maid go, they will pay her for at least for five years worth of work, at the rate of 750 rupees a month: 45,000 rupees. Bharat Bhushan Arora agrees but declines to put anything in writing. 'You write it,' he says to me.

He does, however, bestow on Ursela a 1,000-rupee note. 'For Diwali,' he says. Silently, I will her not to take it, not to cede the higher moral ground, not to accept the relationship that taking the money will seal between them: he, the master, the payer of tips, she, the servant, the recipient of largesse at someone else's discretion. Like a scene in a movie, I want her to fling the note in his face, to say, 'You think our child can be bought with a tip?' But, after demurring, a few times, with an embarassed smile, she takes the crisp note. She has been hosting and feeding Irma for months. She needs the money. And then we leave.

February comes and goes and a new deadline is set, for the summer. Nilima goes to speak with the local police, but finds that Bharat Bhushan Arora has beaten her to it. The police have a statement on which Irma's daughter has put her thumbprint and which Bharat

Bhushan Arora and a neighbour have signed as witnesses. 'I have been working here for ten years and I want to stay here,' says the statement, in which Irma's daughter says she's twenty-four. 'Two women called Ursela and Nilima from an NGO are trying to take me away. Please protect me.' The letter makes no mention of her mother or the salary she's earning at the time, and the police don't seem to have asked any questions.

The next time she visited, in April or May of 2013, Irma says she tried to act with more firmness. It is a decade that her daughter has been working in the city and she is tired of the promises the Aroras kept making. At the Arora's home, she put her hand on her daughter's arm and made as if to leave. 'Daughter, let's go,' she said. 'If you are my daughter, then come home.' If she drew up her courage and met her daughter half way, perhaps her daughter too would be brave and leave with her. But that's not what happened. Not at all. 'She bit my hand,' Irma tells me, her eyes wide in wonder. 'She bit me.'

That is when she gave up hope of reclaiming her daughter. When Irma tells me this, she is no longer staying in the city. Instead, we are meeting in her village, Annabiri, to which she returned after giving up hope of uniting with her daughter. To get to Annabiri, you take National Highway 78 southeast out of Ranchi towards the Chhattisgarh border, and then bear northwest along the Sankh River, as the paved two-lane state highway slowly turns into a barely paved road. Large piles of stones on either side of the road suggest road work has been planned but halted—or maybe thwarted. This is Maoist country. The day after we visit there is a news report of villagers having found five bodies in a ditch in the district. Police issue a statement saying they suspect these may have been Maoist killings but they have not been able to go investigate because the deaths were reported after dark and they don't dare venture into these villages then.

About 40 kilometres from Annabiri, phone signals vanish for all except the state-run network. In one small village we pass the only signs of enterprise around here: two mobile shops. One has a sign with the words 'billpay' 'BSNL' and '3G' brightly hand-painted upon it, while the other advertises repairs. Wait, there's one more: a shop carrying cement and other construction materials. At a window of a concrete building, men and women sign up for government work. All around on the vast plains that occasionally bump into tiny forested hills, the stalks of the rice cut in November and December have turned silvery-grey, and a few cattle graze here and there. This is the Indian economy, writ small.

When Irma first recounted her visits to try to reclaim her daughter, sitting in Ursela's room in a Noida tenement, I couldn't help thinking that the efforts seemed few and far between. But having made the journey, I understand better the reasons for her sporadic visits from Annabiri, the village she married into many, many years ago. To get to Annabiri you must leave the paved road at a point about 12 kilometres from the nearest town. A 5-kilometre drive on a winding dirt road follows—it must be impassable in the monsoon—before we reach the hamlet of perhaps 450 families.

Irma's daughter went to Delhi after Irma's husband died, more than a decade earlier. Her in-laws put pressure on Irma to remarry but she refused, believing that she would have to forego her son's claim to her father's share of the family land. Instead, she took her children to stay at her brother's place, two or three kilometres away over the fields. Recently, her in-laws have given Irma and her son a portion of the ancestral land and both of them have moved back to Annabiri and plan to build a hut soon. Irma says wistfully, if her daughter had sent money over the years, she could have bought a bullock and farmed the narrow fields she theoretically owns through her husband, but which are lying fallow because it takes equipment and an animal to get anything out of them. Even now, if her daughter had another job in the city, and could send money from time to time, it could help so much, perhaps even pay for the hut to be built.

Right now, Irma and her son live off daily labour that pays them in unhusked grain—husked and dried, it will give them four kilograms of rice. She lost her rights to the subsidized rice the very poor are entitled to receive after government workers didn't find her in the village when they came to update the poverty rolls; at the time, she may have been in Delhi working, or staying with her brother. For money, she sells the firewood that she collects from the foot of the hill in the distance; a bundle of thirty stout sticks can sell for perhaps 100 rupees at the weekly market. One February afternoon, she returns from the hill bearing two slim tree trunks on her head to find me waiting for her. Her neighbours gather around us, providing translation and additional details, as we sit on the dirt in front of the wooden fence that cordons off the shack she is renting for the time being.

Not long after Irma's husband died, she tells me, a couple around Annabiri was collecting girls to take to Delhi, sometimes by permission, sometimes by stealth. Irma told me in Delhi that she came home from working in someone else's fields one evening to learn that her daughter and several other girls were at the home of this couple, who would put them on a train to Delhi. It was after dark and it was not safe to go from her own village to the other one. By morning, the train to Delhi had departed. Some of the other families made a fuss, and some of the girls came back. In one telling, the girls are brought back by someone. In another telling, they escaped and ran back. But not Irma's daughter. The female half of the broker couple was from Irma's birth village and she told Irma she would find her daughter a job in a good home. 'They must have spoken to her sweetly and convinced her,' the neighbour who is translating for me suggests.

People in Annabiri whose daughters were born just before or after Irma had her daughter, put her age at around twenty-seven in 2015, and maybe fourteen or fifteen when she first went to the city to work. Many girls that age were leaving to work in the city as housemaids, supporting their families from far away. But when her daughter didn't send money or come home to visit, Irma went to the broker to ask why this was.

'I don't know,' was the reply.

'Did you sell her?' Irma asked.

'No, no, I didn't sell her.' But Irma still suspects otherwise. Even so, after years of efforts, she appears to have accepted there is nothing more to be done. Months before Irma and I meet in Annabiri, Nilima too gave up hope, after the events at a meeting with the Aroras presided over by the Noida Sector 50 Residents' Welfare Association chief, Vimal Sharma.

This is how those events unfolded. In August 2013, Nilima heard from Ursela that the Residents' Welfare Association had called a meeting to discuss Irma's daughter's situation. By the time Nilima heard about this from Ursela, it was the morning of the meeting and she had to rush to Noida. When she got there, the meeting had already begun, and RWA Sector 50 President Vimal Sharma was speaking rather loudly to Ursela and another woman, the broker who had originally brought Irma's daughter to the city. The broker was by then no longer working as a recruiter but as a maid. 'I'll put you inside. Don't come around here again,' the RWA chief said to the women.

Mr Sharma later confirmed Nilima's account. 'I was ready to put them behind bars. With a lot of begging and pleading, promising they wouldn't come here again, they managed to go away,' recollected Mr Sharma, when I met him in January of 2015, at the time of his Gandhi-inspired clean-up drive. 'When I called the police they started folding their hands and crying.'

At the meeting, he says, Irma's daughter told him that she was happy with the Aroras. 'She is getting the love of a mother and father,' he said. He said that when he asked her if she was getting paid, she produced a bank statement. I see on voter lists for the state that she has had a voter card made out with the Arora's address—she would have turned eighteen while living with them, and she would have needed a photo ID to comply with the RWA's verification efforts. Her paper identity, as part of the Arora household, was solidifying.

The RWA chief said the young woman told him that if she was sent away from the Aroras, she would be sold again. Irma, her mother, was not at this particular meeting, an absence no one was able to explain. Bharat Bhushan Arora said that Irma's daughter accused the agent who brought her to Delhi of having sold her. Which begs the question, if there was a sale, who, in this gathering, was the buyer? And was that not a crime? But in this gathering, the women who were trying to help Irma were the ones who were seen as the criminals by the mediators.

'They are cheaters,' said Mr Sharma, of the women. He believes the women were trying to remove Irma's daughter from the Aroras so as to get a share of her final pay settlement—or else they intended to place her somewhere else and earn a new commission as well as collect her future earnings. 'There's 20 per cent or 30 per cent commission for the NGO, the people who supply domestic servants.'

Nilima's group is a bona fide welfare organization that has worked for years with other non-profits on improving the situation of domestic workers in the city, mainly funded by grant money. On visits to its office, I've often seen many of its employees copiously documenting the activities on which they have spent these monies. And yet, I understand why Mr Sharma—why many people—believe that non-profits that claim to be helping maids are actually on the make. There are at least two Delhi groups run by nuns that place women with verified employers for a fee as part of their welfare efforts, with strict rules that the women be allowed to attend church on Sunday, as well as a requirement that they come to a weekly meeting to air any problems they are facing at work. The fees don't go to enrich the nuns, but the fact that they charge money blurs the lines, at least in the eyes of some employers, between these aid groups and other entities that have similar sounding names but are entirely for-profit agencies.

And the maid brokers and traffickers, who aren't stupid, make sure to muddy the waters further. They don't call themselves Stolen Girls Services or Slaves 'R' Us. They don't make it easy to distinguish the avaricious from those who are genuinely trying to help. They use names that manage to convey trustworthiness to families trying to get jobs for their daughters, while also signalling to employers the availability of humble, Christian women from remote areas. Some years ago, a cable news channel conducting an undercover investigation caught on tape a broker who was trying to sell the baby of a teenage maid who became pregnant after being assaulted. The name of the broker's outfit? Tribal Welfare Organization.

Groups like Shakti Vahini and Bachpan Bachao Andolan say that for this reason they work with the police as early as possible, and that their priority is to register criminal complaints. They don't sit around with employers discussing money or trying to reach settlements. Such requests for back pay, made directly to the employer and without the presence of law enforcement, can easily, in a later retelling by the employer, become an accusation of extortion. Because when employers pay their maids meagre wages, it's just market forces at work—but when maids try to collect their dues, invariably it ends up being called extortion.

Mr Sharma's account doesn't tally exactly with the details I am given by Bharat Bhushan Arora, with whom I speak for just a few minutes the same day. He is just about to pull out of his driveway, and I awkwardly crane my head through his car window, reminding him we have met before and telling him I am writing about his maid and would like to clarify a few things. As we speak, his wife eyes me suspiciously from the gate. He says that his servant told a magistrate that she is happy with them. How much do you pay her now, I ask. He is vague at first, but then answers, must be about 1,000 rupees, he says. In her own bank account? I'm going to open one for her, he says. A year passes before we meet again.

I am a little nervous when I go to meet them by myself. But they couldn't be nicer to me. Now that I am not here as a tagalong to a gaggle of tribal women, they present an entirely different version of themselves than the one I previously saw. No plastic chairs are brought out. I am immediately invited to sit on the sofa. Neeta Arora makes me tea herself. And this is true, with one exception, of all the people alleged to have brutalized their maids, including a woman documented on videotape doing so: the face shown to me bears no resemblance to the one they (allegedly) showed their servants.

The Aroras tell me that they had always intended to send their maid back with her mother, except for that first time, which they say was very poor timing. 'The first time she came my father had expired. He had not even been cremated yet,' says Bharat Bhushan Arora. 'So that time we sent her [mother] back saying, "This is the situation." I said to come back another time and take her. And I gave her the money we owed,' he adds, saying they gave Irma about 5,000 or 7,000 rupees.

But then she didn't come for years and years, he says. 'I thought maybe there's been a flood in Jharkhand or something. She never came in those days, and we got no information.' Despite the advance of telecommunications across the country, cell phones are unevenly distributed and communications with the hinterland can still be surprisingly difficult. Even when I go to meet Irma, I am unable to call her beforehand to warn her of my arrival, and it is just by luck that we arrive in Irma's village shortly before she returns from gathering firewood. A relative tried to get word to her by calling someone else in the same village but I don't know if that message ever made it through. At the beginning of 2015, in a country of 1.2 billion, there are more than 900 million cell phone subscribers—but Irma is not one of them.

When Irma finally came back, they say, they were willing for their maid to go with her mother. It was the young woman herself who seemed to have changed her mind, they say. 'At first we thought we should send her,' says Neeta Arora. But then they noticed she appeared to be reluctant. 'Once someone else came to take her. She said, "I won't go with anyone else. I'll go with my mother,"' Neeta Arora says. They say their maid was excited to see her mother at first, but that on subsequent meetings with her mother and the women helping Irma, her enthusiasm diminished. 'When the mother came, she saw her mother's behaviour, she noted some things, and then she hesitated. Then she said, "I don't want to go." That's where the problem started.'

'She said I don't want to go with my mother. My mother has fallen in with some bad women. She could even sell me, or do anything,' Neeta Arora continues. 'Now you tell me, when the daughter was saying this, then what were we supposed to do? I didn't have any option. She helped me so much with my mother-in-law, that I couldn't just discard her and say, "Go with them".'

Their maid has told them about a troubled life in the village, the Aroras say. The uncle the family stayed with after their father's death used to drink and fly into a rage, forcing the children to flee to other people's homes to sleep. Sometimes they didn't even have clothes to wear, she has told them. Her mother became deeply depressed, their maid told them, telling her children to look out for themselves, and not to count on her. This account is why, the Aroras say, they began stalling. Then, says Neeta Arora, her husband got a disturbing phone call from a woman regarding the matter. He told the woman that he considered his maid as a daughter, and the woman on the other end tartly responded she didn't care 'whether you make her your daughter or your wife'.

'Such horrible words those ladies used. Which no one in our family, in our society, in our circle has ever heard,' says Neeta Arora. So she urged her husband to involve the residents' association. 'I told him to go to the society and clear this matter up because things were taking a very wrong turn. We'll get into a jam,' she recalls.

On the advice of the RWA, they took Irma's daughter to a local magistrate in charge of enquiring into labour issues such as bonded labour. The magistrate spoke to Irma's daughter for a few minutes and sought a report from local police. The police reported back that Irma's daughter seemed happy where she was. Their report to the magistrate said nothing about wages, working hours, or time off.

Since then, the Aroras say, they have applied for her to get the paperwork required for a bank account and a voter's ID. Online voter rolls show that she was recently issued a voter's card at their address. And what does she earn now, I again ask? They have been saving her money in their own accounts, they say, vague on the details. They seem a little puzzled that I keep harping on this salary business when the person to whom it ought to matter the most does not, at least according to a story they tell me.

'She has such a good heart. Some time back we were having financial problems and we were discussing it in our room, that our son wanted money, about 10,000 rupees. [My husband] said, "Son, right now I don't have 10,000 rupees,"' says Neeta Arora. 'She heard it, she must have been passing on the way to or from the kitchen. And the child said, "Bhabi, take it out from my account if brother needs it."'

They also say they paid the agent for more years than they previously told Nilima, for four years not two. And they gave Irma money a couple of times, they say, at least a few thousand rupees. But now they have made a start on putting their maid's salary into a separate bank account. Bharat Bhushan Arora shows me a bank passbook for Irma's daughter issued by the local State Bank of India, with 48,000 rupees in it, the sum Nilima and the Aroras had discussed more than three years ago. It is more than two years since the meeting at the RWA office, when Irma's daughter reportedly said she was getting paid and had her own bank account. But on the front page of this bank statement book, the date of issue and of the sole deposit is from October 2015, two days after I resumed actively pursuing Bharat Bhushan Arora and the RWA for an interview about his maid and her salary situation.

And what of the money that should have accrued since then? The Aroras tell me they have had serious financial difficulties, which is why they have not been able to pay their maid's salary of 1,000 rupees a month. Bharat Bhushan Arora had joint pains and they had to spend as much as 80,000 rupees on his injections. 'He couldn't pick up a cup,' says his wife. 'He was in tears.' And in addition, they have to settle their son, who wants to start his own video-game business. So all their resources are going to that right now.

'If I'm not being able to do that much for my own child then she is a child from outside isn't she?' says Neeta Arora. 'Now she's become part of our home. But we are not being able to stand up [settle] the child who is born from us, so we will have to think about her after.'

Bharat Bhushan Arora adds that when they have the means to put more money in her account, they will be more generous.

'It could be 3,000 or 4,000 rupees a month even,' says Bharat Bhushan Arora, who runs a business but doesn't answer my question about what kind of business it is. 'It could be more than that also. There's no limit.'

Then they call Irma's daughter to speak to me. These are not the ideal circumstances in which to understand how she truly sees her own situation and so I restrict myself to queries that would allow me to trace her arrival in the city or confirm or deny the account given by her mother but refrain from queries—about salary or work conditions—that could get her into trouble. She at first looks petrified when she sees me, but slowly begins to answer some questions.

She is bundled tightly in a colourful shawl draped over a pink kurta with a black pattern of fairies hovering over large mushrooms. She is wearing red leggings and the flesh-coloured socks with a seam at the toe that puts me in mind of a Punjabi great-aunt of mine. She tells me that her mother sent her to work. She tells me, as the Aroras just have, that she doesn't want to go back to the village because her uncle used to drink, and when he drank he would get into a rage, and then she had to run away and find a safe place to sleep for the night. She says that before the Aroras she worked with another family, whom she didn't like, but she likes it here.

'So you're just going to keep staying here?'

'Yes,' she says.

I ask that most Indian of questions: what about meeting someone and getting married? Starting your own life?

'What for?' she responds, with the most feeling she has shown so far. 'I'm not interested.' Then she vanishes to another part of the house.

The Aroras show me her room upstairs, opposite the larger

household temple where marble statues of gods and saints, including Sai Baba, are housed under a marble canopy decorated with fresh flowers and golden cloth. The temple is located here, opposite a bedroom, so that when Bharat Bhushan Arora's mother was ill and bedridden, she could still face the temple and pray. Irma's daughter doesn't sleep on the platform bed of course. Her mattress and covers are folded in a neat stack on the floor next to the bed, waiting for her to come and unfurl them at night. A metal plate, spoon and glass, and a plastic bottle of cooking oil, are arranged neatly on the floor next to the mattress roll, waiting for her to come and have her next meal.

'Aren't we doing something good for her?' Neeta Arora asks. 'Have we done wrong? Maybe other people will judge us, but I don't think we have done wrong.'

LUTYENS' DELHI

WHEN I MET THE MP Dhananjay Singh in late 2014, there was little he could tell me about one of the most highly publicized cases involving alleged harm done by employers to their help, although he and his wife were at the heart of it. At the time, the charges on which they were to stand trial had not yet been set, making it, according to their lawyers, a poor time to talk to a journalist (or worse, to be noticed by the judge to be talking to a journalist). Yet, despite the lawyers periodically telling reporters, 'Yeh sab judas [sub judice] hai'—the matter is before the courts—the preferred way in the Indian legal world of saying 'no comment', details made their way into the newspapers. And, as the trial began and proceeded before the court, even more details made their way into court orders, creating a public record of the inner workings of the South Avenue bungalow allotted to the Singhs.

Dhananjay Singh had just flown home from his district in November 2013, where he had hosted a basketball tournament and received Diwali calls from constituents, when he received a phone call from his wife, Jagriti. She informed him that one of their live-in help, a woman called Rakhi, had died. Before setting off for the bungalow, he called the police. The officers who arrived at the home noted multiple bruises and wounds on the body of the dead woman and deemed the death suspicious. Two days later, the police arrested the politician's wife on suspicion of murder. The politician, although absent when the death occurred, was arrested on suspicion of concealing evidence related to the death.

Despite the Singhs denying having done anything wrong, in the court of public opinion, from the day of the arrests, the case became a stark symbol of the state of relations between the powerful and the powerless. The employers lived in the heart of VIP Delhi, from where you can see the curved dome of the Rashtrapati Bhavan. The female servants came from impoverished villages in West Bengal, and were placed in the bungalow by a mysterious 'agent' operating out of a Bengali corner of Karol Bagh. Men with rifles, paid for from public funds, sat at the bungalow's gates to prevent unauthorized entry. Or exit.

At the residence allotted to her husband, Jagriti Singh had been living almost on her own, as relations between her and her husband were strained, court records showed and newspapers reported. She attributed their marital rift to her husband's unsavoury acquaintances and checkered past, which included multiple trials for disturbing the peace and other charges under the state's Gangster Act. Her husband, meanwhile, told a court in a bail application that it was her anger issues that had 'eclipsed the marital bliss' and led him to file for divorce months before the death of their worker. In the application, he said that soon after the birth of their son in 2010, a 'sudden change occurred in the behaviour and temperament' of his wife. Among other things, paranoia over her son's welfare led her to ask her husband to have CCTV cameras, nearly two dozen of them, installed all over the house so she would know how he was treated when she was away.

Ram Pal, the young man from Varanasi who had been working in the home for a year, told the police in a statement that sometime in 2012, a few months after he began working in the house, Jagriti Singh began hitting him and the two women from West Bengal, Rakhi (as Golbanu bibi of Doparia village was known) and Meena, who had been hired through the same broker. Rakhi met this broker through a woman in her village who worked in Gurgaon. Meena's introduction to the Karol Bagh broker came via a relative, a twice-married itinerant vendor of herbal painkillers who dabbled briefly in maid-brokering. Between the three of them, they were responsible for cleaning, cooking and taking care of the Singhs' young son.

Another woman from West Bengal who previously worked for Jagriti Singh, and who was still at the bungalow when the new workers arrived, said she remembers that madam became very irritated when she saw one of them violating one of the house's most important rules: you can only talk on the phone after 9 p.m. when all your work is done. Madam could see on the CCTV cameras that Meena made phone calls during the day as well. 'That's why she took her phone away,' said the former maid, adding that she herself didn't have problems with the MP's wife—except once. 'She liked me quite a bit,' the woman says, 'but she did hit me one time.' Her husband, the painkiller vendor, interrupts her indignantly. 'That wasn't a beating! Just a slap.' Soon after, though, he took his wife away.

The fast-track process put in place for rape hearings now assures both victim and accused something approximating a speedy trial. The trial of Mae's employer took, from beginning to end, six weeks. But after the death of the Singhs' maid, the wheels of justice ground exceedingly slowly. Each time I checked in, no matter how many months had elapsed, the wheel had rolled forward by just a tiny measure.

Six months after the arrests of the couple, lawyers were still arguing over the charges the couple should face before a judge in a courtroom housed in a white building complex that once belonged to a Punjabi maharaja. The judge had to decide whether the prosecution had made its case that the woman, a dental surgeon, should be tried for murder, or a lesser charge. The arguments hinged on the term mens rea, Latin for 'a guilty mind', or intent. One of the lawyers told the judge that the prosecution filings mention that the politician's wife called doctor friends of hers to examine the maid and administer medicine. Clearly, there was no intent to kill; she was trying to treat the woman not kill her, the lawyer argued.

'So generous,' said the judge.

The defence also argued that since, according to the prosecution, the employer had been beating her maids for months, without the maids dying of it, she could not possibly know that these injuries, this time around, would be fatal. Ergo, no intention. Ergo, not murder.

The judge riposted, 'Was she a drum that she had to keep beating her?'

Seven months after the arrests, arguments regarding the charges were continuing, pending the results of forensic tests. The court heard a petition for the imprisoned Jagriti Singh to be allowed sunblock, a dupatta and TRESemmé shampoo for her falling hair. It agreed to the shampoo.

Eight months after the death of the maid, the court closed for its annual holidays. At the nine-month mark, the forensic results had still not come. Ten months from the arrests, the test results were still awaited, leading the court to call for a senior police official to come and explain the reason for the delay.

A year after the death, a new public prosecutor was appointed to the case and at his first appearance he asked for a three-week recess to get up to speed. By the time the next hearing took place, in December, lawyers had embarked on an indefinite strike, demanding that the ceiling on the value of civil cases that lower trial courts are allowed to process be raised. No defence lawyers appeared for any cases that day. Fifteen months after the death, the jocular judge was transferred to a different bench and a new judge was appointed, who would have to hear the arguments on the charge again.

Along the way, everyone was serving time, in one form or another. As a murder suspect, Jagriti Singh did not qualify for bail, and this was understandable. The gaunt-looking investigating officer who first had responsibility for the case, also spent hours at the courtroom waiting around as a hearing was rescheduled from morning to afternoon, and then adjourned in a matter of minutes because a vital piece of information, not always in his control, hadn't arrived. By the time the trial finally began, the number of hearings the police officer had attended added up to nearly a month of work lost by his new unit, the economic offences wing. Perhaps this was understandable too. The case was brought by the state, and he was a servant of the state.

But meanwhile, Meena and Ram Pal, who were the prosecution's key witnesses, were not at liberty either. A judge had ordered that they be kept under police protection till they had testified and been cross-examined, to keep them safe and prevent pressure being put on them. They could not go home to see their families until they had testified. This was for the public good, for justice for their fellow worker, but this seemed a lot to ask of the impoverished for the public good. About a year after the arrests, when I visited Meena's village, her family members asked when she would be back. A grandmother pointed to her six-year-old grandson and said, 'He's always asking for his mother.' He hadn't seen her in two years. Another year would pass before he would.

It wasn't until the public prosecutor filed a petition before the

High Court to cancel Dhananjay Singh's bail that things began moving along. The High Court judge declined to withdraw bail but ordered that the trial court record the testimony of the two main witnesses without delay. In July 2015, getting on for two years after the arrests, the trial finally began. Jagriti Singh was to be tried for murder, assault, wrongful confinement and forced labour, among other charges. Mr Singh was to be tried for concealing evidence in order to shield a lawbreaker. Both pleaded not guilty on all counts.

My efforts to seek an interview with Mrs Singh through the lawyers she had up until the start of trial weren't successful. A request to the jail administration for an interview with her went unanswered. But one day in court, when we found ourselves sitting next to each other, we chatted briefly. A diminutive woman, who had developed dark circles under her eyes during the pre-trial proceedings, she said to me between bouts of coughing into a peach-coloured hand towel, 'Why will I kill a servant? What have I to gain?'

I asked her why both her servants said she beat them often. She didn't say anything at first. Then she said that it was only now that she realized that she was not well, that she was overwhelmed by life, by the stress of her unhappy marriage, the stress of rising at 4 a.m. to go to her job, which she started less than a month before Diwali.

'You are so stressed and you come home and ask for a cup of tea,' she said. 'And it comes after forty-five minutes.'

What would she do differently, I asked her, if she could rewind the clock? She would seek psychiatric help, she said. She would do good works. She would open a dental clinic for people with mangled dentition and fix their smiles, replacing their crooked teeth with straight ones, so that they too could get married, despite marriage, clearly, not being a foolproof route to happiness. About the dead woman, she said nothing.

Three years after that death, when the city was again sliding towards festival season and newspaper readers and cable television news addicts had forgotten about the Singhs, Ram Pal and Meena came to court to describe what life in a Lutyens' Delhi bungalow was like for them. When Ram Pal turned up, he was easily a foot taller than the woman who was on trial for enslaving and torturing him. But despite the fact that they were three and she was one and they could have united against her, they didn't seem to have questioned her authority. But then again, according to statements documented in court orders, the three workers grew up in a country that for some reason made them perfectly able to believe their employer's threat that the armed guards at the gate—also servants of the state—would shoot them if they ran away.

Their testimony was given behind closed doors, but it echoed the statements they had previously made to the police. What they told police right after their employers were arrested was that it was perhaps six months before their fellow worker's death that their employer had begun beating them, and the violence escalated. In the days ahead of Diwali, which fell on a Sunday that year, everything just seemed to make their employer angrier. A few weeks ahead of the festival, she had secured a job as a dentist at a government hospital, but this didn't make the atmosphere at 175, South Avenue more peaceable. She got into the habit of rising at 4 a.m. to get to her shift on time. If she was woken as much as ten minutes late, she flew into a rage. When she returned home, she would fly into a rage at their perceived failings. Sometimes Rakhi was beaten for cooking too slowly, Ram Pal told police. Sometimes Meena was beaten because madam accused her of having an affair with her husband, she told police. Once Ram Pal was beaten when she blamed him for fusing the pump of the aquarium.

On the Friday ahead of Diwali, Mrs Singh kicked Rakhi many times, Ram Pal told police. When Rakhi didn't finish the work she had been assigned to do on Saturday in time, she was beaten again. When, after a day of not eating, she asked for a roti, she was hit. When she crept into the kitchen to make herself a roti, she left an unlit burner on in her haste, leading her employer to accuse her of trying to murder her with a gas leak, Meena said. On the night of Diwali, video footage showed Mrs Singh beating the partially naked woman with the stick that usually lay under the kitchen counter, as well as kicking her in the chest. At one point, the video recording showed her assaulting Rakhi's private parts with a knife. Ram Pal told the court that to him it seemed that Rakhi was beaten almost continuously between Friday and Sunday. Meena says Rakhi sometimes spoke up in defence of the other two, tried to reason with Mrs Singh when she was in a rage. Perhaps that's why she bore the brunt of the beatings.

Or perhaps the other two were beaten less because they cooperated more with their enraged employer. The two testified in a closed courtroom that they also beat their deceased co-worker—an admission verified in the footage according to the court order—leading Jagriti Singh's lawyers to argue that they should be tried along with her for the maid's murder. But the judge rejected this plea, after the prosecution argued that the workers were following Mrs Singh's orders out of fear, and that in any case they had already been granted immunity in exchange for their testimony.

That night, the eve of Diwali, when Rakhi was finally alone, she pulled on an old green-and-white pullover and lay down in the Porta-Cabin in the backyard of the house where she slept at night. While the days were still warm, a slight nip had entered the air at night. She was whimpering in pain when her employer brought friends out to the Porta-Cabin to look at her. Her employer pulled the blanket back so that the visitors could see the bruises around her chest. Her left eye was swollen shut. In the morning, Ram Pal came in to ask if she wanted water. She gestured him away. Later, he came to check on her again; when he touched her hand, it was cold. There was no one with her when she breathed her last.

Far away in Doparia, the phone call to Sajan Ali came in the middle of the night, as these phone calls do. 'Your mother has had a heart attack,' a man told him, Ali recalls. His mother, Rakhi who was also Golbanu bibi, had two mobile phones when she first went to Delhi, but it had been many months since she had spoken to the person she cared most about in the world.

After the death of Golbanu bibi, many people went to the home of the weaver whose wife had taken her to the city to work and warned him they would beat his wife if she returned to the village. The weaver said that he was beaten up himself. He took his daughter out of school and sent her to stay with an uncle, leading her to miss her exams and lose a school year. Eventually, he said, he was allowed to come back along with his son and daughter-in-law. But his wife was still afraid to come home. 'Even if I die she won't be able to come back,' he said.

After a second post-mortem, Golbanu bibi's bruised body was claimed by a small group that included her brother-in-law and a local politician from the Trinamool Congress, Doparia. Neither of her children were present. Sajan Ali was flown by the lawmaker Dhananjay Singh to Delhi for a few brief days, but soon fled back to his village. He says he became fearful when he realized his mother's employer was a politician and so he did not return for the funeral. His sister was married and now lived with her in-laws. For her, a journey to a distant, sprawling city full of strangers, to bury her mother was out of the question. In any case, a burial was a job for men.

Now that she need no longer be Rakhi ever again, the group of men from Doparia took her to be buried in a small Muslim graveyard near the Jhandewalan metro station that amateur photographers love to take snapshots of, for its juxtaposition of a gigantic statue of Hanuman, bearing a mace, with the silvery speeding train. There were no women in the small group to bathe Golbanu bibi seven times. Instead, local women who perform these services for the destitute and the solitary were called to the private graveyard, surrounded by high walls of brick, painted green on the outside. At the graveyard's entrance, where men sometimes leave their rickshaws when they go to offer namaaz at the adjacent mosque on Chamelian Road, the women made a makeshift private bathing area by hanging sheets and saris around the peepul tree.

The women washed the body with warm water as best they could, which was not very well. Golbanu bibi had lain in a morgue for ten days and now little strips of flesh fell away during the ablutions, the distressed women attendants confessed to the burial party later. The gravediggers happened to be from Bengal too, migrant labourers from Malda and other parts. They dug the grave in no more than half an hour and set stone all around it. In the mosque, the imam had prayed over her body. Then, the body, shrouded in cloth the burial party had purchased for 2,000 rupees at a local market, was lowered into the ground.

The grave in which the body lay, perpendicular to Mecca, was on the same axis as the old movie theatre Filmistan down the road, parallel with the brick wall of the cemetery that bears the words the mourners would utter as they scattered the first fistfuls of dirt into the grave, by Golbanu bibi's head. *Minha khalaqnakum, wa fiha nu'idukum, wa minha nukhrijukum taratan ukhra* (From the earth you came, and into it we return you, and from it you shall rise once again).

VASANT KUNJ

IN THE SUMMER OF 2013, a stray comment made by an official with India's human rights commission about what a pain it was just to get to Assam stuck in Ravi Kant's head. 'It took three days,' the man told Mr Kant, of the rescue group Shakti Vahini. 'We were jolted the whole time.' If that was the case, Mr Kant and his brothers wondered, how was it that the lead police officer investigating Mae's allegations against her employer had travelled to Assam and back in four days? Details about the detective's journey to Assam in November, including the times he checked in and out of his police station, had been included among the masses of information, much of it apparently irrelevant, that they had collected from a series of information requests. On that journey, the detective had verified the school certificate with Mae's birthdate that had been found by a defence lawyer for her employer.

For months after the 2013 verdict in the Rajan Sahni trial, the three Shakti Vahini brothers were despondent. After investigators recommended that three of their employees face trial, they gave up hope that they could count on the police to clear their names, despite their history of working with the police force. But, as with a rape allegation, where there is often no forensic evidence to either exculpate or incriminate, how do you establish your own truthfulness or someone else's dishonesty? They began carrying out their own investigations, filing dozens of requests with police under the Right to Information Act, a then eight-year-old transparency law that covers most government bodies, in hopes they might stumble upon some information that could prove that Mae had been persuaded to change her testimony, or at the very least, that something had gone awry in the investigation. Now it seemed they might have picked up a trail.

They checked the Indian Railways schedules for the fastest trains between Delhi and Assam, and found that it was impossible for the detective to make it to Mae's village and back at the times he checked in and out of his police station for the trip, carefully recorded in the police registers. So he flew. What of it? Ah, but this detective was not entitled to fly. Rank and status are signalled constantly in Indian government employment, including in the police, through everything from the category of house you are allotted to the type of travel the government is willing to reimburse you for. (It's why former MPs are so reluctant to leave the government-allotted bungalows in central Delhi when they lose elections: it's a physical confirmation they've been shoved from their coveted spots in the innermost inner circles of Indian life.) This detective only qualified for train travel, so who paid for his flights and why?

Ravi Kant filed an information request in July with the detective's police station in Punjabi Bagh asking for information about the detective's travel arrangements and expenses. The same month, two of the Kant brothers decided to travel to Assam to retrace the police investigator's steps and to look at Mae's school records themselves. Very quickly, they found their efforts rewarded. In Assam, the schoolteacher whose name was on the certificate told Shakti Vahini that he had created it at the behest of a relative of Mae's and another man who had told him that the young woman had met with an accident in Delhi, and that the certificate would help her get free medical care. He provided the Kants with an affidavit that said he had then authenticated the fake certificate when the police officer turned up, accompanied by another man.

In September, Ravi Kant filed a complaint with the anti-corruption department of the Delhi Police asking it to investigate who paid for the detective's flights. In response to enquiries made by the anti-corruption branch, the detective readily admitted to having flown to Assam. He said that due to personal problems that required him to get back to Delhi, he decided to fly to save time and paid for the tickets personally—about 17,000 rupees round trip—with some money his wife had. He said he believed Shakti Vahini was trying to smear him to save themselves from perjury charges.

In February the following year, the Punjabi Bagh police station finally responded to Shakti Vahini's questions about the detective's flights with a singular lack of information. The police station had no

information about how much the detective's travel arrangements to
Assam had cost or how he had paid for them. The following month,
the anti-corruption department completed its report, and provided
a further shot in the arm to Shakti Vahini's suspicions. As part of
its enquiry, the anti-corruption department had obtained booking
information and flight manifests from SpiceJet, the airline the police
officer travelled on. They found that the same travel agency had booked
tickets for the detective and another man, just minutes apart. Both on
the way to Assam, and on the way back, the detective and this man sat
together. An email from the travel agency listed a phone number for
the man, who appeared to be travelling with the detective, a number
that Ravi Kant had seen somewhere before.

He looked through Mae's case file and saw the same number. It
was among the mobile numbers provided by Neera Varma when she
reported to Shakti Vahini that her maid Chutki had been receiving
several phone calls from someone urging her to get her niece Mae to
stop cooperating with authorities. The number had been included in
the complaint letter Shakti Vahini sent to police. In its investigation,
the police anti-corruption division had asked the telecom company
providing service to the number for its customer details. The telecom
company provided a business name and an address in a mall in West
Delhi: Lifecycle Technologies Pvt. Ltd.—Rajan Sahni's company.
The police report said that the man who appeared to have travelled
with the police officer investigating Mr Sahni was Mae's employer's
brother-in-law. Despite this curious finding, police officers from the anti-
corruption branch never spoke to the brother-in-law for their report.
The man 'was telephonically requested to join the inquiry but he did
not', the report states.

It wasn't the silver bullet that Shakti Vahini had been hoping
for. It didn't prove, for example, that anyone had approached Mae
in the shelter or that her changed testimony was untrue. But it was
something. At the very least, the information that a relative of an
alleged suspect accompanied the lead detective raised serious doubts
about the independence of the investigation. Delhi Police opened an
enquiry into the fake school certificate and into the actions of the
police who had investigated Mae's case, which is ongoing. Reassured
that they were making progress, the brothers returned with renewed

vigour to their rescue work. Almost a year after Neera Varma first got in touch with them, they received a fresh tip-off about a maid in trouble from Vasant Kunj, a prominent South Delhi neighbourhood that used to be called 'Murder Kunj' for its vast open areas that once made great dumping grounds for bodies but which have since been parcelled out into new housing developments for the city's upper ranks.

After its investigations, Shakti Vahini decided the tip-off was credible and reached out to the local police. This time, they did things a little differently than they had done a year earlier when rescuing Mae. Rishi Kant went personally to the police station, and led the rescue, accompanied by a young woman who had been part of Mae's rescue as well. Before heading to the house, Shakti Vahini also asked the city's state-run women's welfare agency to depute its social workers, so they would have the necessary backing to remove the woman, and speak to her away from her employer. The group made a little convoy—a Delhi Police jeep followed by Shakti Vahini's Santro and a van driven by the man representing the Delhi Commission for Women—and arrived at the Vasant Kunj home shortly after lunch time. Soon the rescue group was gathered in front of the home about which Shakti Vahini had received the call.

The man representing the Delhi Commission of Women, despite having a patently Hindu name, had grown up in a largely Muslim slum on the banks of the Yamuna and studied at a school run by a mosque, thanks to the intervention of a foundation started by the senior police officer Kiran Bedi. When his slum was torn down ahead of the Commonwealth Games, he had started again on the outskirts of the city, employing himself and several others, including his wife, through a non-profit he founded. Like the Kant brothers, he focused first on health—tuberculosis treatment—but as funding and grants grew in other sectors, particularly women's welfare, he segued into aiding women in crisis, eventually garnering a contract to provide transport services to women calling a distress hotline. This was his first rescue.

Soon, a crowd of onlookers formed. A member of the local residents' welfare association arrived on the scene to see what was happening (it was not the RWA that had called in the information though). Representing the other side, maids and drivers began to gather.

The elderly woman inside the house, alarmed at the crowd that had gathered, refused to open the door. Not till my daughter comes home, she said, before retreating into the semi-darkness of the house. Senior police officers from the local station arrived, some of them made phone calls to the woman's daughter, Vandana Dhir, a spokesperson for the Indian arm of the Alstom Group, a Paris-based infrastructure conglomerate, and told her that they were investigating the alleged brutalizing of a maid in the house. One of the police officers who spoke to Dhir that afternoon described her phone manner as that of 'someone in a terribly important post'. 'I've only heard very senior police officers speak like that,' the police officer said.

A little after eight that night, a woman with short hair and a very tall, thin man approached the house. Vandana Dhir was one of four brothers and sisters. Like the Kant family, their father was also a civil servant who worked for a public sector bank and they had grown up all over India. The Dhir siblings went into the private sector. One of her brothers set up his own outsourcing firm, living in the US for several years before coming back and working for a top Indian steel firm. Like many upper-class Indians, Dhir is deeply spiritual—often appearing with the red tika on her forehead that denotes recently offered prayers. She wears her spirituality not only on her forehead but also on her sleeve—a large tattoo of Shiva, inked in blue, covers an entire forearm. She has made more than one pilgrimage to Vaishno Devi in Kashmir, a site dedicated to the worshipping of goddess Mahalakshmi, another version of Shakti. This form of Shakti represents the powerful goodness of motherhood believed to be personified, like the goddess Lakshmi, in the ideal Indian housewife. But here, on this day, everything is inverted. We have a man invoking Shakti against a woman who may have failed to embody that ideal.

Dhir spoke to the cops. 'Let me tie up my dogs,' she said. A senior police official agreed. About fifteen minutes later, Dhir opened the door and the group trooped in. Two police officials, Kant, and Dhir sat down in the drawing room. The tall, thin lawyer stood protectively behind his client. Despite the initial protests of the police, Kant continued recording the proceedings on his phone. The next day, some of the footage circulated on television channels. While the others were sitting, three of the women went into the room where Dhir's mother was, along with the person they were seeking. A couple of minutes later Kant and another of the rescue team went in too. The three women of the rescue team were in tears. The first thing the man from the Delhi Commission for Women noticed was a putrid smell coming from the girl. Then he saw what appeared to be a hole on the crown of her head and numerous scars on her neck and arms, some of which, he thought, looked like bite marks. Her hair was cropped close to her scalp. She didn't speak.

In a photograph taken that day, the young woman dressed in a red kurta and salwar is shown squatting on the floor with her arms clasped around her legs. She looks wizened and her face is pinched. Her hair is cropped short, and there are many bald patches, especially towards the front of her head. There are dark, swollen pouches under her eyes, and nicks and cuts all over her body. Many of the scabs are the bright pink of newly healed wounds, but there are many older partially healed bruises visible too.

Most striking of all are her ears. They are huge and swollen, closed in on themselves, sealed off. They are hardly like ears, in fact, not the usual whorls and grooves that protect the dark passage to the inner ear. On her medical report, carried out a few hours later, the doctor noted she had 'cauliflower ear', an injury that is a source of pride for boxers. It results from repeated blows to the side of the head, such as those usually sustained in a boxing bout. Blows to the ear, from a hand or a fist, cause the tissues in the ear to separate. Over time, from repeated trauma, the ear fills with pus and almost folds in on itself defensively, offering a smooth, polished, cavity-less exterior to the brutal world, rather like a snail secreted away into its shell. Her other ear had not yet progressed so far on this journey. Although it too had ballooned much beyond its normal size, a whorl here and there offered clues to what it had once been. She didn't look anything like the girl she had been just two years earlier when she left her village, Athgama, and her mother, Suruj Kujur, to come to Delhi to work. This was Fullin, Kujur's oldest daughter.

When Fullin was first asked about her injuries in her employer's home, she didn't blame her employer, people who were present say. 'I fell in the bathroom,' she reportedly said. When the Shakti Vahini workers insisted on taking her to a hospital, she turned to her employer,

'Aunty, should I go?' But later, away from the Vasant Kunj flat, she told Shakti Vahini counsellors and the police that her employer made her sleep in the bathroom and fed her off paper plates, that she had been hit repeatedly with a knife and a hot pan. She says that the wound on her head was caused by repeated beatings with a jharu.

When Fullin emerged from the house, the crowd got a look at her. After the police left, some members of the crowd went back to their own homes in the colony. Others in the crowd, the maids and drivers of families of the area, were so angered by what they saw that they smashed the flower pots of the house. Those flower pots, like the two dogs that belonged to Vandana Dhir, raised questions. It was Fullin who walked the dogs, and no doubt Fullin who watered the plants. Whatever the cause of her injuries, whether a broom held by her employer or a fall in the bathroom, why did the majority of people of this neighbourhood—particularly the resident welfare association officers who were vested with the power to make sure all was well in this tiny corner of the world—do nothing when they saw a dog walker go by with scars and wounds that appeared never to heal?

In 2014, Dhir was put on trial for assault, to which she pleaded 'not guilty', maintaining that Fullin hurt herself in a fall. She declined requests for an interview, saying at one point outside the court that the she didn't trust the media, and that journalists had 'hyped' her story. While the case is still in court, Fullin lives in an educational facility set up for trafficking victims in her home state. Periodically, she goes home to her family in the north of the state, which is where we meet on one of my visits. Her face has filled out, her hair has grown, and many of the scars on her body and face have faded. On her scalp though, a smooth hairless patch remains.

As these things go, this was a successful rescue, much more so than Mae's, whose whereabouts are now unknown. Sometime in 2014, about a year after her employer was acquitted, she left the women's shelter. She did not return home. The shelter's director said she did not know where Mae was now. For the longest time, Neera Varma blamed herself for how things turned out. She didn't know, when she called directory assistance and asked for a list of non-profits that help find missing girls, that in the end Mae would be more missing than ever.

'I don't even know now whether that was the right step, to help that girl out of that place. Maybe she would have lived there all her life, maybe she had accepted that situation, I don't know,' says Neera. 'Sometimes I am laden with these questions and I feel bad. There was a stage when I started feeling guilty, that I am responsible for this...'

Of course, people had tried to warn her as she became more deeply enmeshed, accompanying Chutki and Pano to hearings on some days. Why get involved? Why give yourself a headache? Think about yourself first, her friends and family entreated her. She has tried to explain to her well-wishers that it was never her intention to launch some kind of rescue operation. But it just didn't seem right that Mae couldn't even talk to her family. How could she just sit by and do nothing? 'They should have that much freedom at least, to talk to their family once in a while. That was all my intent was,' says Neera. 'And it took such an ugly turn.' Chutki and her sister had been chewed up and spat out by the legal system, or at least that is how it felt to them, and to Neera.

It has been more than two years since Mae left the shelter and no one in her family has heard from her. But if Mae were in touch with her family, she would know that she now has not only an aunt but a brother in Delhi. In 2015, a village agent offered to take Pano's second child to be a cleaner in a Delhi home, just like his sister six years earlier. He was eager to go, his mother says. He told his mother not to worry about him. He won't end up like Mae, he said. 'I'll go safely and I'll come back safely,' he assured his mother. Where in Delhi is he? Pano doesn't know. 'I've only spoken to him on his employer's phone,' she says.

PART VII

Snakes and Ladders

LADDERS

WHEN YOU MOVE TO A new country or enter a new social class, which can involve similar kinds of psychological dislocation, it is tiny, unexpected things that are sometimes the most disorienting. Not attitudes to sex, drinking, marriage or children, life's most important things arguably, which people expect other nations and classes to negotiate radically differently. Instead, it is casually uttered phrases and attitudes to inanimate objects, even, that can distinguish someone born in the upper class from someone newly migrated to it. That at least was Sonal Sharma's experience. He's reminded of it when I visit him at home, in the servants' quarters area of a government housing neighbourhood, and awkwardly accept the invitation to sit on his bed as we chat. 'It took me a long time to understand this bed thing,' says Sonal, a fairly new member of India's one per cent.

A clean-cut, light-eyed, delicate-featured young man of slight build, Sonal is a sociologist at one of the country's most prestigious think tanks, the Centre for Policy Research in Chanakyapuri, where he carries out research on labour and urbanization. He works alongside public intellectuals whose arguments frequently appear on the opinion pages of leading dailies, and whose philosophies shape the discourse in India on caste, on social welfare programs, on religion and secularism, on what India is and what it should try to become.

In some years, Sonal's name will likely increasingly appear on those pages too. Even though he is only in his mid-twenties, and this is his first job, he has already experienced the international academic circuit, speaking at seminars on labour and space in Switzerland and Italy and organizing similar conferences in Delhi. On his bookshelf sit works of theory, with some surprises here and there. Not far from literary theorist Pierre Bourdieu's *Political Interventions*, sits a copy of *Bridget Jones's Diary* ('I've never read it,' he says. 'Someone lent it to me.') On the wall behind his bed hangs a framed design of an Indian multi-armed goddess, except this deity holds not deadly weapons but brooms and mops in her many arms, a present for Sonal from a graphic-designer ex-boyfriend, and a nod to the importance of his mother in his life. As I look at it, Sonal invites me to sit. There is nowhere to sit but on the bed. He sees me hesitate, smiles and urges me again to sit.

Among the upper classes there's a shared understanding that the bed—and the room it's housed in—is a place of special privacy and intimacy, open only to its owner, and perhaps a few chosen intimates who know they may walk in and sit on the bed without asking. If you think you have to ask, you probably aren't one of that select group. It's an attitude the Sonal is aware of, now that he is, in the ironic lingo of upper-class Indians, a PLU: People Like Us. But he doesn't share it himself, at least not yet, having grown up in a one-room home in the middle of the city, thanks to his mother's work as a housekeeper for senior government doctors at AIIMS.

When Sonal comes home after work, he heads towards the boxy cream and red-brick two-storey government homes in the AIIMS residential campus and enters an alley behind one of them, where the servants live. In this neighbourhood, each apartment comes with two servants' quarters, and one such quarter, consisting of a room large enough for twin beds to be arranged in an L-shape, a kitchen, and a courtyard, is home to Sonal and his family.

These are not the new servants' quarters that real estate developers nowadays build, which are more like cells than rooms where a person with outstretched arms can touch the wall on either side. The housing Sonal has lived in since he was seven years old is from a different era, and was built by the government. It was as close as Delhi got to public mixed-income housing, admittedly sharply segregated. The civil servants' homes look out on to a park and well-paved colony roads devoid of traffic. The servants' homes are in the back, where electricity cables loop messily and the pavements are often missing bricks. An occasional paper stuck to the wall here advertises that 'Doctor Sahib' is looking for a driver.

As in most such homes that I've visited, bed and chair, bedroom and sitting room aren't sharply delineated. Yet, although there are hardly any spaces where someone might go and shut the door on the rest of the family, Sonal does have something in the way of a bedroom, a private space that is his alone, a physical marker of the way in which his social class is no longer the same as that of the rest of his family. He has a 'bedroom', the space we are chatting in, which has been fashioned out of the quarter's courtyard, with a tin roof and a 'wall' that consists of seven or eight of his mother's old saris hanging next to one another to create a rainbow-hued partition from the rest of the home. The rest of his family, his parents and two younger brothers, all sleep in the remaining room, an acceptance perhaps that Sonal's status has been elevated from their own. It isn't always the case that a family or household rises up the class ladder together; the uneven development visible across the country can be reflected within a single household.

'It's more about one's individual status than household or family status. I'm pretty much middle class,' says Sonal, of the realization he began to come to perhaps three years earlier, soon after he finished a bachelor's degree in 2009. 'My brothers' class levels are very different than mine, frankly, because of education levels. And also, the kind of access I have to people, spaces, is very different. Unless I disclose, you know, what my parents do.'

As Sonal travels into a different class, his life is increasingly unintelligible to his brothers even though they live in the same home. His brothers, neither of whom has gone to college, are contract workers at a government-run hospital, impermanent jobs obtained through the interventions of his mother's employer—but ones that carry the hope of being made permanent one day. His brothers go to work, come home, eat an evening meal with their parents in the bed-sitting-dining room as they have done since they were children. It is the life of most Indian families. They don't understand why Sonal is increasingly not there for that family life, why he is so often out in the evenings. And though they are terribly proud of him, sometimes when one of Sonal's younger brothers boasts at the hospital about his brother, the hi-fi researcher at a hi-fi office, people ask an awkward question: why Sonal and not him?

'And then he'll try to cook up a story that my father was not working, that's why [he] couldn't go to school. Which is not true,' says Sonal. 'They failed in Class 10. Repeatedly. That's when they had to start working. But they love to believe in the other story.'

His brothers believe that Sonal has excelled more than they have because their parents favoured him in some way, perhaps because he was the first-born son. Their narrative, according to their older brother, is one of suffering from inequality within the home. But Sonal sees if differently: if at times his parents spent more on him out of their meagre resources, it was because they saw he was already doing well at school. In the long term, there would be a greater return on their investment in him.

It was also because they somehow recognized, albeit a little slowly, what Sonal seemed to always know about himself, that he was able to figure out the rules of a game that baffled millions of others. He could see how to get from one square to another, could see the little ladder that connected a lower spot on the board to a higher one, and knew just how to put his foot on that first all-important rung. And then the next one. And the next one. The ladders differ depending on the player, and they are finite. For one, it might be a family property that catapults him or her to the next level. For another, it might be marrying the right person. It might be securing an entry-level government or army job. Or it might be getting into college—the right kind of college—that helps a young boy get to where he thinks he ought to be.

◆

'I always looked at things differently, even when people of my age, my cousins, they thought I was being...like, I just had too many dreams,' says Sonal. 'I always thought I was different from others—people in my school, people in my locality—that I was not one of them.'

It took some time for his parents to understand that. When he was a boy, his mother thought she would find a way to settle him in a job by relying upon her employer's goodwill and his networks. This was her responsibility, she felt. Her husband, with his failing eyesight, didn't work and was on poor terms with several in his family, making it difficult for him to contribute to either the family income or Sonal's future. So, when Sonal was eleven or twelve, his mother encouraged him to babysit the toddler of a young medical resident who was a family friend of her own doctor employers. The young resident often called Sonal to come play with his child, saying it was difficult for his wife to tend to the baby all the time. 'Come play once in a while,' turned into a daily affair after school. But they gave him lunch, and it seemed to Sonal's mother like a good relationship to foster with an eye on the future. Sonal remembers that home differently—it was the place that taught him exactly what it meant to be a servant, something that he could not, of course, learn in his own home, where he was among equals.

When he felt hungry and asked the couple's cook for food, the cook admonished him. 'First, the sahibs will eat. Then we will eat.' When he and the cook did eat, it was in the kitchen on the floor, while his 'playmate' was fed at a table in another room. When he went on outings with them, and got bored or tired of holding the baby and tried to hand him back, sahib would stop him, saying his wife was too tired to carry her child. Madam is entitled to get tired, but the twelve-year-old child of a maid is not.

When the couple was set to move to Hyderabad and expressed an interest in taking Sonal with them, perhaps promising to re-enrol the boy in school in the new city, his mother was for it. But Sonal had an unusually clear sense that if he went with them, he would be landing on a snake. At best, he would gain lifetime employment in the doctor's medical practice, which he could hold on to in the deferential and self-effacing way his mother had always approached her job and her employers. At worst, he might be let go after a few years, when he was older and less compliant, and would find himself, in his early twenties, with a partial education and no job.

So, he resisted. Often in the years to come, he found himself having to sidestep the snakes that appeared on his path, usually disguised as a good opportunity or well-meant advice, although that same advice would not be offered to the sahib's own children. When people told him that going to college by correspondence was just as good as going to a real college, he resisted. When he began to think of doing a master's degree and people told him or his family that he had studied enough—wouldn't it be better to get a job now?—he resisted.

Sonal was a dreamer, it's true, but he was a practical one. 'I had plans, and most of those plans have materialized,' he says. 'There were things I wanted to have, and I worked towards some of those things, like speaking English, like getting into a different school, a good school.' In middle school, he found out about and took an exam to move from a local government school to a different one that was among a small group of high schools for gifted children set up by Sheila Dikshit during her first term as chief minister of Delhi state. At that school, Sonal participated in extra-curricular activities not available at all government schools that would serve him in good stead. When Sonal didn't do as well as he would have liked on school-leaving exams, scoring in the mid-80s while marks of above 90 were required for the programme he wanted to get into, a teacher at the school told him to try another way: the debate quota. Indian teachers can be uneven in the attention they pay students. They can appear very uninterested in those they have little hope of success from, but if they have a good student they will lavish attention on him or her.

He set his sights on one of the hardest programmes to get into—Economics Honours—at the country's most prestigious grouping of undergraduate colleges, Delhi University. Several colleges had debate team quotas; he auditioned for these slots, and had his first proper taste of linguistic and class snobbery. The elite St Stephen's undergraduates of the 1950s and 1960s might have mocked an upstart with cutting remarks and sarcasm shaped by P. G. Wodehouse. But the young people presiding over the debate auditions in Sonal's time knew nothing of Bertie or Jeeves. Although just as snobbish as the previous generation, they were shaped to a far greater extent by Star World and veejays and reality television, and their unkindness was refracted through these cultural experiences.

'The people who auditioned at Hindu [College] were treating it like *Indian Idol* auditions. Like, "You. Go." As in, get out of here. They were terrible people. Snooty in a particular way.'

At these colleges, kids made no bones of the fact that they found the Hindi speakers funny when they tried to speak in English. At Kirori Mal College, which had both English and Hindi debating teams, the English teams couldn't hide their laughter over the florid style and rhetorical flourishes of the style of debating taught at Hindi-medium government schools—quite different than the fact-based logical progress of argumentation the English debaters had learned. 'They were giggling constantly when other Hindi speakers were also speaking,' he said. But they stopped laughing, and were impressed in spite of themselves at the way Sonal answered one question they put to him: would he accept admission if it were offered to him in one of the college's less prestigious subjects, and not Economics? 'No,' he said, surprising both himself and them with this proud answer. 'Have you already got admission somewhere else?' 'No,' he repeated. He found out soon after that he was selected for one of the four debate slots—two Hindi and two English—for which 250 kids had applied at Kirori Mal College.

His first year was a nightmare. He had begun to study English at school in Class 6, and didn't understand most of what was said in lectures. He scraped through his first year. He worked harder at English, making a point of speaking it as much as possible, despite the fact that it sometimes made him the butt of jokes. Once, he pronounced the word 'vocabulary' as 'vocab-lerry'. A girl who heard him say this burst into laughter and asked him to repeat himself, so she could burst into another fit of giggles.

'That was a shocker...I just didn't know how to deal with people who were speaking such fluent English, who looked at basically my accent, my pronunciation, as something worth laughing at,' he says. 'Now I realize they were really young. People don't really know what is funny, what is not, what hurts and what doesn't.'

He switched to debating in English, made English-speaking friends and volunteered at a non-profit for youth interventions, around issues of social justice, conflict and identity. It was something he was exploring as well, trying to understand who he was and where he fitted in terms not only of class but also sexual identity, because he is gay. At the non-profit, after a long time, he felt he wasn't being judged by others; they were listening to what he had to say when he spoke, not cataloguing the mistakes in his English. He began circulating in queer groups too, as he came out more publicly, expanding his networks through groups like the collective Nigaah, where he often felt as if he was the only person present of working-class origin.

After college he kept working at the non-profit, taking charge of student activities, and slowly noticed a change in himself. 'I was mentoring people who were middle-class...I was part of these meetings, people listening to me, I was able to speak in English,' he remembers. 'I think that's when I started feeling like I was part of a different class.'

He went on to complete a master's in sociology at one of the city's newer humanities institutions, Ambedkar University, near Kashmere Gate. Through friends and activists in his political and other circles, he began to hear about one opportunity or another. He did part-time translation work at MIT's Poverty Action Lab that paid one rupee a word. Later, a friend who was a budding academic a few years older than him, and who was a kind of mentor to him, put him in touch with a revered economist at the Centre for Policy Research. He applied for an opening and got it. His own value among his peers rose exponentially thereafter. College acquaintances began getting in touch with him to ask him to please keep them in mind if he heard of any further openings at CPR. These were people who hadn't spoken to him during their three shared years of college.

When Sonal was not at home in the evenings, he was socializing. This was the most important ladder of all, he had come to realize, not just becoming a PLU, but knowing many, many other PLUs, and being known to know them. There is no unkinder cut in Delhi than to say to someone at a party, 'You've been lying low', or even worse, 'I thought you had moved abroad', hinting at all the social opportunities in your circle that you have not been at, or worse, didn't even know about. At this level of the class system, Sonal realized, you are more likely to hear about a coveted job opening at a party than anywhere else. 'You have to socialize, you have to know about other people's work,' says Sonal. 'I mean, like, okay journals do send out a call for applications, but the papers that actually get published are those in which editors know people, and they'll say, "Hey, why don't you send in something?" Similarly for jobs. People don't get jobs because there's an ad and then you send a résumé. No, you don't get jobs like that. Somebody has to introduce you. This is something I learned recently, that that's how it works.'

Not that, Sonal is quick to add, having a good network of PLUs means you get amazing jobs handed to you on a platter. What it means is your resumé doesn't end up in someone's trash folder. 'You can keep sending your CV to a company—and one doesn't get a job because you have come through someone—basically you have to, you need networks so that somebody could have a look at your CV seriously, right?' he says. 'These networks are important to signal, basically, that this person is worth considering.'

Two years into his job at CPR, Sonal began applying for doctoral programs overseas. He had noticed that the people at the top in academia in India had very often studied abroad, often at just a handful of schools. Columbia. Yale. Duke. Harvard. Cornell. It was the next ladder, the next stage in the expansion of his world and its ever-rippling circles: acquiring both the skills and the social cachet of a PhD from a top American university. New humanities institutions have opened in India in recent years, seeking to create an indigenous answer to these schools. But scholars from pre-existing 'indigenous' universities grumble that it is still the people with PhDs from America who get top billing at these places.

Sonal's decision to apply overseas marked a turning point in his relationship with English. Taking the GRE and writing personal essays for unknown American readers was daunting but achievable. To my ear, his is the English of the upper-class Indian that I can easily pick out even in the midst of a crowd of English speakers of all kinds on a New York City subway platform. There is none of the mixing up of 'v' and 'w' noticeable in many Hindi speakers when they acquire English, no mispronouncing 'hotel' as if it rhymed with 'total'.

Sometimes, some of Sonal's friends suggest, ever so subtly, that he's too focused on this whole English thing. They tell him his Hindi is so beautiful, he shouldn't lose touch with his roots, he should speak Hindi more often. Why not even do some of his academic writing in Hindi, they suggest? But, as he's learned to do before, he resists these innocent-seeming suggestions. Where, he wonders, is he to deliver these Hindi lectures, and which of the journals that his peers follow the most closely, will publish such Hindi essays should he choose to write them? At the roundtables at CPR or Delhi academic conferences that almost always take place in English? 'Because this is the language that's close to power, I've chosen to write in English,' says Sonal. 'Why do I have to wear this burden of writing in Hindi for the masses? I love the language, I love to translate, but I think I have to learn English. And the more I write, the better it gets.'

And yet the better he got at English, the better he got at recognizing the differences that remained, even if ever so slight, between his English, and the English of those who have grown up with it. 'This is where those fine markers of class become apparent,' he said. 'Like people whose grandparents were doctors, lawyers, they are elite, they are not middle-class, they can make out those differences and point [them] out.' They have, for example, the ability to understand the meaning of a string of words like, 'I'm about to turn into a pumpkin', and to know without any effort that it is both a reference to a particular childhood tale and a comment on the lateness of the hour. 'I didn't grow up reading English novels and stories like Cinderella which you know many people, many of my friends [did], when they talk to each other, I cannot participate,' he said. 'Earlier I used to pretend that I knew what these things were but then gradually I've stopped pretending. It's not worth it.'

He also discovered the elite, and not just callow undergraduates, but even those who are scholars of class and caste, can be both confident and curiously possessive about English. Much as they say it's theirs (which is why they feel affronted when a well-meaning foreigner compliments them on their English), they sometimes act as gatekeepers of someone else's fortress. The way they judge true ownership over the language is by judging whether someone like Sonal is saying the word as close to the way someone in England, speaking standard British English, would say it. From time to time, even Sonal's closest friends, to whom he has come out about this class background (he says the experience of trying to disclose his class origins to upper-class friends is not dissimilar from the experience of coming out as gay) behave in this way. They correct his grammar, publicly. They make little 'jokes' about his English. Here's one: 'How do you know that Sonal is drunk?' Answer: 'His grammar is suddenly perfect'.

It will be a relief, I imagine, to study abroad and speak English somewhere else for a change, where people won't have the ear to distinguish between his English, and that of the Indians who are judging him. In the fall of 2016, Sonal left for Baltimore to start a doctoral programme at Johns Hopkins on a scholarship. It's enough, he hopes, to be able to send a little money back to his family, which they'll need once they have to leave the AIIMS campus and rent a place of their own, which is likely to happen when his mother's employers retire.

◆

In 2014, when Sonal was in Hyderabad carrying out research, his mother urged him to go meet the doctor family whose child he played with all those years ago. Sonal was not very keen. He always saw the relationship differently, and felt it would be awkward. But his mother told him, 'No, no, you should go and visit them. They'll be very happy to see you.' Even his father chimed in, 'They really love you.'

'I never thought, like, they love me,' says Sonal. 'But I was like, 'Okay, I'm in the city. I'll just go.' So he called the family up. Immediately he sensed the reluctance. Sonal had been useful, as he suspected, not loved, as his parents imagined. 'This woman was not really interested in meeting me because she thought like, oh, maybe I was expecting something, a job or some sort of financial thing,' he says.

He arrived at the appointed time. There was the awkward bestowing and receiving of a gift, imparted with thoughtlessness by the giver; it is burdensome to the recipient, much like the drab fabrics that Lovely's madam would give her and Lovely would spend money on to make a suit she didn't like very much so as not to offend madam's feelings. Sonal thanked her for the T-shirt, which was clearly new, but not attractive. 'I could see she just bought it for the sake of it, like I have to give you something,' he tells me. 'I could see that.'

The toddler was now a teenager in high school, talking of college, and even graduate school already. These were things Sonal was also thinking about, and knew about. But he felt constrained from saying the kinds of things that he might volunteer in a gathering with whom he had no personal history. In a different setting, he might without hesitation say, 'I know this professor at such-and-such university that has a good programme in what you're interested in. Should I put you in touch?' But there he felt awkward. He did, at one point, suggest the teenager consider studying abroad in China, and mentioned a friend who had done the same whom he could put him in touch with. But again he felt a constraint, perhaps from them, perhaps from himself, perhaps on both sides, that he had transgressed. He intention was to be helpful but his words could be taken, he realized, as showing off, or even as usurping a role that his hosts should be playing.

'The assumption in these relationships is that they are the ones with the contacts, they are the ones with resources,' he says. 'If I

present myself as somebody who can be resourceful in this way...
they don't know how to make sense of that.'

Sonal is aware there's an irony to the discomfort he's feeling in
this home, since as part of his work he has been trying to figure out
how domestic workers perceive and adhere to boundaries in their
employers' homes. How do they know where to sit, and where not to?

'So I was sitting on the same sofa as she was, right?' says Sonal.
And it dawned on him, he didn't really know if that was okay by
his hostess, or if he was making her uncomfortable. 'When I was
a child, I was like any other child and nobody thought I'd be doing
what I do today, so I think for them, also, they would not know how
to interact,' he says. 'I was constantly thinking what to say and what
not to say, you know? What is it that is okay, and what is it that will
be perceived as transgression? He felt that if he put a foot wrong,
the welcome mat, modest as it was, could be pulled away suddenly.

These people remembered him as a servant's child, and it was hard
for them to immediately recognize and adjust to the fact that he was
now their social equal. But he could not behave in accordance with
how they had known him and the rules he had been taught by their
cook all those years ago, because he was no longer that person. If
social mobility is disorienting for those who are on the move, it is no
less disorienting for the people they encounter who might once have
felt themselves to be superior but no longer can do so. In that brief
meeting, the Hyderabad family glimpsed Sonal's changed status. Back
in Delhi, though, his mother's employers have already understood it
and tiny changes in their behaviour reveal this to Sonal.

When Sonal was younger, he had often helped his mother do her
chores at her employers' house or filled in for her when she wasn't
well, washing dishes and sweeping and mopping. His brothers, the
ones who have secured their jobs through the doctor, still run errands
for the family when they get home from their hospital shifts. But now,
when the doctor's wife raps on the window of the quarter that looks
into the back garden of the bungalow to ask one of his brothers to
photocopy a letter or lift a suitcase, she declines if they are not home
and Sonal is offered in their stead. 'Sonal is here, I can send him,' his
mother might say. But now the response is, 'No, don't send Sonal.'
Suddenly, they are squeamish about accepting chores from him, or

behaving as if they have a right to his time and help, by virtue of employing his mother.

That change, noticed by both Sonal and his mother, reminds me of a story told to me about a family member about interviewing maids. When she asked one of the prospective maids where her children went to school, the woman answered 'Shri Ram', the very same school her own children went to. The prestigious school had made a genuine effort to enrol students from lower-income families, in keeping with an education law passed in 2006 to, among other things, ensure that schools that had often benefited from subsidized public land contributed to the project of making class boundaries more porous. 'I just couldn't hire her after I heard that,' she said. It was too odd to stomach that the mother of one of her children's schoolmates—whose parents she regarded as her peers—should be her servant.

SQUARE ONE

'CAREER OBJECTIVE: TO ACCOMPLISH RESPONSIBLE, challenging suitable position in the organization where I can utilize my skills in the department and achieve the organizational growth.'

The sentence that sits at the top of the one-page summary of Lovely's professional accomplishments reads like a parody of résumé-writing. A friend of hers, who helped her compose and print it, appears to have strung together a series of buzzwords that human resources professionals love. The sentence, pretty much devoid of meaning, doesn't tell you who Lovely is and what she can do—but it is far from the main problem with her résumé.

Recruiters usually scrutinize résumés looking for work histories that convey an erratic approach to work; résumés, like smiles, are marred by gaps that are too numerous or too wide. A single small one is acceptable—no more than that. Lovely's résumé unfortunately has the opposite problem: it shows you she has had too early and consistent a relationship with the world of work. She is only nineteen, and her résumé lists five years' worth of work experience. And that's after leaving out about half her working life. That means she couldn't possibly have a Class 12 school certificate, which automatically disqualifies her from the consideration of the managers who hire for the kinds of jobs Lovely yearns to have.

Her top choice is to be sales girl in a clothing shop at one of the nearby malls that cluster on a road named for Mahatma Gandhi, a man famed for his austerity. A close second choice is a job working as a cashier at McDonald's. She sees both of these jobs as a huge leap forward from the work she has been doing since she was about eleven. 'At the end of the day, no matter how nicely ma'am treats me, I'm still a servant in someone's home aren't I?' she says one day.

I imagine Lovely could easily do a cashier's job even without that all-important certificate. She has basic reading and writing skills—how else would she Whatsapp and Facebook with all her many friends. And she knows her numbers—you have to when you're responsible for a household of four plus a family back in the village. She's an extrovert and knows how to win over a crowd. I see it happen when we go to the local Aadhaar centre for her to register for a photo ID, her first ever, and her mimicry of the broad rural accents of the customers at a Sohna Road clothing shop where she briefly worked gets a trio of Bengali girls laughing. If she were working at youth clothing retailer Forever 21, she would love to wait upon an indecisive shopper, explaining why this top looks great on her, and why those trousers wouldn't suit.

We are already in a post-writing world, many say. Soon we may be in a post-reading one, or a least one in which video instruction, speech-to-text and other options diminish the differences between those with a high school education and those without one. It seems a shame that a piece of paper stands in the way of her entirely reasonable aspirations; this is not brain surgery, after all. But then, that's not the employers' problem.

It is also easy to sympathize with the gatekeepers' insistence on some kind of piece of paper that makes it easier for them to select a chosen few from a vast pool of applications. Millions of Indians join the labour force every year. In 2014, an estimated 66 million students were pursuing a high school certificate. Some of them likely continued on to college, but many more would have fanned out looking for work. How would you choose one of the hundreds if not thousands who apply for openings every year? By instituting basic, not unreasonable, requirements that weed out many hopefuls quickly.

Women make up nearly half of those 66 million students—and of these, perhaps just a third will seek work, but that still provides companies with millions of choices who look better on paper than Lovely. That piece of paper is why Lovely's friend Renu can get a job in McDonald's or at a call centre days after she shows up for a walk-in interview, but Lovely cannot. And so, sometimes getting a leg up requires turning to deception, giving the dice a little nudge when no one is looking, pretending you rolled a six, not a five, so that you can land on a ladder and not on a snake. At least, that is what one helpful neighbour advises.

'If you want a mall job, you have to tell some lies,' says a young man who is trying to help Lovely get work at a nearby branch of the discount supermarket Big Bazaar, which also requires school certificates from its job applicants. He tells her to revamp her résumé, creatively. 'I want to see at least a year of shop experience. And nothing about cooking.'

The résumé rewriting is part of Lovely's efforts to reinvent herself, which she began in late 2015 at the age of twenty after she suddenly found herself unemployed. One September day Lovely went to the apartment complex where she had worked for six years—a job described as 'Chef' in the version of her résumé rejected by her neighbour—to find the apartment locked. Ma'am had been saying for some time that she intended to go to Saudi Arabia to join her husband, whom Lovely understood to be a financial adviser to a Saudi prince, and now she had left. 'You'll always be like a daughter to me,' ma'am texted Lovely by way of farewell. Lovely deleted the text.

Lovely used to sing ma'am's praises but the relationship had frayed in the past year, which is perhaps why she now refers more formally to the woman she used to call 'aunty'. Earlier, when ma'am used to travel, she would leave the keys to her home with Lovely without even seeming to think about it. But recently, Lovely said that ma'am had begun recounting stories about maids employed by her family members, who were ever so trusted but who turned out to have been thieves. She told these stories in a rather meaningful way, Lovely thought, offended. 'She tells me how the woman who works in her mother's house, one day when her mother wasn't there, she stole something and left. So she thinks, "What if Lovely becomes like that",' said Lovely. 'She was telling me that the police came. So I told her, "The person who's going to do wrong, only he'll feel afraid, so I'm surely not going to be worried about such things." Then she said, "No, beta, I'm just telling you what happened." But she's making a point, isn't she?'

In recent months, Lovely felt ma'am was more irritable with her and found fault with her work. If Lovely's work wasn't as good as before, it was because she had more of it. The cleaning lady had quit and not been replaced; instead, Lovely was doing the cleaning as well.

Previously, Lovely had done light cooking and top cleaning, and kept ma'am company. Ma'am was the employer she had always spoke of with great affection, describing their many chats over juice and snacks. But Ma'am's son had returned home from his studies overseas and perhaps as a result Lovely had been consigned to her proper place, her role as a quasi-family member diminished. You don't need someone to be 'just like family', when you have actual family around. Instead, the servant part of her role had increased. (The fraying of a warm relationship of long standing isn't uncommon between maids and madams. When I ask one nun who helps tribal women find work as maids why she thinks this happens, she mulls it over a few moments and then says, 'Menopause'.)

The few days before ma'am left for Saudi, Lovely was feeling so upset with her employer that she didn't go to work. Perhaps she also didn't realize the departure was quite so imminent, since ma'am had spoken of moving to Saudi Arabia in the past, but had invariably returned after her trips. The reason for the upset was that Lovely had overheard ma'am talking to her husband, repeating things Lovely had shared with her in confidence. 'I was in the kitchen and I was going to go ask her something and by chance she was talking about me to her husband at that time. I went to the door and the way she was talking me about me, in one moment my face fell,' Lovely told me in the days after ma'am's departure. 'I share things of my heart and then she talks about it with someone else in not a nice way... She didn't understand who I am,' she said, shortly.

But Lovely didn't remain downcast for too long, as she was one of those people who was always trying to not just better herself but others as well. For example, when she went back home to her village in 2013, and went to get her eyebrows shaped at a beauty parlour that had opened in the nearest town, she gave the proprietor, a migrant returned from Delhi, a slew of styling tips. 'You can't cut hair just straight across,' Lovely admonished the parlour-owner. Her own hair falls gracefully, in steps. 'Don't you know about layers?' Lovely suggested that customers would like it much better if the parlour kept fashion magazines with the latest hairstyles so they could point to actress Aishwarya Rai's blow-out or Deepika Padukone's tresses to show what they wanted. The lack of magazines or even haircutting skills may not have been as much a hindrance to the parlour's fortunes as Lovely worried. Most Indian women, whether at a fancy hotel in Delhi or a parlour in rural Bengal, wear their hair very long and very straight. Nine times out of ten hair stylists hear this: 'Just a little off the ends.' But that was Lovely's personality—forever an optimist trying to better her own family's and other people's fortunes.

The rooftop of the tenement where Lovely lives, in Gurgaon's Chakkarpur area, is where people of the building hang their clothes to dry, fall in love, and find jobs. A month before she heard about the Big Bazaar opening, a man on the roof asked her if she wanted to work in a spa. What's a spa, she asked? Men come there to be massaged, he told her. She asked: Do women have to do bad things there? Well, that's up to you, he said. She declined. Meanwhile, her friend Renu's husband, who sometimes works as a maid broker, tells her he can place her in a home. Once he collects the plaçement fee, she can run back to Chakkarpur where they'll never be able to find her, he says. They can split the fee. She turns down that offer too. These are the opportunities that come her way through her social network, which is not as robust as Sonal's, or that of a housekeeper working for a more elite Delhi family. As she tells me about these rejected offers, she asks for advice about how to draft her résumé and collect the supporting documents that will enable her to move up in life.

'This guy is saying to just go get a fake Class 12 certificate made,' Lovely says. 'Shouldn't I be honest with people?'

I want to say 'yes', but then it occurs to me, it's not remotely possible that everyone she is competing with is honest. Of the millions of Indians who are armed with certificates, degrees, and diplomas, at least some are certainly not the real deal. The person who may beat Lovely to that Big Bazaar job may have obtained their certificate through hard work and study. Or not. Just months earlier, newspapers reported that the capital's law minister had fabricated his degrees. A 2013 article in *Caravan* describes how 'a pandemic of fraud among job applicants' has spawned a booming new industry: résumé detectives who go in person to check out the schools and companies a candidate claims to have been part of. The fraudsters try to stay one step ahead, staging a home with the signboard of a fictitious business mentioned on the résumés created for several customers. It's very likely that

Lovely is competing against people who may themselves have faked school certificates and degrees. Perhaps that occurs to Lovely as well, for she muses out loud.

'What if I use one of the girls' school certificates?' she wonders. 'Would that be the right date?'

The sisters don't share names, so it might seem implausible for Lovely to use one of her younger sisters' documents. But that discrepancy could easily be explained away—many Indians irritate government officials by producing certificates and identification that show multiple names, usually explained as appellations bestowed upon them formally versus the ones they use within their families. However, her younger sisters are four years away from completing Class 10 and six years from finishing high school—if all goes well. Once they've finished school, that trick might work. But not now.

For the time being, we look at Lovely's résumé with a view to dressing up her experience while remaining as truthful as possible, translating her descriptions and explanations into even more HR jargon. Following the neighbour's advice, I suggest she cut 'cooking' from among her hobbies, more suitable to a matrimonial CV, and put down 'Facebook' instead. It is perfectly truthful and suggests literacy and tech-savviness—modernity—in a way that cooking does not.

For perhaps a week, in the months since she lost her housekeeping job, she worked at a clothes shop on Sohna Road. The customers, most of whom seemed to be relatives of the shop-owner, had a ton of money, she says. The women would pull large bundles of notes out of their salwars. Fifty thousand rupees. A lakh of rupees. 'Bundles upon bundles,' says Lovely. 'I showed customers fabrics,' she tells me. 'And I would help them make a selection from the menu.' Menu? A pattern book is what she is referring to. I suggest this can appear on her résumé as, 'Proactively assisted customers in making purchase selections' and 'Recommending suitable cuts and styles from store catalogue'. Did you fold things, I ask? Yes, that too, she says. I suggest she add 'restocking supplies' to her list of job responsibilities.

'It wasn't even my job to put the fabric back but the helper who was supposed to do it ran away. She said it was too much work,' says Lovely.

Lovely gets into the spirit, and asks if it wouldn't be better to add a fancier-sounding job to the résumé, or else inflate the amount of time she worked at the clothing shop. They may ask you about your work in an interview, so it's better if you rely on an actual experience than a completely made-up one, I say. And, I add, you shouldn't make up fictitious dates of employment at the shop, but perhaps it's better not to specify that it was just a week, which really doesn't help you much at all. Just list a year—2015—without elaborating, and then list the name of the shop and what you did there. That way it's not an out-and-out lie and you can always be honest if they ask—which they probably won't.

Her mother, meanwhile, is not very happy with Lovely's efforts to move into a different line of work. With the four sisters surviving just on the salary of Lovely's younger sister Rina, who works as a nanny, no money is making its way back to Jahanara in Malda. 'Why do you have to work in a mall?' Jahanara has said to Lovely more than once. 'Just find another kothi.'

It's always money, money, money with her mother, Lovely says. Send her money, and she loves you. Don't send her money, and you may as well not be her daughter. By Diwali, Rina is reporting to her oldest sister that Mother has said, 'Lovely is dead to me.'

'Well, she's dead to me too,' says Lovely. 'She should understand my dreams.'

Instead, her mother tells her she should be embarrassed to live on her younger sister's salary while she indulges in her fantasies. This, Lovely thinks, is a bit rich.

'It's only been two months,' she says. 'Didn't Mother live off me for ten years?'

I don't get to see the revamped résumé. But weeks later I hear Lovely has secured some kind of a marketing job for a packaged snacks company based out of Old Delhi. I'm slightly alarmed when I first hear about this job. The other people she works with are all men. She has to work quite late, and it's an hour by the metro back to her home in Chakkarpur. But she seems hopeful about it. It can be quite hard to tell in advance whether a particular job will end up a blip on her résumé, like the job at the clothing shop in Sohna Road, or a launching pad. But even as she teeters between her past as a servant and a possible future in retail, she is in some intangible way, already living on a different planet from many women she knows. It's a difference I notice the most in the way she talks about marriage and men. When she gets married, she says, she won't be a caged bird. 'After marriage, why can't girls go out? If you have to go to the market, why do you have to ask for your husband's permission? Friend se milna, ijazat chahiye. Yes, okay, you should say, I'm going here or there, but why should he say don't go?' says Lovely. 'Why? I can't understand it. I think marriage should be like this. If I say to my husband, I'm going to see a friend, he should say, "Cool". He shouldn't say, "Why are you going? You would rather be with your friend than with me?"'

Another time, she complains that a city-bred cousin of hers is mired in 'petty village thinking' after he tries to get Lovely in trouble with people back in Malda by reporting that he has seen her photo stored on the phones of male friends of his. What of it, Lovely retorts. She has put photographs of herself on Facebook. Some boys may have seen her photo and saved it to their phones. 'If a fan downloads a photo of Shahrukh Khan, is it his fault?' she asks me. She Whatsapps this boy or that, none of whom she ever graces with the name boyfriend. She has no interest in having one, she says. Another time she falls out with a friend who wants Rina to date her brother-in-law. But her stance on boyfriends softens in the years I know her. In the beginning, she tells me she will beat up her sisters if they turn up with boyfriends, mimicking her older brother's stance. But later she tells me, no, she wouldn't do that. But they must bring them to meet her so she can approve of them. And while she personally wouldn't be against a marriage with a Hindu boy, she says with a laugh, 'Mother would beat me.'

Her independence, though, is financed in no small part by money. If she had to depend on the earnings of a brother or her parents, she could not live according to her own rules and her own thinking. Her household's earnings are precarious and all it would take for her to lose her perch as an upwardly mobile city girl is for one thing to go wrong. For her to contract her brother's tuberculosis, say. Or for her younger brother's asthma to require such frequent dispatches of money to Malda that she falls into debt. But then again, all she needs is for one of the many things she has invested her time in to go right. One sister whom she's cajoled and bullied into staying in school to clear her Class 12 exams and get a job at McDonald's or Starbucks.

Or clear college and get a white-collar job. Or maybe her own job could lead to a promotion and a raise and a career. Or, by practising a little successful deception, she just might get one of those coveted mall jobs herself, from where she can work her way up, piling real achievements on that first fraudulent one, and eventually erasing it.

LANDED

IN FEBRUARY 2015, I HEAD one morning to Trilokpuri to attend a housewarming puja and lunch hosted by my friend Vijia. By the time I arrive at the newly-built four-storey house and pass through a doorway studded with decorative tiles overhead, the ceremonial first boiling of milk in the kitchen under the auspices of a priest has already taken place. A fire has been lit between bricks and all around it sit large shiny thalis filled to overflowing with bananas, coconuts, and flowers. My hostess, Vijia, a short, chocolate-coloured woman who is resplendent in a blue silk sari with a gold paisley border, is receiving more of these offerings from various friends and relatives. Other thalis contain saris and packets of candy in shiny wrappers, piled into neat pyramids.

Vijia and her husband and four sons live on a 25-square-metre patch of land in this neighbourhood of first and second-generation migrants to Delhi. The solidly middle-class status of the families isn't immediately visually recognizable to outsiders, whether Indian or foreign—when I bring a friend who has recently been in South Africa she says the neighbourhood resembles a shantytown. But though there is rubbish strewn in its narrow streets and the drains are open and sometimes choked, the homes of the families who live here rise up three and four floors, and many of them have a motorbike parked out front. Almost every child here will study at least till Class 10. On one block there are families from Rajasthan—my Defence Colony maid lives here, around the corner from Vijia—another block houses families from Uttar Pradesh. Sikhs used to live here too, and a large gurdwara is still a landmark for the neighbourhood, but most of them left after they experienced pogroms in the wake of the assassination of Prime Minister Indira Gandhi by her Sikh bodyguards in 1984.

Vijia's own block and those surrounding it are populated by Tamil Chettiars. She migrated from Kallakurichi in Tamil Nadu as a child with her mother. Her father had another family, and, in any case, died while Vijia was still a child. The home in which the housewarming party is taking place sits on land allotted to her husband's family in the 1970s, when the city was carrying out one of its many resettlement programmes that periodically picked up people from one crowded part of the city, in a bid to cut down on slums, and put them down somewhere else. Vijia's in-laws were picked up from Jangpura, where they were living in tarp huts over a covered drain. The city gave them the right to live indefinitely on the parcel of land that they were allotted in East Delhi, where farmland was then being turned into apartment buildings by cooperatives of professionals, such as young diplomats, who were priced out of Delhi proper, and who would one day in retirement hire the resettled slum inhabitants as maids and drivers.

Vijia's in-laws built a simple hut at first (which is all people can afford to do when they are first resettled) expanding it a little every few years as they managed to save money. Vijia's mother lived not far away in a tiny neighbourhood formed from huts abandoned by construction workers who had built a private school in the area. Vijia lived with one or the other of the families whose children she had taken care of since she was about eleven, or sometimes with her mother, until her future in-laws spotted Vijia at a local wedding when she was about twenty.

Slowly, as Vijia and her husband, a municipal plumber, clambered up the class ladder, their property shifted shape to reflect this. When Vijia was pregnant with her third child, sometime around 1999, she and her husband added two more floors to what was then a one-room home. Bricks cost 1.5 rupees each at the time and although they had the money to hire two bricklayers, they had no money for masons. Instead, they mixed the masala to cement the bricks, and ferried the bricks and cement back and forth themselves, saving the 150 rupees they would have had to pay a third labourer.

Fifteen years and one more son later, when a crack appeared in the wall over the front door to the house, they decide to tear the whole thing down to make a foundation strong enough to add another floor: one for each of their four boys. This time, they don't do any of the construction themselves. Instead, they hired two bricklayers and three masons, paying the bricklayers 500 rupees a day, and the masons 300 rupees a day, at a total cost of 2.5 lakh rupees.

Because these plots were originally bestowed as 'leaseholds'—which means technically they revert to the government after a very extended period—rather than 'freehold', which gives full ownership and no restrictions on sales, banks are loath to lend money for home redevelopments or purchases here. In 2013, Delhi granted residents of some forty-five resettlement colonies, including this one, the right to apply for freehold rights, but with fees for the conversion pegged at existing tax rates, it's a costly endeavour. Vijia amasses the money for the redevelopment through savings and quid pro quo financial arrangements with people she has cultivated over years of attendance at weddings and funerals, and through the savings groups she runs, also known as chit funds.

The committees work like this. If twenty people join, it lasts for twenty months; if thirty people join, it lasts for thirty months, and so on. The point of the committee is forced savings. Each member has to give a certain amount every month to the kitty, say 3,000 rupees, which makes for a monthly pool of 60,000 rupees for a group with twenty members. Each month, one woman gets that amount, minus some deductions to the other members, and Vijia's 'agent' fee. The amount of the deductions is established through a kind of auction. It's complicated. Vijia has to show me her ledger, which she keeps locked in the Godrej cupboard in her home, several times before I fully understand the process. The longer you wait to collect on the pool, the fewer deductions there are, and you get very nearly the full amount, minus Vijia's service fee of 300 rupees.

Vijia runs perhaps four of these groups each month, with bid meetings usually set for between the sixth and tenth of a month, by which time the women—cleaners and cooks, and sometimes manicurists—will have been paid. Vijia's aplomb in the face of handling lakhs of rupees in a neighbourhood prone to robberies, and where she sometimes has to pursue the savers quite firmly for their monthly contributions, suggest to me she ought, by rights, to have occupied a prominent niche in the formal banking system. 'It's a lot of risk,' she tells me. Should one of her savers suffer a tragedy, particularly one who has collected their lump sum already, it will be up to her to make good on their contributions.

Once, a brand-new member to the fund tried to take out her money in the third or fourth month, despite the fact that Vijia had explained very clearly at the outset that as someone with no financial history with her, she could only collect in the last month of the savings fund. A squabble ensued. The woman insisted she had not understood these rules and would make good on the coming payments, but really needed the money immediately for a payment on a property. Vijia wasn't comfortable taking that chance and the woman agreed to be reimbursed for her contributions thus far, and to leave the fund.

Another month, a chit fund member suddenly died of a heart attack. Vijia went to the home to investigate. The woman's husband was known to be violent and the blood seeping out of the woman's ears did not seem typical of a heart attack, which he claimed was the cause of death. 'Why didn't you take her to the hospital?' she asked him. Neighbours told Vijia they heard the sounds of a scuffle and some of them decided to make a report to the police.

Sometimes larger forces make themselves felt. In 2006, municipal officers threw their zeal behind a 'demolition drive', tearing down construction and forcing the closure of businesses that trespassed on streets and pavements. Not long after the drive began, one of the fund's few male members attempted suicide. He had lost his job after municipal officers shut down the shop that employed him. He began paying for his family's monthly expenses with the help of a moneylender, and as he saw the debts pile up, he decided to help his family by hanging himself. In the nick of time, his family rushed him to a private hospital, which saved his life and doubled his debt.

Sometimes Vijia makes mistakes, as when she hands over the pool money to the husband of one of her members after the man tells her his wife has dispatched him to collect the cash. Despite keeping her ear close to the ground, Vijia saw no reason not to agree to this request. Later, the irate wife turns up to berate Vijia—she and her husband have not been getting along well and now he has absconded with the savings.

In 2016, Vijia has one of her most stressful months ever. She has collected the cash from her savers and is set to make the pay out when the government suddenly announces 500-rupee and 1,000-rupee notes are no longer legal tender. She can't use the money to make the payment and must find a way to deposit the sum and withdraw it in new notes, without getting classified as someone who has been hiding earnings and avoiding taxes. Vijia and her husband are actually part of the formal banking system as well, and she is able to convert the now worthless chit fund cash. She has a bank account in her own name as does her husband, as do many neighbours. In addition to their savings through the committees, her husband also has a retirement fund through his government job with the Public Works Department, to which the agency contributed, and from which they were able to borrow for the house redevelopment. The house is also helping pay for itself: two families who each wanted to rent a floor fronted her a year's rent each towards the rebuilding. When the lease ends, she will pay them back the amount they lent her, but no interest. Instead, the interest she would have had to pay if they were simple interpersonal loans—tallied at 6,000 rupees a month—would be set off against the rent owed to her. All told, with demolition and labour costs, and materials, Vijia spent about 16 lakh rupees on the house.

While construction was on, Vijia and her family lived in a barebones lean-to, using one edge of the nearby municipal park as a wall, and constructing a hut against it. The construction project led to more bickering with a neighbour next door, a woman about Vijia's own age who grew up here and returned to the neighbourhood after an estrangement with her husband, and now ran a small shop on the corner. The animosity was inexplicable to Vijia: hadn't she taken the woman to hospital when she was in the accident that left her lame and embittered? But even so the woman yelled and shouted at Vijia or at the others when she was in a bad mood, which was often.

At first their fights were small, with the woman trying to needle Vijia by throwing dirty water on her doorstep or muttering profanities as she passed. Then she began to threaten to set herself on fire and implicate Vijia's husband for it so as to get him thrown out of his government job, or worse. During the construction, this neighbour accused Vijia and her husband of throwing bricks at her, an accusation Vijia hotly denies. The police came and locked up Vijia's husband and they had to pay the cops 5,000 rupees to release him. We talk on the phone from time to time about how stressful the rebuilding is, particularly with a neighbour like that, who is watching the new house go up like a hawk. 'She's just jealous of you,' I tell her.

By the end of 2014, the house is finished, complete with flourishes adapted from all the upper middle-class homes Vijia has worked in, including my mother's, which is where we first met, when she cooked for my parents after they retired and moved to this part of Delhi, to a complex where domestic service is dominated by the Tamil residents of Trilokpuri. That was just about her last job as a cook and she didn't stay with my parents long, since the financial groups she ran were taking up more and more of her time. But it was long enough for us to become friends after a fashion, as much as people can be across deep class and cultural lines.

I would drop in on her house unexpectedly, but she would not take the same liberty with me. She has always been after me to get married and even as I promised to work on it, I concealed from her the fact that I lived with my boyfriend, even though I thought she would like him very much. I didn't agree with her that the women in her neighbourhood who wore low-cut tops necessarily had bad characters, but didn't make a point of saying so when she complained about them. We were fond of each other and so over our decade-long friendship we learned what to talk about and what to avoid.

When I first began visiting Vijia at home, her house was still the one built in the 1990s, with each floor consisting of two rooms. On the ground floor, the back room is a bedroom with a double wooden bed mounted on bricks, which is where she usually invites me to sit. Then she makes coffee, and piles a plate with murukku or biscuits. The bedroom is full of gadgets—in one corner of the room is a large television, while next to the bedroom door there is a red fridge. A large steel-grey Godrej cupboard for locking up valuables, the savings group accounting ledgers, and the cash deposits from the savings group members is in the corner. A ledge runs along the wall above the head of the bed, crowded with pictures and statues of gods and goddesses, lit up with fairy lights and festooned with artificial flowers. A silver double-photograph frame displays Vijia's four sons on one side and on the other side Vijia and her husband, Uttarawati.

The new home, apart from standing on the same spot and still maintaining two rooms per floor, bears no resemblance to the old one. The kitchen is tiled in white ceramic tiles with a sprinkling here and there of patterned tiles with motifs that include a teapot and cherries. The ceilings are ornamented with moulding around the ceiling fan and again at the four corners. The landings and the exterior of the building have floor-to-ceiling textured tiles of faux beige and grey pebbles. The kitchen cabinets have modular drawers that slide out. Each floor has its own bathroom.

That February morning of the housewarming lunch, there are people sitting on every floor being served dosais, vadais, idlis and then halwa on banana leaves, women on one floor, men on another. Vijia hired a cook to cater this lunch, to which she invited more than fifty people. Vijia's sons and their friends—who represent a broader mix of Trilokpuri's many communities than the older guests, and include several pretty teenage girls—troop up and down the stairs in excitement. I meet Vijia's extended relatives, many of whom still work as housekeepers. One woman tells me she works for a Dutch family which runs bicycle tours of Old Delhi. They give her Saturday and Sunday off, and stole all the attention from the bride and groom when they came to a wedding in Vijia's family.

It's fairly easy at a gathering like this to tell the ups and downs of a family's fortunes with a quick glance at the throat and ears of the woman of the house. Two twinkling gold nose rings, plus a pair of such studs at the ears and a mangalsutra or thali at the neck means all's well. Little sticks to keep pierced ears open or a thread at the neck mean something's been pawned. This isn't necessarily bad—it could be to take a loan to build an additional floor of a home, or to buy a piece of land down south, or to buy gold coins for a wedding. Or it could be to pay health costs, in which case the money will never be recovered. Despite all their recent expenses on the house, Vijia has on the yellow gold flowers she always wears on her ears, and two similar studs on either side of her round nose.

The Indian government's interventions are sometimes brutal— after all, when it flings people into resettlement colonies, it doesn't give them money to build a home. Yet, Vijia and her husband, and millions of others, could not have gotten as far as they have if not for these interventions. Those who are able to stick out the experience of urban homesteading, like Vijia's in-laws, do get a leg up. For one, it means they never have to pay rent. Vijia's husband also landed a government job, which came with fixed hours, paid time off, savings contributions from the employers, and assured raises approved by the government. A steady income and a home of their own, both of these came to them thanks to spending by a state whose tax collections are relatively puny.

In the US, individual income taxes accounted for nearly 40 per cent of the federal budget in 2015, according to the National Priorities Project, a US non-profit that carries out federal budget research. In India, a little under 13 million individuals and families paid income taxes in 2011, according to the *Wall Street Journal*, in a report citing Indian tax-return data. These direct tax payments account for just 15 per cent or so of a typical Indian national budget (but corporate, service and other kinds of taxes also support spending). As the government seeks to be more fiscally prudent and efficient, the kinds of benefits that helped Vijia and her husband become middle class are available to a far smaller share of Indians.

The number of people qualified to apply for a government job has grown over the decades since Vijia's husband was first hired, while the number of such jobs has declined. Between the mid-1990s and now, India lost 2 million government jobs, going from 19.5 million to 17.5 million central and state employees, a recent official labour survey showed. Competition for the government jobs that remain is fierce, and not just for those that allow applicants to one day end up running the country. When a staff job as a cleaner opens up at a public-funded library named after India's first prime minister in 2015, 25,000 people apply. It takes a week to interview all the shortlisted candidates staff at the library tell me. The job pays around 12,000 rupees, around the middle of the scale for this rank of government staff, which tops out at around 20,000 rupees. Eventually the selection is made, and the job goes to a man with a hearing impairment who applied via an affirmative action category for the disabled.

When it comes to resettlement programmes, which still exist, the city has more people to resettle and fewer unoccupied, well-located areas to relocate them. People who are removed from public land and now resettled get as little as 18 square metres, or even 12.

As a result of all these changes, Vijia realized that she will have to look to private enterprise, rather than government employment, to settle her sons, and the rebuilding of the house was especially planned with them in mind. Over the next decade she'll be looking for wives for all of them, and it will help if a prospective bride's family likes where she'll be living. In the redesigned home, each couple will have two rooms, and a bathroom to themselves. Vijia is a bit worried about whom her boys will marry. They have gone to school with and befriended north Indian girls. She wouldn't be surprised if at least one of them asks her to arrange a marriage to a girl who is not Tamil. She said she doesn't mind but her husband has said that he would have nothing to do with any son who goes down that route and she knows many neighbours would take a similar stand. Should she allow her sons to assimilate, and marry a local girl if it means losing the goodwill and social network of their relatives and friends in this tight-knit community?

Still, that dilemma would be a happy problem. No girls will be interested if her sons don't have jobs and aren't earning well. Vijia and her husband have pulled themselves far, far forward from where they started as children. Vijia herself lived, essentially, on the street at times before she married. But it's not clear whether their children will pull themselves even further up than their parents, or whether the family's upward momentum will stall. Or, perhaps Vijia's children, like Sonal and his brothers, will end up at different points in the system.

In 2007, not so long after Vijia and I first met, her oldest son was fifteen and an aspiring Bollywood dancer. This was a matter of some concern. 'In our caste we don't dance,' she explained. But she didn't stop Kumar when he began spending all his evenings practising Bollywood dance moves to a crackly tape with a neighbourhood friend in a nearby park. Maybe he could get on television, Kumar hoped, or win a reality show. That didn't happen. Instead, by the time of the rebuilding, he is twenty-two and has finished high school with great difficulty. Vijia blames herself for his poor education. Kumar had to be taken out of school when she fell ill with jaundice so her husband could pay the doctor. 'It was my life or his education,' she says. He likely won't go to engineering college, his current dream, or get a white-collar office job.

Her second son finished high school in 2015, but his marks were low, even though he qualified for an affirmative action quota. A lawyer contact who lived in a nearby apartment complex offered to help him get into a private law school if in return Vijia's son worked for him for free for the duration of the five-year course. Another neighbourhood contact promised to help him get admission through a quota into one of the Delhi University colleges. His marks looked too low to me for him to qualify even that way, but somehow he's in. He works at a law firm when he's not studying. Her third son dropped out in Class 10, although she urged him not to. Her youngest boy is still studying at a school run by a Tamil society, a pretty decent one.

A year after the housewarming, I arrive to see shelves lining the front room of the ground floor, a counter and a weighing scale. Big sacks of rice sit here and there, and in the back room, a sign leaning against one wall proclaims 'Vijia Shop'. Vijia has started her own business, specializing in South Indian masalas and pickles, and cheap dal and rice. A shopkeeper in Old Delhi to whom she has gone for years to stock up on Tamil groceries, pointed out one day that she was in a perfect position to start a shop, given her built-in customer base through the savings group. At least forty women come to her house every month, after they have just got paid. Vijia should try selling them stuff, he suggested. He told her a cheap place to source goods from, which would allow her to offer a price point 10 or 20 rupees a kilo cheaper than other people. She decided to also make dosai batter and chutney, offering it to women who come home tired from cooking all day at their jobs, but who still have to make a fresh dinner for their husbands and children. 'I mix it up when I'm making it for the house,' she says. Right now she's not really turning much of a profit, maybe just 10,000 rupees a month after expenses. After demonetization, she has to allow many people to buy on credit. But she's not too worried she says. 'First, let me build up my market share.'

Vijia encourages her oldest two sons to come in with her; they can accompany her when she goes to buy provisions or man the shop when she has to go somewhere else. She's trying to create a fall-back option for them. At some point, if the kind of job he aspires to is not forthcoming, her oldest son may realize that running a grocery store isn't such a bad option. In fact, it's a rather good one. Indians still do almost all their cooking at home and about half their spending is on food—the last item of spending to be cut when families are being frugal. If the shop does well, it can easily provide employment for at least two of her sons.

At around the same time, Vijia begins taking on more debt—she comes to me for a loan as well, and after some consideration, I agree to give her some money. She's buying a next-door house that has come vacant because its owner is moving back to Tamil Nadu. Two adjacent houses among four brothers will secure a better selection of possible wives than one house among the four.

During one of my visits, I notice that she's had painters in. Here, a maroon wall, there, a golden wall—a suggestion from her oldest son. We climb from floor to floor—each painted a different colour. We look out of the window from the third floor. It towers over the home of the volatile, quarrelsome neighbour. It towers over all the homes, in fact, and from her roof I can see my parents' apartment building. 'Aren't you afraid?' I ask, referring to the neighbour opposite who so often picks fights. I already believed her to be jealous before of Vijia's husband with a government job and four sons. Now, there's this new and beautiful house. But Vijia just smiles, a contented, happy smile. 'She ought to be jealous,' she says, 'I've given her something to be jealous of.'

SNAKES

IN INDIA, IT IS POSSIBLE to go up, but it is just as easy to go down, to lose your unsteady footing on the particular rung you have climbed to by dint of sheer hard work, and carefully cultivated networks. The most common way for this to happen is the death of a parent, particularly a father. A death like that can swallow up a whole family's fortunes, dashing their dreams, sending their children back to square one. For all that the father in question may be a less than stellar human being or a below-average breadwinner, his presence alone offers something, a kind of protection. The next worst catastrophe is to be cut off from networks, which is why people are so careful even today to marry the right way, to be careful not to offer slights, either by not extending invitations far and wide through a clan or community, or not accepting them. It can take generations before it's clear which way the trend line of a particular family is finally going and, as with stock markets, past performance is no indication.

Which is why it's surprising to me to find in members of the Indian one per cent, a certain complacency about where they are in life. As if there is something extraordinary in them as individuals, that has led them to a post as partner, professor or vice president of something or the other. When actually, they—and this is perhaps true everywhere in the world—are where they are in large part through luck and having the right ancestors. It ought to be sobering and vertiginous to think of how many other people could be where you are, doing exactly what you do, if everything in India was just a little better. Although many people in India, in Delhi, complain that 'everything is getting worse', that feeling is due to the fact that on some level, things are actually getting better. Hundreds of thousands, if not millions, of Indians, like Sonal or Lovely, are living more ambitious lives than their parents. And yet, when you probe a little further, these stories of mobility aren't quite what they appear to be. That is, they don't represent movement in only one direction, a clear upward trajectory on an X-Y axis, plotting a neat 45-degree ladder to the top of the graph. One particular generation's life might, if plotted, look that way. But if you step back, the progress appears a lot more winding and slithery. What might look at first like a completely new member joining the middle or upper classes is actually a hard slog back to a perch lost by a previous generation.

Sonal's grandfather—his father's father—was a low-level government clerk. From that position, and the stability it comes with, it's possible to fund a good education for your children, good enough that they ought to have been able to try for the civil services or prestigious colleges or become doctors. If Sonal's grandfather was a clerk, and his father an IAS officer or IIT graduate, Sonal would very likely have grown up in a house his parents owned, perhaps gone to an Ivy League college abroad for an undergraduate degree. Instead, that grandfather died young, leaving his eight children to fend for themselves; some of Sonal's aunts and uncles maintained their spots in the class system, but his father didn't. His father didn't study beyond the eighth grade. On top of that, he had poor eyesight and difficulty getting and keeping a job; he tried his hand at various business ideas that didn't go anywhere. He hit thirty and wasn't married, a sure sign of failure for most men in India.

That downward mobility happened on Sonal's mother's side of the family as well. Sonal's mother grew up in a government colony in central Delhi, where her father was a cook in an Air Force mess, a reasonably good job, and one that could have also afforded connections for clerical jobs for his sons. But he died young too, when Sonal's mother was just sixteen. She began cleaning to get by. Five years later someone brokered a match between her and Sonal's father, although the two were of castes at opposite ends of the spectrum and a decade apart in age.

Given where Sonal is in his late twenties, headed to Johns Hopkins University in the US for a PhD, it might seem like the dip in fortune experienced by his parents, while tough on *them*, didn't make a huge difference in *his* life. But the same is not true for his brothers. Sonal may have returned to where he ought to be because of a combination of intelligence, hard work and luck. But what he managed to do is unusual and difficult, which is why it's admirable, and also why his progress can't be taken as a benchmark. Just because some people who are raised by parents with little money or education grow up to be highly educated and affluent doesn't make that a reasonable expectation for the majority of people who grow up in scarcity. Sonal's brothers might have done better than they have if they had had the opportunity to grow up with a certain amount of money and in a social class where the expectation is that you will finish high school and go to college whether you're academically gifted or not. Most of us, after all, are ordinary achievers—we do quite all right when growing up without hunger and if we go to decent schools, and don't do well when the opposite is true, and expectations of us are low.

Lovely's family history is also one of zigzags. Her father's parents had land, which they left to him. But without an aptitude or interest in farming, he couldn't make a go of it. Between drinking and odd money-making ideas he ended up selling much of what he started with. His cousins, some of whom bought land from Lovely's father, have done much better. When Lovely's mother takes me to her husband's village and we meet his cousins, I see that they are actually quite well-off. One cousin has a large home, with many rooms and a television. The day I visit, hired woodworkers are sitting at what will be its main entrance, chiselling timber into floral patterns for an ornate door. A central hall is stacked nearly to the ceiling with 50-kilogram bags of rice that will fetch tens of thousands of rupees in the market—farming has been good for them. This family eats well, with fried potatoes, fish curry, homemade chutneys and massive mounds of rice put out at lunch. Lovely's branch is clearly the poorest branch of the family.

But then, in a span of a few years, it could all switch around. A boat that seems to be safely pulling in to harbour can run aground, one that is tossed about at sea can return to safety. And if future professors and entrepreneurs can come from the ranks of families working as domestic help, then a job as a nanny or cook can often also be the unhappy landing place for people who expected to do much, much better.

In January 2015, I visited one of the graceful homes in central Delhi, the residence of another business family, similar and not far from the Khoslas on Prithviraj Road (but far wealthier). When I arrive at the bougainvillea-covered gate of the mansion, I tell the seated guard the name of the person I am here to meet and his manner turns surly and suspicious. First, he mutters, 'There is no such person', pretending not to know a man he surely sees every day. The logo on his uniform shows that this guard is not an employee of the household but, instead, has been placed here by a well-known global security company. Perhaps because he is employed by a company, he considers himself superior to the man I have asked to meet. Or perhaps, having seen that I drove myself here rather than being driven by a chauffeur, and that I am asking to meet a servant and not a family member, he has slotted me into the ranks of 'not a sahib', and feels he can forego the usual deference in his dealings with me.

Eventually he ushers me along a tree-lined path to the tastefully maintained nearly century-old home. I had visited this home once before for an interview and when I had said I was there to meet a member of the business family, the guard on duty that day had shown me in with much greater alacrity. But this time, I am here to meet the cook. Or rather, *a* cook, as there is more than one.

I wait in a sort of anteroom that looks very similar to an old-fashioned receptionist's room in a government office, with files and an old typewriter, and in a few minutes, the gentleman I am here to meet appears. He is in his fifties, dressed in a rumpled T-shirt of red, yellow, and blue stripes, with a smattering of white stubble on his face. His eyes are bleary, possibly from awakening from a nap. We are meeting during his afternoon break. As a cook he works in the morning until after lunch, and again from the early evening to after dinner.

Although he has been at this particular home a fairly brief time as old-timers go—about a decade—his employment with various branches and relatives of this business clan comes to some twenty-five years of collective service, with a brief break in between. He works for one unit of a joint family that includes perhaps a dozen adults. The oldest generation is in its sixties, the youngest generation, the grandchildren of the former, have just started school. In this home, the maids, cooks, drivers, gardeners and other workers number around forty.

We do not go to the staff quarters, instead we go to one of the wings of the family home, perhaps of a family member who is travelling. First, the cook must resolve the matter of the seating arrangement. We cannot sit together on adjoining sofas, as I did when meeting his employer. So I wait to follow his lead. From the kitchen he fetches a low stool for himself to sit on and directs me to a much higher seat. Sitting this way isn't very conducive to a good interview, even if it might be a little less awkward than the occasions where a worker ordered by her employer to speak to me remains standing in a doorway, while I sit in a chair sipping tea. I cast around and eventually perch on a footstool to establish some kind of parity; but it has a swinging mechanism built into it and I nearly fall off. I abandon it for a pristine white sofa instead. If we were stick figures, a spectator peeking in at the window would still be able to identify sahib from servant just by how we're seated. And so we begin.

Very early in our conversation it becomes clear that disappointment has set in deeply and long ago for this man and it emanates from him now, escaping him with every word he speaks in a low voice. He was never going to be a servant; that was never the plan. His two older brothers began working in their teens to support his efforts to study and get an office job, hopefully as a government peon, which may not on the face of it seem a lofty goal, with its duties of filing, answering calls, and a lifetime of kow-towing to senior bureaucrats. He finished high school, an astonishing achievement today, and even more so three decades ago. He even completed the first year of a bachelor's degree—putting him in a miniscule minority back then. At the start of the 1980s, less than three million people were enrolled in higher education of any kind, according to the World Bank. (Almost forty years later, nearly 35 million students were enrolled in a college or another form of graduate education in the 2015-2016 academic year, according to India's human resources ministry.)

He was competing against a tiny pool of people. But the number of jobs available was not great, and having grown up in a remote rural area, his contacts in the urban world (where most of the jobs were to be had) were limited. If in his extended circle, there had been someone ensconced in a company or a university, he might have been able to get a toehold somewhere. But he and his family members didn't seem to know enough people like that. So he filled out forms many times for government jobs seeking high school graduates. So many forms, he remembers. But his name never appeared on the lists of selected candidates. He even tried paying money to a distant relative to help him bribe his way into the army; the relative was unsuccessful and, with more integrity than one could probably expect today, returned the bribe money. Despite being among the privileged few in his village to have a higher education, his seemingly upward trajectory stalled. In those days, as today, an education on its own was not enough to land a job. At last, at the age of twenty-five, he was open to anything. When a man with ties to his village, who worked as a cook in Delhi, said that his master's relative was looking for a kitchen worker, he raised his hand. 'I accepted defeat,' he says.

The home was on Sardar Patel Marg. He didn't know anything about wages and so he didn't make any demands about what to be paid. In any case, that wasn't really how it worked back then. He left his salary up to his employers and he feels they paid him decently enough of their own accord. He earned 300 rupees a month, in 1987, or about 3,000 rupees today. In 1986, by contrast, a peon's pay was about 1,075 rupees, or nearly 11,000 rupees today. At the time, the highest paid Indian civil servant earned about 5,500 rupees post tax, about twenty times the cook's salary.

(Clearly, servants at the Mughal court, nearly 400 years earlier, were paid obscenely high amounts. According to one Mughal-era memoir, female servants in the zenana, many of whom may well have been the daughters of noble families, were paid 200 rupees a month. Today, though, there is more parity between a cook's salary and a top bureaucrat or elected official, excluding any alternative sources of income. The prime minister's salary and allowances come to about 160,000 rupees, or about ten times the earnings of a well-paid nanny or cook.)

In the late 1980s, if he spent nothing on himself at all, it would have taken the cook two months on a salary of 300 rupees to save enough to buy a bicycle, or ten months to buy a television. But he did not buy a bicycle. For one, he had no need of one, living as he was in his employer's home. For another, he had married at fifteen and by this time had two daughters and a wife waiting for his wages in his village on the border of Uttar Pradesh and Bihar, a bus ride from the town of Gorakhpur. He didn't bring his family to the city because then

there would have been no one to wait upon his parents. His two older
brothers had moved away, taking their wives and children with them;
they had sacrificed their youth to help him get ahead, and when it
didn't happen, they perhaps felt it was his turn to sacrifice. So he left
his wife and children—three daughters and a son eventually—behind
to cook, clean and help on the farm.

Even today, in his quarters in Delhi in the servants' compound, he
does not have a television. Instead, he goes to the room of another
servant, a man senior to him because he is the long-tenured cook
in the home's main kitchen, the nerve centre of the house, when
he wants to watch TV. This man's family has also remained in his
village, and the two ageing men, both Brahmins unlike many of the
other help, lead the lives of bachelors rather than long-married men,
usually spending the afternoon rest hour watching television together.
In the servants' housing area, many others have brought their wives
and children here from their villages. In such cases, the children go
to local government schools, and the wives often also work, either
for this household, or nearby, in jobs found for them, at the homes
of politicians or other businessmen known to this family.

In 2015, the cook is earning about 6,000 rupees a month, which
is substantially on the lower side, given the wealth of his employers.
Still, the cook says his employers are nice, they speak to him politely.
They have loaned him money for his second daughter's wedding, for
which he plans to spend 2,50,000 rupees. He says he has made peace
with the job he never wanted, but that is difficult to believe. His face
is full and plump, puffy almost, and his eyes are bleary, off-colour.
This is not the look of broken sleep—it is a look I've seen in other
disappointed men of all different classes, particularly men who drink
too much, beginning at the point in life when they realize they are
not, after all, going to reach the destinations in life they once believed
to be in sight. In spite of a daily morning walk, he has the midsection
girth that health articles warn is a sign of looming diabetes and heart
trouble. Finally, he tells me that, actually, yes, there is something that
bothers him about his job.

'When everyone gets done for the evening, then my work starts,'
he says. 'The office worker, the driver, all these people become free.'

But, there's no point dwelling on his own disappointments, he has to think of the future. His son will soon finish school. He is still at an age when he is not yet ready to accept defeat; soon, he will be looking for an office job. What are his chances? His father is not sure. On the one hand, there are many more jobs today that his son could try for than there were when he himself was a young man: computers, call centre, mobile phone repair. But there are limits to how many young people these new industries can absorb. India's technology services firms, for example, employ only around 3.5 million people directly, according to the leading industry body.

On the other hand, the jobs today are not what they once were. More than half of Indians who work describe themselves as self-employed. Formal jobs with protections make up only a very tiny percentage of Indian employment. Many of those who do get a job do so on 'contract' basis, not permanent; these vacancies no longer come with all the things that used to distinguish a man in a job from a servant. Perhaps instead of a job his son may apprentice with some kind of trader or repairman. 'He'll have to live in a shop and learn a trade,' says his father.

We have been speaking for an hour and only a little of his break is left, so I take his leave. Outside, as I get into my car, I see a man come around to the red brick wall of the home, overhung with green vines, face it, and urinate. It is a simple act, one done by many men working all over the city, but I am struck by seeing it happen to this house, with its multitudes of staff, and its guard seated at the gate to prevent just this kind of desecration by the masses. And then I notice something else. This is no random passer-by. The man peeing on the brick walls that gate this beautifully tended mansion, and enclose the bonsai version of the class system inside it, is the same surly guard tasked with protecting it from the world outside. And his act, at once insignificant and meaningful, is yet another reminder of the subtle tremors unsettling our homes, much like the seating arrangements of a now-distant Goa holiday.

ACKNOWLEDGEMENTS

Before I lived in Delhi in my thirties, I thought of writing books as the pursuit of erudite people I didn't personally know and couldn't relate to. In Delhi, I met so many writers, budding and established, literary and pop, and was infected by their passion for telling a wide variety of stories. I'm extremely grateful to all the people who by their example (and often their encouragement) put the idea into my head that perhaps I too might write a book one day.

At Aleph, I'd like to thank David Davidar for reaching out to me, and for helping me to turn the wide-ranging and unwieldy idea I had into a slightly more manageable one. I'm also glad he rejected several dishevelled versions of this manuscript that I tried to turn in, and for kind words at the right moments. I'd also like to thank Marysia Juszczakiewicz for her helpful conversations and waiting out a long process. Simar Puneet has been a patient, diplomatic, and sharp-eyed editor. Thanks to her the book has far fewer false notes and errors than it otherwise would have had. Mahesh Rangarajan granted me permission to work temporarily at the Nehru Memorial Museum and Library, which was a wonderful place to write. Nilanjana Roy responded speedily to cris de coeur and all sorts of questions about contracts, agents and aesthetics, all along the way.

So many people made this book possible by giving me precious time and answering intrusive questions. There isn't any way to thank all of them by name but I'd like to mention a few. In Delhi, Lovely Khan and her sisters gave me many hours when I dropped in on them after they'd had a tiring day of work or school; Prabeen Singh was her frank self in a way few others would have been; Yamini Aiyar helped me take a peek inside a Lutyens' home; Gauri Singh offered me a unique perspective on the elite as employers; and Neera and Pavan Varma helped put together the pieces of an important story.

Also in Delhi, Sonal Sharma and Vijia were eloquent on the topic of social mobility. Vijia, in particular, over the years allowed me a close look at the very hard work involved in upward mobility and made me want to write about her experiences, which is what eventually led me to this book. In Jharkhand, Karmi Hansda hosted me in her home, no questions asked, and helped me get a sense of the rhythms and economy of that village. She explained a lot to me about life, food, and earning in Athgama, as did Basudeb Gorai and Manik Soren.

Apart from Vijia, I didn't interview anyone who had had a work relationship with my family or me. But many other people I have known because of such relationships planted the seeds for this book too with stories and remarks: Rogelia, Jaya and her son Nelson, Sona, Guddi, Vandana, Nandu, Bharti, Khuku, a different Guddi, Babli, Prem and Vinay.

I wouldn't have known how to do this book without working as a journalist first. Richard Vega (Boomer) encouraged me to quit my job at the *New York Times* website and go to India to experience a more pavement-pounding style of journalism. At AFP, editors encouraged us to leave our desks often for features.

The place I learned the most at, though, is the *Wall Street Journal*. Paul Beckett, a dear friend and a great journalist, took a chance on me in 2010, and that allowed me to work with the amazing people who made up the New Delhi bureau that year. They included Amol Sharma, Shefali Anand, Vibhuti Agarwal, Krishna Pokharel, Eric Bellman, Tom Wright, Anirban Roy, Will Davies and Margherita Stancati. Later I was lucky to work with Joanna Sugden, Aditi Malhotra, Saptarishi Dutta, and, a great partner on tough stories, Preetika Rana. Gordon Fairclough, Sean McLain and Suryatapa Bhattacharya were always encouraging and asked after the book—just the right amount. If I took the time out to list all the great things about working with each of these people, it would severely try the reader's patience. But I know that no one will grudge me singling out Paul to say what a special place he made the Delhi bureau.

Heather Timmons has been a wonderful friend and a true mentor, shepherding me towards things that I would naturally be inclined to keep a good distance from—but that I would have regretted terribly not doing.

To the High Hats (or Haaths?), and to Tanya Luther and Mitali Saran for rallying these wayward troops, thank you for the music and the golgappas when I really needed to take a break.

Somini Sengupta and Menaka Guruswamy have been the source of intellectual ferment and also merriment in Delhi. Anjali Puri has been a great friend (as well as relative) with whom to talk books, as well as a provider of gin-and-tonics, journalism gossip and sometimes, unwittingly, a place to work. Mishi Saran, so many thanks for the pep talks and meals during the last mile. Patricia Codina, everyone should have a lifelong friend such as you, especially for last-minute cover consultations and conversations that can pick up just where they left off months earlier.

My dearest Smithies: Nivedita Chakravorty, Lule Demmissie, Melissa Myambo and Jaya Shah. I have probably had more conversations with each of you, collectively and individually, about class, race/ethnicity, privilege, fairness and unfairness than with almost anyone else I know. I'm both excited and frightened to have you read this book. Nivi and Jaya, thank you for being warm and loving, and helping me think I could do this (and also for your company, respectively, in seeking out spider crab rolls and cute Park Slope bars). Gabriela Betancourt, my longest lasting (and last) roommate, you are pretty much one of my Smithies. Melissa, I have had so many exchanges of ideas with you in college and after, about life and the universe, and nemeses and crises of confidence (and many other things), that it's probably been a whole additional education. But few conversations could have had the impact of that one we had in a Northampton shoe shop where we fell into talking about whether it is or isn't okay for another person to wash one's underwear.

Mashis (what can I do, now you have a collective noun): thank you. Aparna, you had brainwaves about places where I could go and work and sourced all kinds of impossible-to-find books for me (I should probably return them to you so you can return them to the source). Anasuya and Ratna, you have made me laugh harder than anyone else in the past decade, barring AB, with your antics. I hope we'll always be laughing as uproariously, and find ways to run, or rather, *smooth over* any problems that come our way. Although no one can choose between mashis, and I certainly would not, Ratna, you especially have been such a wise counselor on this book so many times: thank you.

Arnab, thank you for constantly reminding me not to worry about offending people with my writing, and for the road trips and mountain breaks, during which I expected to feel very guilty for not writing but didn't at all. And for being so contagiously chilled out that I could actually believe you when you told me everything would get finished and it would all be just fine. When you first read a portion of a very early draft you noticed that my writing style was kind of unfocused, dropping the plot and haring off wildly in some other direction just when things were starting to happen. Kind of like my approach to time management. I'm sure I wouldn't have ever got the book done if you didn't keep patiently repeating this useful approach: don't spend your day doing all the least important things first.

There isn't any way I could sum up what it's meant to have my sister Smita through our wandering life. You always have known just what to say to me in the depths of despair, and how to perfectly distill the essence of a thought I'm trying to express. You are the best, that's all. (John, my excellent brother-in-law, thanks for hosting me for long stretches during my book writing. I regret not making good on my promise (threat!) to come and live with you guys and be Uma and Surya's nanny in return for room and board—it would have been much more fun.)

Last but not least, Ma and Baba: Despite my bitter complaints through childhood (and sometimes adulthood) about the many failings of your parenting styles, the truth is I am so, so grateful to have had you for my parents. Thank you for all the books, for being such decent and upright people, and for the unconditional love.

NOTES AND REFERENCES

3   **Two-thirds of all domestic help employed by families are women:** National Sample Survey Office (NSSO), Ministry of Statistics and Programme Implementation, 'NSS 68th Round: Employment and Unemployment Situation in India 2011-2012', January 2014, Table 27, pp. A-329-A365.

3   **These days, it is one of the most common jobs that women do outside the home:** Ibid.

4   **In India, the large numbers of help in the early twentieth century:** Swapna M. Banerjee, *Men, Women and Domestics: Articulating Middle-Class Identity in Colonial Bengal*, (New Delhi: Oxford University Press), 2004, pp. 40-44. Banerjee cites Rudranghshu Mukherjhee's essay '"Forever England" : British Life in Old Calcutta' in Sukanta Chaudhuri (ed.) *Calcutta: The Living City*, Vol. I, (New Delhi: Oxford University Press), 1990, pp. 45-51, as the source of this information.

4   **'diminishing fortunes of the [very] richest':** Abhijit Banerjee and Thomas Piketty (eds.), 'Top Indian Incomes, 1922-2000', *Top Incomes: A Global Perspective*, (Oxford University Press), 2010. Accessed online at https:// books.google.co.in/books/about/Top_Incomes_A_Global_Perspective. html?id=eGaVAwAAQBAJ.

4   **India, for example, had 1,070 people with \$100 million or more in assets:** Private email communication with Boston Consulting Group's wealth management division, 26 June 2015.

5   **If Britain saw the numbers of servants drop from 250,000 in 1951:** Lucy Lethbridge, *Servants: A Downstairs History of Britain from the Nineteenth Century to Modern Times* (London: W.W. Norton & Company), 2013; and Lucy Delap, *Knowing Their Place: Domestic Service in Twentieth-Century Britain* (London: Oxford University Press) 2011, p. 136.

5   **the number of servants in India shrank by half:** Census of India, 1951; Census of India, 1971.

5   **There are now more than 40 million female domestic workers:** 'Domestic Workers Across the World: Global and Regional Statistics and the Extent of Legal Protection', (Geneva: International Labour Organization), 2013, p 20. Downloaded from ILO website on 3 May 2015.

6   In the decade after liberalization in 1991, the number of maids, drivers
      and nannies in India doubled: Census of India, 2001.

12   These days young people are rising up so fast: All the material in this
      section is from recorded interviews with Om Prakash Verma and family
      on 18 May and 21 May 2014. Permission to quote from these interviews by
      name requested on tape during second interview with the family.

12   In recent decades, millions of families have moved into the terra firma
      of the upper ranks: Christian Meyer and Nancy Birdsall, *New Estimates of
      India's Middle Class: Technical Note*, (Washington, DC: Center for Global
      Development, Peterson Institute for International Economics), 2012.
      Downloaded 30 January 2013.

13   Yet despite this apparent demand-supply problem: NSSO, 'NSS 68th
      Round: Employment and Unemployment Situation in India 2011-2012',
      January 2014, Table 27, pp. A-329-A365.

13   the share of working women in cities who are employed as nannies,
      maids and cooks in private homes: NSSO, 'NSS 61st Round: Employment
      and Unemployment Situation in India 2004-2005', September 2006, Table
      28, pp. A-239-A251.

14   The head of a new government skills council: Suryatapa Bhattacharya,
      'How India is Trying to Improve the Lives of Its Millions of Maids', *Wall
      Street Journal*, 30 March 2016.

14   that the female workforce in urban India—where domestic workers are
      concentrated—is about 22 million: NSSO, 'NSS 68th Round: Employment
      and Unemployment Situation in India 2011-2012', (New Delhi: January
      2014), Table 27, pp. A-329-A365.

14   There are about 18 million households in India whose monthly
      spending: NSSO, 'NSS 68th Round: Implementation Level and Pattern of
      Consumer Expenditure 2011-2012', 2014, p. 85.

15   The number of women in cities of working age increased some 40 per
      cent between 2001 and 2011: Census of India 2001; 2011.

15   As one Bengali woman pointed out in a 1924 essay: Ipshita Chanda
      and Jayeeta Bagchi (eds.), *Shaping the Discourse: Women's Writing in Bengali
      Periodicals 1865-1947*, (Kolkata: Stree), 2014, p. 60.

15   In the third book of the Mahabharat, Draupadi retires with another
      woman, Satyabhama: Pratap Chandra Roy (trans.), *The Mahabharata: Vana
      Parva* (Calcutta: Oriental Publishing Co.), 1972, pp. 506-508.

16   for a woman, caring for her husband, mainly through caring for her
      home, is the route to spiritual freedom: I. Julia Leslie (trans.), *The Perfect
      Wife: The Orthodox Hindu Woman According to the Stridharmapaddhati of
      Tryambakayajvan*, (New Delhi: Oxford University Press), 1989.

16   A   2014   Organization   for   Economic   Cooperation   and
      Development   report: http://www.oecd.org/gender/data/

balancingpaidworkunpaidworkandleisure.htm

17   'There were eight maidservants in the house, but all of them lived outside the household,' wrote a woman: Rassundari Devi, *Amar Jiban* (Calcutta: Writers Workshop), 1999.

17   One 1933 headline proudly reported that four landowning families: *Harijan*, 25 March 1933, Volume 1, Issue 7, p 5. Accessed online www. gandhiheritageportal.org on 01 March 2017.

18   In her autobiography, Flora Annie Steel, the wife of a Scotsman in the Indian Civil Service: Indira Ghose, *Memsahibs Abroad: Writings by Women Travellers in Nineteenth Century India,* (Delhi: Oxford University Press), 1998.

22   Nowhere is that more true than in Delhi: 'Delhi's per capita income 3 times the national average: Govt', *Business Today*, 30 December 2016.

33   The wheat and rice harvests wrested from these small parcels: 'Pathna Block Below Poverty Line List 2002-2007', Government of Jharkhand. Downloaded from http://sahibganj.nic.in/en/BPL_List.html.

40   Usha Pal's father operated by the philosophy: This section is based on author interviews with Usha Pal and Renu Pal that took place on 14 June and 15 June 2014.

52   At sunset, as Christmas Eve approaches, men wearing military fatigues and masks walk into five Santhali hamlets: The opening of this section is derived from Delhi Solidarity Group, 'Recent Militant Violence Against Adivasis in Assam: A Fact Finding Report'. Accessed at https://abdulkazad. wordpress.com/2015/02/04/fact-finding-report-on-assam-massacre-december2014/ on 24 July 2015.

53   Mae came to Delhi sometime between the third and fourth cycles of ethnic violence: This girl's whereabouts are presently unknown. She was in a government home until late 2013 or so. I travelled to Assam in December 2015 and met her family. My information about her in this chapter is from public court records and recorded interviews with her mother and neighbours in the village, as well as social workers who assisted the family. (The name 'Mae' is a pseudonym.)

68   At these remarks, Mr Srivastava, a chubby-faced young man in his twenties clad in shorts and a yellow T-shirt: Information in this section is from an interview with Santosh Srivastava by the author.

73   'The difference between picking up a lace nightgown versus unravelling a pair of crumpled jeans...': Timothy Aeppel, 'Why Robots Still Can't Fold Your Laundry', *Wall Street Journal*, 24 February 2015.

76   a laundering practice that dates back at least to the Victorians: Lethbridge, *Servants*.

78   No one seems to think it odd that this internet discussion is taking place on a website run by nursery school chain Shemrock: Shemrock website. Maid Agencies Placement Consultants and Services list in Delhi NCR.

TRIPTI LAHIRI

Accessed at http://www.shemrock.com/blogs/maid-agencies-placement-consultants-and-services-list-in-delhi-ncr/ on 17 December 2014.

78   In 2007, an outfit calling itself the Adivasi Sewa Samiti, or Tribal Welfare Society, brought a teenage maid to Delhi: *Child Welfare Committee vs. Govt of NCT of Delhi* in the High Court of Delhi at New Delhi, 3 September 2008.

89   In the early 1800s, Mary Martha Sherwood, a clergyman's daughter: Indira Ghose, *Memsahibs Abroad: Writings by Women Travellers in Nineteenth Century India*, (Delhi: Oxford University Press) 1998, pp. 197-198.

119 Such suspicion can be widespread, at least in the minds of those tasked with investigating crimes: When something happens to a child, though, it is sometimes the case that the first person on whom suspicion falls is the guilty party. In 2009, a Standard Chartered bank cashier and his wife, an AIIMS nurse, hired a young nanny from West Bengal for their younger child. Months later, in November, the husband called home around lunch to speak to the nanny and got no answer. Alarmed, he arrived home and found his son was missing, as was the nanny. The distraught father remembered that months earlier a mason had done some work at his Mayur Vihar home. The mason and the nanny were often seen talking together, a guard at the housing complex later told the *Indian Express*. The father spoke to his local contractor who had sourced the mason and two days later, the nanny and child were found in Uttar Pradesh's Etah district, with a relative of the mason. The father of the missing child said the mason and his uncle had sought a 5 lakh-rupee ransom. In 2013, a court convicted the nanny of kidnapping (police were unable to find the mason). Taking into account the duration of the trial and the nanny's young age, about twenty-three at the time of conviction, the court sentenced her to time served.

138 In a memoir Prabeen later publishes, she reminisces: Prabeen Singh, *Life was Like That Only*, (New Delhi: Academic Foundation), 2017.

150 In her 1998 book on the culture of the chair: Galen Cranz, *The Chair: Rethinking Culture, Body and Design*, (New York: W. W. Norton & Co), 2000.

202 Jharna's employer was the India distributor of high-end Japanese car audio systems that ranged in price up to 20,000 rupees: Shelley Singh, 'Alpine offers insurance for car stereos', *Indian Express*, 19 January 1998.

202 Mrs Pandit said later she was only able to get the employers' number after asking Mrs Sen several times: Affidavit submitted by Kalpana Pandit before the Delhi High Court on 23 May 2002, in connection with *Kalpana Pandit vs. State*.

203 In September 2000, less than a month after Jharna had gone missing, a woman filed a police complaint of kidnapping: FIR 584/2002. Submitted by counsel Aparna Bhat before the Delhi High Court as an annexure to an affidavit on behalf of her client Kalpana Pandit on 5 October 2002.

203 **Mrs Sen, though, says things didn't happen the way Mrs Pandit says:** Author interview with Sunita Sen.

204 **They couldn't provide any details about him or where he was from:** Status report filed by Delhi Police before the Delhi High Court.

208 **Like Ms Pandit, Hembahadur wasn't always the most cooperative client:** Author interview with Bhuwan Ribhu, head of Bachpan Bachao Andolan legal department, on 5 February 2015.

208 **In September 2014, the government of Delhi finally issued rules:** Government of National Capital Territory of Delhi Labour Department. Delhi Private Placement Agencies (Regulation) Order, 2014. Downloaded from http://www.delhi.gov.in/wps/wcm/connect/doit_labour/Labour/Home/ on 25 September 2015.

214 **After discovering where Mae was, a Shakti Vahini worker:** Copy of letter on behalf of Shakti Vahini submitted to SHO Punjabi Baghi on 5 October 2012.

215 **For the trip, Pano pawned three-fourths of an acre of land:** Interview with Pano Kishku conducted in Kokrajhar, Assam, on 22 December 2015.

216 **She had told the Shakti Vahini workers and then child welfare agency officials that in her third year of work, the head of the family, Rajan Sahni, began to rape her:** I sent detailed requests for an interview via registered mail and also visited the Sahni family house in person to make the request. They did not want to speak to me for the book.

249 **In September, Ravi Kant filed a complaint with the anti-corruption department of the Delhi Police:** Letter from Mr Meena to Delhi Police vigilance branch.

273 **In 2014, an estimated 66 million students were attending high school:** NSSO, 'Implementation, Education in India, NSS 71st Round January-June 2014', (New Delhi: March 2016). Page A-57.

250 **The police report said that the man who appeared to have travelled with the police officer:** Copy of Delhi Police vigilance report.

273 **Women make up nearly half of those 66 million students:** NSSO, 'Education in India, NSS 71st Round January-June 2014', March 2016, p. A-55.

276 **A 2013 article in Caravan describes how 'a pandemic of fraud among job applicants':** Aditya Kumar, 'Chequered Pasts', *Caravan*, 1 April 2013.

288 **Between the mid-1990s and now, India lost 2 million government jobs:** Economic Survey 2012-13 Statistical Appendix, (Ministry of Finance, Government of India), p. A-56.

296 **At the start of the 1980s, less than three million people were enrolled:** 'India: Country Summary of Higher Education', World Bank, 2007. http://siteresources.worldbank.org/EDUCATION/Resources/278200-1121703274255/1439264-1193249163062/India_CountrySummary.pdf

Accessed on 2 March 2017.

296 **Almost forty years later, nearly 35 million students were enrolled:** Department of Higher Education, Ministry of Human Resources Development, 'All India Survey of Higher Education 2015-16', 2016, p. 11. Accessed online on 2 March 2017.

297 **At the time, the highest paid Indian civil servant earned about 5,500 rupees post-tax (not including bribes or dowry money, of course), about 20 times a cook's salary:** Surjit Singh, *Wages Down the Ages*, (New Delhi: Lancer Press), 1988, p 116.

BIBLIOGRAPHY

'Symbol of Arvind Kejriwal's party is loaded with many meanings', the *Times of India*, 7 August 2013. http://timesofindia.indiatimes.com/edit-page/Symbol-of-Arvind-Kejriwals-party-is-loaded-with-many-meanings/articleshow/21866359.cms?

Anonymous, *Enquire Within Upon Everything*, Kindle edition. [The Kindle edition is the 89th edition, originally published in 1894 by Houlston and Sons.]

Baker, Sophie, *Caste: At Home in Hindu India*, London: Jonathan Cape, 1990.

Banerjee, Abhijit and Piketty, Thomas, 'Top Indian Incomes, 1922-2000', Atkinson, A. B. and Piketty, Thomas (eds.), *Top Incomes: A Global Perspective*, Oxford: Oxford University Press, 2010.

Banerjee, Swapna M., *Men, Women and Domestics: Articulating Middle-Class Identity in Colonial Bengal*, New Delhi: Oxford University Press, 2004.

Beeton, Isabella, *Mrs. Beeton's Book of Household Management*, Beeton Press, 2013, Kindle edition.

Borthwick, Meredith, *The Changing Role of Women in Bengal, 1849–1905*, Princeton: Princeton University Press, 1984.

Bowles, Cynthia, *At Home in India*, New York: Harcourt, Brace and Company, Inc., 1956.

Burnell, Arthur Coke and Hopkins, Edward W. (trans.), *Ordinances of Manu*, New Delhi: Oriental Books Reprint Corporation, 2nd edition, 1971.

Chanda, Ipshita and Bagchi, Jayeeta (eds.), *Shaping the Discourse: Women's Writing in Bengali Periodicals, 1865-1947*, Kolkata: Stree, 2014.

Chatterji, Bankimchandra, *Debi Chaudhurani, or The Wife Who Came Home*, Lipner, Julius J. (trans.), Oxford: Oxford University Press, 2009.

Chaudhuri, Nirad C., *The Autobiography of an Unknown Indian*, London: Macmillan and Co, 1951.

———, *The Autobiograpy of an Unknown Indian*, Berkeley and Los Angeles: University of California Press, 1968.

Delhi Solidarity Group, 'Recent Militant Violence Against Adivasis in Assam: A Fact Finding Report'. Accessed on 24 July 2015. https://abdulkazad.wordpress.com/2015/02/04/fact-finding-report-on-assam-massacre-december2014/

Deshpande, Kusumvati (trans.), *Ranade: His Wife's Reminiscences*, New Delhi: Ministry of Information and Broadcasting, Publications Division, 1963.

Devi, Rassundari, *Amar Jiban*, Calcutta: Writers Workshop, 1999.

Diaz, Abby Morton, *A Domestic Problem: Work and Culture in the Household*, Kindle edition. [Originally published in 1895].

Doniger, Wendy and Smith, Brian K. (trans.), *The Laws of Manu*, London: Penguin Books, 1991.

Gait, E. A., *Census of India, 1911, Volume I, India, Part I–Report*, Calcutta: Superintendent Government Printing, 1913.

Ghose, Indira, *Memsahibs Abroad: Writings by Women Travellers in Nineteenth Century India*, New Delhi: Oxford University Press, 1998.

Gopalaswami, R. A., *Census of India, 1951, Volume I, India*, Calcutta: Government of India Press, 1954.

Government of Jharkhand, 'Pathna Block Below Poverty Line List 2002-2007'. http://sahibganj.nic.in/en/BPL_List.html.

Hutton, J. H., *Census of India, 1931, Volume I, India, Part I–Report*, New Delhi: Manager of Publications, 1933.

International Labour Organization, 'Domestic Workers Across the World: Global and Regional Statistics and the Extent of Legal Protection', Geneva: International Labour Organization, 2013. Accessed from ILO website on 3 May 2015.

Khan, Ahmad Hasan, *Census of India, 1931, Volume XVI, Punjab and Delhi*, Lahore: Printed at the Civil and Military Gazetter Press, 1933.

KPMG Advisory Services Pvt. Ltd., 'Human Resource and Skill Requirement in the Domestic Help Sector', New Delhi: National Skill Development Corporation, Ministry of Finance, Government of India. Accessed from Ministry of Skill Development and Entrepreneurship website (www.skilldevelopment.gov.in) on 17 April 2015.

Leslie, I. Julia, *The Perfect Wife: The Orthodox Hindu Woman According to the Stridharmapaddhati of Tryambakayajvan*, New Delhi: Oxford University Press, 1989.

Lethbridge, Lucy, *Servants: A Downstairs History of Britain from the Nineteenth Century to Modern Times*, London: W. W. Norton and Company, 2013.

Lowell, Thomas, 'At the Shrine of the Fish-Eyed Goddess!', *India: Land of the Black Pagoda*, New York: The Century Co., 1930.

Manucci, Niccolao, *Storio do Mogor or Mogul India 1653-1708, Volume II*, Calcutta: Editions India, 1966.

Marten, J. T., *Census of India, 1921, Volume I, India Part I–Report*, Calcutta: Superintendent Government Printing, 1924.

Mehta, Aban B., *The Domestic Servant Class*, Bombay: Popular Book Depot, 1960.

Meyer, Christian and Birdsall, Nancy, 'New Estimates of India's Middle Class, Technical Note', Center for Global Development, Peterson Institute for International Economics, November 2012. Accessed on 30 January 2013.

Narayan, Shriman (ed.), *The Selected Works of Mahatma Gandhi, Volume 1, An Autobiography*, Ahmedabad: Navjivan Publishing House, 1968.

———, *The Selected Works of Mahatma Gandhi, Volume 5, Selected Letters*, Ahmedabad: Navjivan Publishing House, 1968.

National Sample Survey Office, 'Employment and Unemployment Situation in India: 1999-2000, NSS 55th Round (July 1999-June 2000)', Ministry of Statistics and Programme Implementation, Government of India, New Delhi: The Government of India, May 2001.

National Sample Survey Office, 'Employment and Unemployment Situation in India: 2004-05, NSS 61st Round', Ministry of Statistics and Programme Implementation, Government of India, New Delhi: The Government of India, September 2006.

National Sample Survey Office, 'Employment and Unemployment Situation in India: 2009-10, NSS 66st Round (July 2009-June 2010)', Ministry of Statistics and Programme Implementation, Government of India, New Delhi: The Government of India, November 2011.

National Sample Survey Office, 'Employment and Unemployment Situation in India: NSS 68th Round (July 2011-June 2012)', Ministry of Statistics and Programme Implementation, Government of India, New Delhi: The Government of India, January 2014.

National Sample Survey Office, 'Level and Pattern of Consumer Expenditure 2011-12: NSS 68th Round (July 2011-June 2012)', Ministry of Statistics and Programme Implementation, Government of India, New Delhi: The Government of India, February 2014.

Office of the Registrar General and Census Commissioner, India, *Census of India 1981, 1991* (accessed on CD from Census office), *2001* (accessed online), 2011 (accessed online).

Office of the Registrar General, *Census of India, 1961*, Delhi: Manager of Publications, 1962.

Olivelle, Patrick, *Manu's Code of Law: A Critical Edition and Translation of the Manava-Dharmasastra*, New Delhi: Oxford University Press, 2006.

Padmanabha, P., *Census of 1981, Series I–India, Part II Special*, New Delhi: Controller of Publications, 1983.

Parks, Fanny, *Wanderings of a Pilgrim, Volume 1*, Karachi: Oxford University Press, 1975.

Planning Commission, 'Report of the Expert Group to Review the Methodology for the Measurement of Poverty', New Delhi: Government of India, June 2014.

Pyarelal, *Mahatma Gandhi, Volume II: The Discovery of Satyagraha—On the Threshold*, Bombay: Sevak Prakashan, 1980.

Rasul, Faizur, *Bengal to Birmingham*, London: Andre Deutsch Limited, 1967.

Ray, Renuka, *My Reminiscences*, New Delhi: Allied Publishers Private Limited, 1982.

Risley, H. H. and Gait, E. A., *Census of India, 1901, Volume I, Part I–Report*, Calcutta: Superintendent Government Printing, 1903.

Roy, Protap Chandra (trans.), *The Mahabharata of Krishna-Dwaipayan Vyasa: Virata Parva, volume 3*, Calcutta: Bharata Press, 1886.

———, *The Mahabharata of Krishna-Dwaipayan Vyasa: Vana Parva, Volume 3, second edition*, Calcutta: Oriental Publishing Co, 1955.

Sarkar, Tanika, *Hindu Wife: Hindu Nation: Community, Religion and Cultural Nationalism*, New Delhi: Permanent Black, 2001.

———, *Words to Win: The Making of Amar Jiban: A Modern Autobiography*, New Delhi: Kali for Women, 1999.

Shekhar, A. Chandra, *Census of 1971, Series I – India, Part II SPECIAL All India Census Tables*, New Delhi: 1972.

Shukla, Vinod Kumar, *The Servant's Shirt*, Khanna, Satti (trans.), New Delhi: National Book Trust, 2009.

Singh, Colonel Surjit, *Wages Down the Ages*, New Delhi: Lancer Press, 1989.

Steel, Flora Annie and Gardiner, Grace, *The Complete Indian Housekeeper and Cook*, Crane, Ralph and Johnston, Anna, Oxford: Oxford University Press, 2010.

Sunderland, Jabez T., *India in Bondage: Her Right to Freedom*, Calcutta: Prabasi Press, 1929.

Thānvī, Ashraf Alī and Metcalf, Barbara Daly, *Perfecting Women: Maulana Ashraf 'Ali Thanawi's Bihisthi Zewar*, New Delhi: Oxford University Press, 1992.

Tillotson, Sarah, *Indian Mansions: A Social History of the Haveli*, New Delhi: Orient Longman, 1998.

Valmiki, Omprakash, *Joothan: A Dalit's Life*, Mukherjee, Arun Prabha (trans.), New York: Columbia University Press, 2003.

Walsh, Judith E., *Domesticity in Colonial India: What Women Learned When Men Gave Them Advice*, Lanham: Rowman and Littlefield Publishers, Inc., 2004.

Walsh, Judith E., *How to be a Goddess of Your Home: An Anthology of Bengali Domestic Manuals*, New Delhi: Yoda Press, 2004.

Yeats, M. W. M., *Census of India 1941, Volume I, India, Part I*, Delhi: Central Legislative Assembly Debates, 1943.